Decline and Revival in Higher Education

Decline and Revival in Higher Education

Herbert I. London

Routledge
Taylor & Francis Group

LONDON AND NEW YORK

First published 2010 by Transaction Publishers

2 Park Square, Milton Park, Abingdon, Oxfordshire OX14 4RN
711 Third Avenue, New York, NY 10017

Routledge is an imprint of the Taylor & Francis Group, an informa business

First issued in paperback 2017

Copyright © 2010 Taylor & Francis

Library of Congress Catalog Number: 2009046341

Library of Congress Cataloging-in-Publication Data

London, Herbert Ira.
  Decline and revival in higher education / Herbert I. London.
     p. cm.
  Includes bibliographical references and index.
  ISBN 978-1-4128-1425-6
    1. Education, Higher--United States--History. 2. Universities and colleges--Standards--United States. 3. Educational change--United States. 4. Educational innovations--United States. I. Title.

LA227.4.L66 2010
378.7309--dc22

2009046341

ISBN 13: 978-1-4128-1425-6 (hbk)
ISBN 13: 978-1-138-50904-7 (pbk)

Contents

Preface   vii

Introduction   1

1. The Tenured Left   9

2. College Life from 1968 to the Present   35
   (The Barzun Perspective)

3. Decline and Revival   61

4. Experiments in the Academy   95

5. Off Track at Specific Institutions   131

6. Sports and Educational Standards   165

7. The Student Perspective   179

8. The Heroes in the Halls of Ivy   213

9. Scholarship and the Curriculum   229

Index   327

Preface

The compilation of articles in this book represents a four-decade history in higher education. In some respects, these pieces embody a personal odyssey from student to professor to dean. More importantly, in my judgment, is that these pieces mirror the evolution of higher education in the recent past.

In some sense, this is a tale of despair since I believe the academy predicated on the free exchange of opinion has been transmogrified into a center for orthodoxies. But there is reason to believe that the essence of higher education can be recaptured through intellectual beachheads, places where the best of our civilization's intellectual heritage is assigned and discussed openly and without prejudice.

Clearly some points in the book are dated, e.g. tuition rates, and just as obviously some events are only to be found in the entrails of the past. Nonetheless, the basic emphasis on the conditions that degraded higher education and the factors needed for regeneration remain intact.

While my professional aspirations have taken me from my professorial chambers to the think tank world, my heart is still very much with the academy. I know what higher education has done for me and I know as well what it can do for others. It is with that spirit in mind that this book is offered to the prospective reader.

—HIL

Introduction

In the interest of full disclosure, I entered Columbia College in 1956 as a largely uninterested student. While I was in the top 5 percent of my high school graduating class, academic work was something I was obliged to do, not something that I really wanted to do. I had one overarching interest: playing big time basketball.

It may seem odd by contemporary standards, but in the fifties the Ivy League produced several great players. But something strange, indeed intoxicating, happened at Columbia that altered my worldview. Yes, I did play on the basketball team. But gradually, inexorably I fell in love with ideas.

Where this started is somewhat hard to say. It may have been the "C.C. Hum" (Contemporary Civilization-Humanities) sequence of required readings—what I have called Columbia's great books program. Or perhaps it was Bill Casey's remarkable analysis of social theory (not to be confused with the Bill Casey who worked for the CIA). Or maybe it was history courses with Professor Metzger and Shenton. All I know is that by the time I graduated I was filled with desire to read every book in Butler Library from Aristotle to Zoroastrianism.

My thoughts moved from the hardwood to dusty stacks. This journey also included a deep appreciation for the cultivation of the mind that went beyond reading; it incorporated thought into the free and open exchange of opinion, into the uncharted terrain of positions I hadn't heard and wanted eagerly to explore.

Columbia at the time had a deep commitment to liberal opinion. Father and son Van Doren (Mark and Charles), the recently appointed Dan Bell, my adviser named Sam Huntington, the legendary Lionel Trilling, and a brilliant lecturer named Amatai

1

Etzioni graced the campus and, more or less, leaned left at the time, albeit over the years several had their political orientation change. Yet there was one constant: These professors eschewed orthodoxies, notwithstanding the fact that in a poll of faculty members Adlai Stevenson won the 1956 presidential sweepstakes hands down.

Different views were welcome. Controversy was invited. "Political correctness" had not yet entered the academic vocabulary, nor had it insinuated itself into debate and chastened nonconformists. I was intoxicated by the sheer variety of thought. For me this smorgasbord of ideas had delectable morsels at each setting. It was at some moment in my senior year that I became enchanted with the idea of an academic career.

The one thing that mystified me was the artificial constraint of disciplinary study. After all, C.C. was history, philosophy, religion, social thought, and psychology. Why weren't all courses multidisciplinary, perhaps even integrated? Was Montesquieu a political theorist, a social commentator, a jurist? Could Homer only be thought of as an epic poet? Was Shakespeare simply a playwright? I was struck by the arbitrary boundaries of disciplines and began to daydream about a university unfettered from what I considered disciplinary restraints.

The subsequent years seemed to fly by. I was awarded a PhD, received a Fulbright to study in Australia, wrote my first book about the liberalization of the "white Australia policy," and, *mirabile dictu*, was offered an appointment at NYU—the same institution that conferred my advanced degree.

I taught with fervor, eager to impress my students and fully cognizant of my Columbia College experience. My goal was to unlock the secrets of knowledge, to excite and hopefully inspire. What I didn't appreciate was the *zeitgeist*. The Vietnam War and the draft elicited an impatience with contemplative analysis. This generation of students wanted action; they were intent on winning an ideological war of their own creation. These students I soon learned were the acolytes of Antonio Gramsci eager to transform the university of learning into the launching pad for social transformation.

One day as I passed Waverly Place on my way to a class I noticed graffito on a wall that captured the spirit of that time and opened my eyes to a new and, from my point of view, degraded academy. It read "Make them teach you only what you want to learn." These it was; the naïve had taken command of the center of learning. I was part of "them" and felt as if I had been transported into Thomas Mann's *Magic Mountain.*

Most of my students didn't want to read. In this new age, they simply wanted to express themselves. Each spring from 1967 to 1973 brought blossoms to Washington Square Park, the start of the baseball season, and demonstrations. Classes were invariably suspended and bacchanalia was in season. I grew despondent about my chosen profession.

At a commencement exercise in 1970 the president of the university delivered an address in which he said, "Seated before you is a graduating class endowed with the talent and knowledge to solve the problems of war and peace, urban woe, income disparity, and third world deprivation." I sat there with a smirk on my face.

As I left the exercise, I ran headlong into the president and couldn't resist blurting out, "you mean to say that these students are prepared to solve the problems you listed when you can't be sure they've even read a serious book?" "What are you getting at?" he inquired. I made it abundantly clear that these students were not prepared to balance a checkbook much less deal with the platitudinous goals outlined in the speech.

To his credit, he said, "What would you do to address this matter?" Needless to say, I was baffled by the question, but the conversation led to my appointment on a newly created Commission on Undergraduate Education. It was on that body that I devised a plan to create a new "experimental" college devoted to the study of great books and removing the barriers that militated against cross-college enrollment. Why, I asked, shouldn't an undergraduate take a law school course if he meets the criteria for admission?

The key to winning acceptance for this college was to call it experimental. To some degree, it was since cross-school enrollment was limited by financial concerns. But the curriculum of eighty-seven great books including the Bible, Plato, Aristotle,

Dante, Aeschylus, Euripides, Shakespeare, Tolstoy, Marx, Dostoyevsky, Freud, etc. are hardly readings one would describe as experimental.

But as I noted at the time, when commencement rolls around I'll be able to tell the president my students have read serious books even if I cannot be sure they'll solve the problem of urban woe.

Now the question that arose was even if my plan made sense, would the faculty council approve it. I received a call from the chairman of this body, Sidney Hook, the eminent philosopher, who gave me the time and place of the hearing.

Professor Hook arrived with five colleagues, but he proceeded to ask the first question. "Tell me Professor London, can you name a great man who attended an external degree program?" By my lights, this was a most peculiar question. It was obvious that Professor Hook misunderstood my proposal. I had no intention of inaugurating an external degree program. Moreover, at that moment I couldn't think of a great person who graduated from a conventional degree program. But as I hastily rummaged through the rolodex in my mind, I remembered that Lenin attended the University of Moscow Extension Division.

With that in mind, I said if I can change the words "great man" to "influential man," I have an answer for you. Hooked nodded and I blurted out Lenin. A strange look crossed his face. "How did you know that?" he inquired. When I provided a source for my reply, Professor Hook noted that further questions were unnecessary. He spoke for the council and said the program is approved. Thus was born a new division at the university based on a path I had anticipated years earlier at Columbia.

Deciding what to call this entity wasn't easy. As fate would have it, I was browsing in the library stacks when I came upon the papers of Albert Gallatin, Jefferson's Secretary of the Treasury and coincidentally founder of NYU. At the time of founding, Gallatin was asked why New York needed another college. After all, Kings College (later Columbia) was in place uptown. Gallatin noted that Kings College was organized for the children of clergymen; he was intent on creating a college for the children of New York's emerging merchant class.

Well, said one trustee, if the students at Kings College are obliged to study Greek and Latin, what will students at this new college study. Gallatin thought for an extended moment as a colleague shouted out, "English." Upon hearing that, Gallatin the Swiss born, but true patriot said, "no in my college students will study 'American.'" The college, my college, now had a name, "The Gallatin School."

Based on my instincts and background, the curriculum was easily determined. At first, I offered seminars on the Bible and Plato. But, in time, I hired faculty members from other colleges. In fact, I "cherry picked," lining up those colleagues I most admired and "buying," in effect, a portion of their time.

To my astonishment the 55 students who joined the program escalated in number to 130 in the second year and, for the first time, I felt confident this school would meet its financial goals.

This newly constituted "experimental" college was considered the progeny of the early 1970s *zeitgeist*. In reality, it was a throwback, an assertion of Newman's definition of a classical college. However, I went along with the misleading claims. On several occasions I was invited to address the so-called higher education experimental consortium, a group of colleges devoted to innovative approaches.

After several of these meetings all that I could attest to is the loonyness that accompanied higher education innovation. On one occasion I was encouraged to push "energy balls" across the Roger Williams College campus. At another meeting I was chastised for insisting that students read the work of dead, white, European males. I responded by noting I would happy to assign alive, black, Zulu, female authors if appropriate great books can be identified. This didn't go over so well with my new found colleagues.

As a consequence of founding a college, I was given the status of dean, a title, I soon learned, that means very little except that the dean is a metaphorical hydrant on whom those above and those below choose to urinate.

However, decanal status offered two privileges: attendance at university senate meetings and participation in the deans' council. Both of these privileges were transmogrified into headaches. The deans met weekly with the university president. While I assumed educational priorities would be discussed, the primary focus was financial. One meeting after another was devoted to this matter. Feeling thoroughly frustrated, I finally spoke up asking if we would ever discuss educational issues. The president replied: "Any other questions or comments?"

I got the message. When I mentioned my frustration to a seasoned colleague who had attended these meetings for years, he said, "I love the Deans' Council; since virtually nothing is at stake, it is the only time during my busy week when I can daydream."

Senate meetings weren't much better. Each one seemed to confirm the Kissingerian view that expression was exaggerated because so little was at stake. When an important issue did emerge, such as divestment of the university's assets in South Africa, left wing opinion was mobilized and contrary views given short shrift.

It became apparent by the 1980s that Gramschiites had come to dominate university life—hiring and tenure decisions were meant to exclude those skeptical of the campus orthodoxy. I remained devoted to my students and committed to the college I helped to create, but the signs of change in a most unwelcome direction produced dismay.

In the mid-1980s I spent interesting meetings with three resourceful professors, Peter Shaw, who taught at the State University of New York at Stony Brook; Steve Balch who had an appointment at John Jay College; and Barry Gross, who was teaching at York College. We shared a common concern about developments in higher education and agreed that a new organization was needed, one that would promote the free and open exchange of opinion in the academy. Initially we called it the Campus Coalition for Democracy, but in time this title with activist implications was changed to the National Association of Scholars. Steve Balch became its president and I was named chairman and editor of its publication, *Academic Questions*.

Since our goal transcended political matters, even though detractors didn't believe that contention, we attracted to our membership C. Vann Woodward, former president of the ADA, and Sidney Hook, self-proclaimed socialist and, yes, the same person who was chairman of the faculty council at NYU. In time, of course, an academic public came to believe we were intent on imposing our conservative principles on an unwary professoriate. This was and is a grotesque description of our goals, but it persists.

My personal fortunes also changed. In the late 1980s and the early 1990s, I pursued a role in politics running first for Mayor of New York City in 1989, Governor of New York State in 1990, and Comptroller of New York in 1994. After my gubernatorial run, I retired as dean and assumed the John M. Olin Humanities Chair at the university. Due to the beneficence of the Olin Foundation, I was able to maintain a university affiliation and still pursue my political ambitions.

What I didn't understand at the time is the John O'Sullivan Law of institutions: "Those that are not avowedly traditional and guarded as such, will soon be radical." One successor as dean maintained that "great books" is an ambiguous phrase that does not take into account the extraordinary contributions of minorities. The great books list I assembled was soon transformed into an affirmative action list. At a meeting with a *New York Times* reporter she noted, "It is more important for students to read Toni Morrison than William Shakespeare." I couldn't believe what my ears had heard. Soon after this episode, I wrote a letter to the president asking him to remove my portrait from the college since I no longer wanted to be associated with the school to which I gave birth.

For me the capture of the institution was complete. From Duke to Berkeley and the many stops along the way, university life was transformed. An ethos of radical sentiment was ensconced. So complete was the victory that university professors hardly noticed. It was simply assumed this state of affairs was the norm. What was once leftist became conventional. Political correctness was correct in the sense that it was a view consistent with the prevailing sentiment on campus and correct in the sense that it was normal, what was in the ideological air one breathes at the university.

In my almost forty-year involvement in higher education I witnessed the complete transformation of the academic enterprise, from my inspired Columbia experience to my dismay with politicization. It was hardly surprising that when asked by reporters why

I would leave university life for political office, I responded as Woodrow Wilson did when he left Princeton to run for governor of New Jersey: "I wanted to get out of politics."

The articles in this book follow not only my personal evolution, but the evolution of the university from the 1960s to 1990s. At one point, the dismay I mentioned led me to the conclusion that the death of the university may not be far off. That claim seems exaggerated, but surely the dramatic transformation of the academy cannot be denied and the perversion of the soft sciences and humanities into forms of relativism and solipsism has moved with alacrity in this four-decade period.

Clearly, the reader will have to determine whether the many articles in this book constitute a valid critique of university life or are merely a personal *cri de coeur*. But as I see it, these musings describe much about the transformation and the present state of affairs in the halls of ivy.

1

The Tenured Left*

with Stephen H. Balch

Like ionized particles transiting a cloud chamber, two quite different campus projects involving tiny fractions of the collegiate population have recently succeeded in precipitating reactions of surprising scope and visibility. While the resulting trails move in very different directions, their vectors reveal much about the dubious atmosphere of American higher education in the 1980s.

The first of these two passages has been that of the divestiture movement, with its demand for the liquidation of university investments in firms with holdings in South Africa. An effort under way for several years, the movement accelerated greatly with the spreading violence in South Africa during 1985. At one level it sought to free the academy of any taint of involvement with apartheid; at another, to intensify economic pressures on the Pretoria government; and at a third, to further that government's progressive delegitimization. Finally, many of its organizers, through an exercise in guerrilla theater, hoped to recover some measure of that radical consciousness that prevailed on campuses during the late 1960s.

*This chapter originally appeared in 1986 as an article in *Commentary*. It set the stage for the counter attack on the radicalization of the academy. Steve Balch, co-author of this piece, became president of the National Association of Scholars and offered extraordinary leadership for a group of academics who believe fervently in the free and open exchange of opinion on campus.

In a variety of ways the divestiture movement is a classic embodiment of the ethos of campus protest born during that decade. For one thing, it assumes that students (or at least an activist fringe) are equipped with the moral and political perception necessary to judge the policies of the institutions entrusted with their education. For another, it understands the imperatives of its cause as conferring a license willfully to disregard university regulations, to seize or obstruct university property, and to be sharply uncivil toward university officials offering resistance. The tactics of the movement have in fact created confrontations and threats of disorder not experienced on most American campuses since the Vietnam War.

Though it might wish to disavow the honor, Accuracy in Academia (AIA), the second recent campus "movement," also bears the stamp of the 1960s in its assumptions and *modus operandi*. Fathered by Reed Irvine at the beginning of the 1985 fall semester as a counterpart to Accuracy in Media, Accuracy in Academia is essentially a "Naderite" enterprise with a conservative twist. Instead of criticizing the corporate world for deceptive advertising, and shoddy merchandise, it levels similar charges at the intellectual products of the academy, which it sees as tainted by a tendentious radicalism. Its informants are not dissatisfied automobile owners or disgruntled nuclear engineers but unhappy academic consumers (that is to say, students).

In both its virtues and shortcomings, Accuracy in Academia has much in common with other contemporary ventures in grassroots muckraking. Among its virtues is a flare for instant controversy, designed to draw attention to the chosen target; among its shortcomings, a certain surreptitiousness invariably associated with "whistle-blowing" enterprises. But whatever may be said of its tact, the efforts of Accuracy in Academia, unlike those of the divestiture campaign, have been wholly confined to the realm of public criticism, neither fomenting disruption, nor toying with the possibilities of violent confrontation, nor obliging university administrators or faculty members to adopt an institutional stand.

In light of this rather fundamental difference, the response of the educational establishment to each of these two projects might strike an observer unfamiliar with the vagaries of academic life as somewhat surprising. For while the divestiture protests have often encountered an embarrassed resistance on the part of presidents and trustees worried about the value of institutional portfolios, or doubtful about the most effective way of combating apartheid, almost nowhere have they been seen (for the record, at least) as seriously threatening those norms of reasoned discourse, or that climate of intellectual tolerance so often cited as constituting the university's special claim to grace. Quite the contrary: on campus after campus they have been accorded the indulgence reserved for activities whose transcendent moral status immunizes them against the ordinary quibbles of law.

Thus, at Harvard, eleven students who conducted an all-day sit-in at the offices of the university's board of governors received only a "formal admonition," the mildest penalty possible and one mitigated still further by a statement complimenting the students for having maintained a "constructive level of civility." (Another group of Harvard students, who had physically blockaded a South African diplomat on his way to address a conservative campus group, had their more severe penalties suspended.) At Cornell, the university dropped charges pending as a result of 1,200 arrests between April and December 1985, on the ostensible ground that the installation of a new disciplinary code required that the old slate be swept clean. At Yale, a decision to remove demonstrators blocking campus buildings produced an anguished petition signed by 156 faculty members deploring the university's "use of force." This was shortly followed by a ruling from a faculty disciplinary committee, slapping the defendants on the wrist and allowing the reconstruction of their shanties.

By contrast, there has been very little uncertainty about the menace to the climate of freedom posed by Accuracy in Academia, and no hesitancy at all in denouncing it in the strongest possible terms. The Committee on Academic Freedom and Tenure of the American Association of University Professors (AAUP), for example, predicted that "the proposed program of AIA, if undertaken and accepted seriously [would] lead toward the deadening of discourse and the stultification of learning." Dr. Bruce Mason, chairman of the faculty senate of Arizona State University (one of whose professors had been an early object of AIA criticism); declared that the organization had "poisoned the faculty student relationship," making "students' innocent questions" seem like "devious attempts to make trouble." Chancellor Joseph S. Murphy of the City University of New York likened AIA's methods to those of a "corps of thought police," and characterized the group as posing a "grave menace to the free exchange of ideas." And falling back on the inevitable comparison, Dr. John W. Chandler, president of the Association of American Colleges, opined that while "two generations of college professors [had] escaped the battles of McCarthyism," the academy would now have to "gird [itself] to resist another round."

Perhaps the greatest irony in the reaction to AIA has to do with the strong defense it has provoked of established procedures of university self-governance. Such a defense stood at the center of a statement issued by the AAUP and eight other higher education associations in November 1985, intended to constitute their definitive rejoinder to AIA. "We believe," the statement ran, that "the quality of academic performance is best judged through peer evaluation by skilled professionals. Chief executive officers and governing boards are responsible for ensuring both accountability and academic integrity while safeguarding the university from undue outside influence. We encourage colleges and universities to resist this assault on institutional integrity by reaffirming established practices for insuring professional responsibility and academic freedom...." Brave words, no doubt, but one may wonder where this determination to protect the prerogatives of "executive officers and governing boards" and to resist assaults on "institutional integrity" fled when it came to dealing with the disruption and intimidation practiced by proponents of divestiture.

The disparity in the reception accorded anti-apartheid demonstrators and the minions of AIA has much less to do with the respective threat each poses to the life of the academic mind than with that mind's most seasoned prejudices. As an enterprise of the Left, the divestiture movement is guaranteed the automatic sympathy of the vast majority of politically conscious faculty and administrators. As an organization of self-confessed conservatives, AIA provokes the instant wrath of this very same group. To be sure, a decent case can be made for the goals, and against the methods, of each of these ventures, but with some honorable exceptions (largely among conservative intellectuals outside the academy) few observers have seemed able to get beyond a fixation on ideological provenance.

The moral of this tale is not that the academy is a bastion of liberalism, a fact which most would take to be indisputable, but that the liberalism of the academy, like much of that beyond its walls, is now hard pressed to recognize its own principles, and even less capable of defending them when they come under attack from the Left. "No enemies on the Left," once the rallying cry of the Popular Front, has become a veritable shibboleth for the majority of the American professoriate, at least when dealing with campus radicalism.

As a pervasive intellectual reflex, this attitude is between twenty and thirty years old. Its origins may be found in the backlash against McCarthyism, its consolidation in the "cultural revolution" of the 1960s. Historically, the development of this reflex coincided with an era of unprecedented institutional expansion within the world of higher education, in which the number of jobs, and the influence of the university on American life, greatly increased. This conjunction created a peculiar opportunity for American radicalism, partially compensating for its failure to establish any sizable foothold within the general population. Deprived of a strong institutional base among elected officials or in the labor movement comparable to that of radical movements elsewhere, the Left in America sought sanctuary in the academy. Given the skewed sensibilities of its liberal guardians, and given, too, the intellectual proclivities and gentrified tastes of many 1960s radicals, the academy provided a safe, even pleasant, haven for ideological rest, recuperation, and regrouping.

Thus it has come about that, despite the sincere desire of most university people to see themselves as exemplars of democratic idealism, the American campus is now the nesting place for a significant population of political extremists. Indeed, with the waning of the more traditional forms of racist and nativist ideologies, the campus has probably become American extremism's principal address.

It is difficult to measure with precision the magnitude of the radical presence within the academy, though enough data exist to allow estimates. In 1984, for example, the Carnegie Foundation for the Advancement of Teaching conducted a survey of the entire professoriate, sampling 5,000 faculty members at 310 2-year, 4-year, and graduate institutions. Respondents were asked to choose which of five labels best described their political orientation, with designations ranging from "Left," "liberal," and "middle-of,-the-road", to "moderately conservative" and "conservative." Reading from "Left" to the aggregated results disclosed percentages of 5.8, 33.8, 26.6, 29.6, and 4.2 in each of the categories. If "Left" is taken as a synonym for "radical," then the first percentage would translate into something in the neighborhood of 35,000 radical faculty, out of a total academic population thought to number about 600,000. (The inevitable rejoinder that the 5.8 percent on the "Left" is almost balanced by the 4.2 percent calling themselves "strongly conservative" will impress only those who equate the outlook of Herbert Stein with Herbert Marcuse.) As with most similar polls, the Carnegie study found the proportion of leftist faculty to be higher at institutions of greater prestige and influence. Thus, while only 3.9 percent at 2-year colleges designated themselves as on the "Left," the figure rose to 6.3 percent for faculty at "research universities," and to 6.7 percent for those at 4-year liberal arts colleges.

The Carnegie survey covers all segments of the professoriate, including faculties teaching in business and professional programs, mathematics and the natural sciences, physical education, home economics, and other fields generally distant from political controversy. When consideration is limited only to those disciplines that set out to analyze and evaluate social and political phenomena, even the semblance of ideological balance vanishes. Needless to say, the largest bloc of academics within nearly all these disciplines describe themselves as "liberal" rather than "leftist," but with the exception of economics, every field within the humanities and social sciences contains a substantial cohort of radicals, dwarfing anything found at the opposite end of the scale. For example, among the philosophy faculty surveyed at 4-year institutions, a full 21.7 percent designated themselves as "Left" and none at all as "strongly conservative"; for the sociologists, the percentages were 37.0 percent versus 0.9 percent; for the political scientists, 19.8 percent to 4.8 percent; for the historians, 12.8 percent to 3.0 percent; and for professors of English literature, 10.2 percent to 2.4 percent.

Except among sociologists, where the Left has grown substantially, these patterns have remained fairly constant since the late 1960s. What has changed decidedly over the last two decades is the extent to which leftist radicalism has managed to institutionalize itself within the academic world. Whereas twenty years ago the campus Left was largely confined to registering its presence through vocal demonstrations and protest, today it is more comfortably ensconced within a network of journals and professional organizations, university departments and academic programs.

Take journals, for example. Before the 1960s one would have been hard pressed to find more than two or three leftist journals with any claim to scholarly standing. Since then, over thirty such journals have appeared (a few to fall by the wayside) in areas as diverse as anthropology *(Dialectical Anthropology),* art criticism *(Praxis),* criminology *(Crime and Social Justice),* economics *(Review of Radical Economics),* geography *(Antipode),* history *(Radical History Review),* and literary criticism *(Diacritics).* And one could easily add to these about a dozen feminist journals (most operating out of a specific discipline) that share the same insurgent perspective.

The journals vary a good deal in style, intellectual quality, and activist commitment, from the sedate, almost antiquarian *New German Critique,* which devotes considerable space to publishing the translated texts of deceased theorists of the Frankfurt School, through more gritty and polemical publications like *New Political Science,* with its topical preoccupations and discussions of movement strategy, to such outlandish periodicals as *Trivia,* a feminist "journal of ideas" whose overall tone of lesbian mysticism is best conveyed in the explanation of its title, a derivation of "*trivium* (crossroads),...one of the names of the Triple Goddess..." describing "the matrix of our creative power, the gathering of wise women in which our ideas originate and continue to live."

Were it not that they are accompanied by a measure of academic respectability, the mere existence of these journals would mean little. None has become a major organ in its discipline, but many have achieved respectable circulations and, symbolically more important, institutional affiliation and support. *Praxis,* for example, is published with the assistance of the College of Fine Arts, the Graduate Student Association, the Division of Graduate Studies, and the College of Letters and Sciences of UCLA. The *Insurgent Sociologist* is produced by an "editorial collective" housed in the department of sociology of the University of Oregon. *Trivia* has been regularly funded from the proceeds of a feminist lecture series co-sponsored by the Women's Resource Center at Smith College. (The Winter 1986 issue, which features articles on lesbian economics, the spiritual legacy of the ancient Amazons, and the five-billion-year long racial memory of womankind, broke with this pattern of feminist support. It was subsidized by a grant from the National Endowment for the Arts.)

These journals play an important role in facilitating communication and maintaining a fortifying sense of intellectual community among the constituencies they serve. But anyone familiar with the nature of contemporary college life will also quickly recognize their practical significance in sustaining the careers of radical professors. In the increasingly bureaucratized process by which academic personnel decisions are made, tenure or promotion frequently turns on rather crude and readily quantifiable measures of achievement. Paramount among these are the number of a candidate's scholarly publications, with each citation representing another point on the scoreboard. By providing respectable scholarly venues for articles too pointedly political, or fantastic, for most mainstream publications, the radical journals help contributors to advance their careers without abandoning their activist vocations.

This is not to say that articles of a radical bent find any particular difficulty getting into mainstream publications. Marxist and feminist scholarship is quite commonplace in most established journals, particularly in fields like sociology, anthropology, and history. Of course, some of these articles, despite their ideological orientation, have real merit and deserve publication. Nonetheless, occasions arise that call into question the capacity of mainstream academics to maintain even an elementary standard of critical judgment when evaluating the work of the Left.

A case in point is the lead article in the December 1985 issue of the *American Sociological Review,* the official journal of the American Sociological Association. Entitled "Mythologies of Work: A Comparison of Firms in State Socialism and Advanced Capitalism," the article seeks to assess the reliability of eight widely-held Western "stereotypes" concerning the relative inefficiency of firms in socialist economies. The method employed is that of the case study, in which the researchers immerse themselves in the lives of two comparable manufacturing firms, one in the United States and one in Hungary, and then describe their impressions.

The result, as it turns out, stands in sharp contradiction to the conventional wisdom. Whether one is looking at the motivational level of the workforce, the capacity for innovation, the influence of workers in organizing production, the degree of bureaucratic rigidity, or at any of the other operational characteristics analyzed, the Hungarian firm emerges as at least the equal, and often the superior, of the American one. This finding leads the investigators to conclude that a socialist firm can indeed be more efficient than a capitalist one, provided it is shielded from direct state control by an intervening level of corporate structure. They also take pains to indicate that it is just in this direction that the Hungarian economy has recently been evolving.

Food for thought, certainly, and all the more so since the premier publication in sociology attests to the authors' credentials. But who are they? One is Michael Burawoy, a widely published Marxist sociologist from the University of California at Berkeley, and, parenthetically, an associate editor of the review. Nothing indefensible here: everyone has biases, and it is appropriate for academic editors to credit a scholar of established reputation with the ability to keep his under control, assuming he is in a position to do so. Unfortunately, however, not all the world's social scientists are in this position. One who may well not be is Burawoy's collaborator, János Lukács, research fellow of the Institute of Sociology, Hungarian Academy of Sciences, and the person largely responsible for the case study of the socialist firm.

Now, the credibility of any piece of purportedly scientific research requires that the investigator be free either to substantiate or to falsify the hypotheses he is exploring, as the evidence dictates. Therefore, to accept "Mythologies of Work" as a serious scientific study, the editors of the *American Sociological Review* had to believe that a Hungarian academician could put his name to a study of a Hungarian firm, for publication in a prestigious foreign journal, which would *confirm* eight negative Western stereotypes about the efficiency of socialism. To say the least, this is rather doubtful. Ironically, in recent years the social sciences have experienced several acrimonious controversies about the extent to which the sponsorship of research by agencies of the American government taints the work of those who participate in it, or damages the reputation of entire disciplines. Judging from "Mythologies of Work," involvement with a Communist regime may not be as troubling.

Max Weber once wrote that the teacher "will beware of imposing from the platform any political positions upon the student, whether it is expressed or suggested....[T]he prophet and the demagogue do not belong on the academic platform." While this caution may be honored more in the breach than in the practice, it expresses the standard by which most professors would be willing to be judged. What distinguishes the majority of radical academics from their colleagues is the view that scholarship and teaching are preeminently, and unavoidably, extensions of politics. For the most extreme, the distinction between teaching and indoctrination altogether evaporates.

When pressed as to whether the purpose of his teaching is to convert students to socialism, Bertell Ollman, the doyen of Marxist scholars at New York University, answers that "a correct understanding of Marxism (or any body of scientific truth) leads automatically to its acceptance." (One wonders about the fate of the dull or intransigent student who cannot grasp the "scientific truth.") Michael Parenti, a Marxist political scientist at Brooklyn College, and a former fellow of the Institute for Policy Studies, defines the mission of the radical academic even more baldly. "Our job in academia," he states, "is not only to reach out to working people but also to remind our students that they're workers...that their struggle is also a labor struggle, [and] that labor struggle is the most profound democratic struggle in our society."[1]

Such statements imply that the university, and the values traditionally associated with it, are regarded as adversaries, albeit adversaries that provide the radical academic with influence, status, and income. And so, to the question, "What does Marxism have to offer the bourgeois university?" Harvard biologist Richard Lewontin replies, in a paper published in *New Political Science*, "preferably, nothing." He explains:

> That is, Marxism can do nothing *for* the university; the real question is what can Marxists do *to* and *in* the university....For the natural and social scientist the answer is very clear. The university is a factory that makes weapons—ideological weapons—for class struggle, for class warfare, and trains people in their use. It has no other leading and important function in the social organization. [Emphasis in original.]

Lewontin specifies three separate ways in which the expertise and academic status of the revolutionary scholar can be used: first, "to demystify and destroy the obfuscation which is part of the ruling-class ideological weaponry"; second, "to create weapons that can be used on our side"; third, to bring about the "delegitimation of the authority of bourgeois ideologues," an activity that must involve "writing, speaking on radio, on television, in schools, in newspapers and magazines." Finally, Lewontin observes, the Marxist professor must create in his workplace "a situation that intensifies contradiction,...that intensifies the class struggle, and... must engage in revolutionizing practice in the day-to-day relations on the job."

Recognizing that present circumstances are not those most propitious for overt revolutionary struggle, many radical academics see their function as laying the intellectual groundwork for that time when, in the words of Frederic Jameson (then a professor of French literature at Yale), "merely abstract doctrine will come back into [students'] minds as a solution to urgent problems." Jameson continues:

> At that point, retrospectively, the things we all taught them, in apparently imperceptible accretions that left no trace, will come back and be activated for the first time. That is, it seems to me, no negligible function for us to play, even if it offers very little immediate personal satisfaction. But I think I have to give an even broader historical characterization of the moment in which American Marxists find themselves and in which our pedagogical work takes its significance. Lenin said that the two necessary [but not sufficient] preconditions for social revolution are a class-conscious proletariat and a revolutionary intelligentsia. If, as intellectuals, we can necessarily play only a marginal role in the development of the former, the task of creating the latter is clearly our fundamental one. To create a Marxist culture in this country, to make Marxism an unavoidable presence and a distinct, original, and unmistakable voice in American social, cultural, and intellectual life, in short to form a Marxist intelligentsia for the struggles of the future-this seems to me the supreme mission of a Marxist pedagogy and a radical intellectual life today.

While these Marxist professors do not dominate opinion in their disciplines, it would be a mistake to underestimate their influence or the influence of Marxist studies. According to Bertell Ollman and Edivard Vernoff, the editors of *The Left Academy* (1983), four Marxist-inspired textbooks in American government were published between 1970 and 1982. Before this period there were none. During the same period three of the most prestigious university publishers, Cambridge, Oxford, and Princeton, issued books on Marx and Marxism, "almost all of them quite sympathetic." Whereas in the 1960s only a handful of courses in Marxist philosophy were being taught, today there are well over 400 such courses offered on American campuses.

When Secretary of Education William J. Bennett recently expressed the belief that "a significant body of opinion" has developed on college campuses, which "openly rejects the democratic ethic," his comment was greeted with mocking skepticism. One academic, John Chandler, replied that "The situation [Bennett] describes was a much more pronounced problem in the late 60's and early 70's than it is today." Chandler was thinking of revolutionary displays by students. What he ignored was the extent to which the practitioners of academic agitprop have vacated the quadrangles for more decorous and strategic roosts behind the lectern. In this sense, Secretary Bennett's concern over radicals at war with society is more pertinent now than it would have been in the turbulent 60s.

The decentralized character of academic governance offers numerous opportunities for faculty intent on politicizing teaching and scholarship. What goes on in the classroom is almost totally under the control of the professor in charge. Faculty members with a special sense of intellectual purpose can usually have a disproportionate impact on course and program development. Even the policies of professional academic associations can be strongly influenced by determined and organized minorities. Consequently, in many institutions, while radicals have not become the dominant force, they have made a deeper mark than their numbers alone would suggest. Their principal effect has been to introduce into academic life a shrill and persistent tendentiousness that frequently succeeds in structuring the agenda of academic discourse while simultaneously cheapening it.

One measure of this effect is the increase in the number of one-sided, question-begging, or highly partisan course descriptions now to be found in college catalogues. Take, for instance, the description of *Black Studies* 145: *Capitalism and Colonialism in Contemporary America* found in the catalogue of the City College of New York:

> White America is described as capitalist and colonialist. Efforts will be made to comprehend the relative importance of the two phenomena for strategies of liberation depending upon who and what is the American and America.

Or take the following account of *Economics 380a. Comparative Economic Systems: The Third World* drawn from the Vassar College catalogue:

> The course will compare capitalism and socialism as alternative strategies of development of Third World countries. The first part of the course will address the central theoretical issues in the literature on the possibilities of capitalist development, socialist development, and autarky. In the second part, we will discuss how different socialist countries in the Third World have dealt with a variety of problems, including government ownership of productive enterprises, agrarian transformations, technological development, population growth, and the status of women. Depending on student interest the course will cover the following countries: China, Cuba, Nicaragua, Chile under Allende, Jamaica under Manley, Tanzania, Angola, Zimbabwe, North Korea, and Cambodia.

Lest it be thought that these examples are uniquely egregious, one might contemplate the lecture series, "America After 1984," organized last year at Bard College by Stanley Diamond, then the occupant of its Alger Hiss Chair in Culture, Society, and the Humanities. Topics in this series have included: "The Underside of Justice in the United States"; "American Cultural Imperialism"; "Anti-Communism in America: Its History and Functions"; "The Origins and Continuity of the American Crisis: A Native American View"; "Radical Ecologists: The Environmental Crisis Heats Up"; "The Gathering Crisis in Public Education"; "Private Education in Crisis"; "The Media Crisis in America"; and "Race and Gender in America."

At the University of Massachusetts in Boston, a Marxist Studies program offers twenty-six courses, including "Food: Politics and Policy," about which the catalogue states, *inter alia:* "[T]he development of a world network of food trade, aid, and finance has created a world food system in which the U.S.'s farm policies, and federal deficits and bank interest rates, fundamentally affect whether Indian farmers will grow more wheat or African peasants will starve."

Descriptions like these tend to parody themselves. More commonplace is the gratuitous introduction of political material into conventionally designed courses—or, worse yet, the use of the vocabulary and apparatus of scholarship to mask an appropriation of a broad swath of the curriculum by a political movement.

The rapid growth of black studies programs in the late 60s and early 70s was the first manifestation of this phenomenon. The essentially political character of black studies, which was regarded by its champions as a means of consciousness raising and by most college administrators as a way of avoiding trouble, has always been an open secret on the campus. While black studies seems to have undergone a contraction from its heyday in the 70s, it is still represented by some 350 college programs, including 141 leading to a baccalaureate, and it is imitated by smaller clusters of programs in areas like Chicano and "Native American" Studies.

Women's studies comprised the second wave, sweeping through the already breached ramparts of academic integrity. As Michael

Levin has written, "At a time when black militants were developing black studies, it was possible for other groups to demand a 'study' of their own on grounds of equality....The women's-studies courses introduced during the 1960's and 1970's did not originate in significant discoveries as did courses in molecular biology or the 'higher criticism' of biblical texts....Nor did women's studies undergo the scrutiny that normally attends even the most modest academic innovation. The very speed with which these courses proliferated suggests that they were perceived as entitled" by historical and political necessity, to a place in academe." As of 1984, there were 476 women's studies programs, of which 125 led to baccalaureates, and the number continues to grow.

The latest variation on this theme has been the rapid diffusion of "peace studies" programs, which at last count had a place in the curriculum at well over 200 institutions of higher learning. The emotionally loaded and propagandistic qualities of similar programs at the primary and secondary school level have already been explored in the pages of *Commentary*[2]; needless to say, they are often duplicated at the college level. What has received less attention is that in many of these college programs, the study of conflict is but the camel's nose of a comprehensive effort at radical indoctrination justified by the purported power of sweeping social change to eliminate the scourge of war. What is more, many of the leaders in this "field" do not view their programs as merely one more academic major but as the kernel of a new type of professional school, designed to train and accredit new generations of movement activists.

The Peace and Social Justice Program established at Tufts University in 1983, and often referred to as a model for others, provides a case in point. Upon opening its bulletin one does, to be sure, encounter a few perfunctory nods toward the ideal of "open intellectual inquiry" and the need to avoid "predetermined ideological perspectives" when dealing with a subject that requires "considerable effort and reflection." But one has hardly read two pages before it becomes clear that peace-and-justice theorists have already made some remarkable scientific strides toward firm arid final conclusions. Indeed, within the space of a single paragraph they are able to lay to rest what might be regarded as the most intractable issue of their discipline, namely, the causes of war. Citing the best of all possible authorities, they confidently inform us that "history shows" that war arises from "greed, competition, and profit...[from] underdevelopment and economic deprivation, from institutional violence, from inequalities and powerlessness, and the denial of human rights...[as well as from] unchecked growth and resource depletion, particularly at the initiation of the developed world."

Perhaps the reason for so quickly stripping away the veil of mystery is to spare the curious student the inconvenience of paying any further attention to the program. Alas, no. Its sponsors wish not only to lure students in, but also to visit their desperately needed wisdom on those obdurately remaining without. In fact, as the faculty members describe their objectives, it becomes clear that the inauguration of a Peace and Social Justice Program is meant to be nothing less than the occasion for a reconsideration of the aims of higher education all across the curriculum. As they write:

> The university is not only well equipped to consider and solve human problems it has a historical imperative to do so. And few of its activities are as intrinsically important as pursuing the specific goals of peace and justice. That the traditions of liberal-arts education imply these objectives is, however, rarely discussed....For example, universities traditionally consider their major responsibility to be providing Information and theories about the world. We would further ask how our education can prepare students to *change* conditions in that world rather than merely accept it as it IS. Further, how can our education instill in students the desire to act, the antidotes for personal despair, and a sense of personal responsibility for improving our world?...If we desire peace we must teach peace and do it how. This will necessitate a new set of priorities and educational aims. [Emphasis in original.]

With such broad ambitions it is not surprising that the program's coordinators imagine themselves spending as much time lobbying colleagues as teaching students. They will seek to build a new sense of "purpose, cooperation, community, and social responsibility that will revitalize the university." Because the goals of peace and social justice require challenging "competitiveness and individualism" and promoting "cooperation and interdependence," this effort will necessarily focus on "personal as well as global change." More specifically, each department at Tufts is to be invited to develop several of the forty-five proposed courses (mostly culled from the catalogues of other universities) which the peace theorists consider necessary for their grand design. The engineering department, for instance, can offer "Appropriate Technology and Community Control"; mathematics, "The Ethics of Mathematic Modeling for Military Use"; American studies, "Racism and Sexism in American Society"; economics, "Introduction to Third World Poverty"; music, "Singing the Blues: Music and Social Injustice"; and so on. Yet even this will not suffice, for peace education should be integrated "as a process, and not merely as a discrete subject...throughout the curricula and into university life generally." Consequently "every Tufts professor" will be challenged "to interject, if they have not already done so, some peace and justice component into *all* their courses" (emphasis in the original). Finally, to ensure that the mind will never have a moment to wander, the whole campus is to be immersed in a swirl of films, conferences, lectures, seminars, and teach-ins, all sponsored by the program.

Here, then, is a plan for turning Tufts into a new, radical bastion of orthodoxy. Appropriately enough, there are also companion projects designed to use the program as an active center for the support of missionary training and proselytism. Thus, the program bills itself as providing skills "that will specifically attract a variety of governmental and non-governmental employers, including organizations in law, peace, education, human services and rights, dispute resolution, community development, international relations." Among its special features are an internship, bestowing college credit for student work with organizations in "broad areas of peace and justice, both on the local and global levels," and an "Alternative Careers Conference" fashioned to "stimulate further ideas for peace and justice careers." Departing from normal academic practice, the Peace and Social Justice Program also throws its core courses open to members of the general public, and conducts off-campus ventures which include "community training projects on peace, justice, and nonviolence."

Most peace-studies programs are not so hell bent on intellectual hegemony as the one at Tufts (though quite a few in women's studies could probably match it in this respect). Nor are most programs quite so intent on explicitly linking the pursuit of peace to the total realization of the Left's agenda. (Most leave the word "justice" out of their formal titles.) Nonetheless, the great majority share in its basic assumptions about the roots of war, the requirements of social justice, classroom advocacy, and the propriety of academic subsidies for political activism.

Scholarly associations, like universities, have usually been conceived of as forums for the exchange of ideas or debate on the merit of rival theories. Their ability to perform these intellectual services has been predicated on an understanding that as institutions they themselves take no position on the matters being discussed. Among those fields regarded as "sciences" there has been the further notion that knowledge is always tentative, subject to falsification through the acquisition of new evidence, and never to be cloaked in the garb of definitive pronouncements. As a result, within many academic associations an ongoing struggle has taken place between those committed to these liberal conceptions and those desirous of turning the organizations into platforms for agitation. It is one thing ideologically to capture a department, program, or even an entire college, but quite another to leave one's impress on a national association with many thousands of members. Still, politics is rich in examples of relatively small groups controlling large organizations by virtue of their energy, discipline, and sense of purpose. Accordingly, while some scholarly associations in the humanities and the social sciences have successfully defended their traditional roles, each has witnessed its struggles, and a few have been seriously compromised.

Almost invariably the attempts to politicize the associations have come from the Left. The size of the leftist component, its organizational base, and the nature of its efforts have, however, varied from discipline to discipline. In the case of economics, for instance, the Left is relatively small and somewhat intellectually isolated. On the other hand, it is fairly well organized, possessing its own association, the Union for Radical Political Economics, which operates both within and alongside the American Economic Association (AEA), and a journal, the *Review of Radical Political Economics,* which reaches an audience about one-tenth that of the *American Economic Review.* While the radical economists have managed to achieve a certain respectability, and have seen a few of their leading lights gain AEA office, their room for overt political maneuver has been comparatively limited. One factor in this is a provision in the AEA constitution, which forbids the association from taking positions on public issues. Nonetheless the union did manage a small breakthrough at the 1985 AEA business meeting by helping to push through a divestiture resolution over the opposition of the AEA executive committee.

Among political scientists the fortunes of the radicals, organized in the Caucus for a New Political Science, have waxed and waned. In 1972 when the Caucus still contained members of both the "soft" and "hard" Left, it missed by a hairsbreadth electing one of its leaders, Peter Bachrach, president of the American Political Science Association (APSA). Two years later, James MacGregor Burns, another of the Caucus's members, was elected president with the endorsement of the APSA nominating committee. Simultaneously, Caucus-endorsed candidates won nine out of the fourteen seats at stake on the APSA's governing council. These events, followed by an annual convention whose scholarly agenda was strongly colored by Marxism, prompted counter-organization on the part of centrist political scientists, and a split within the Caucus over the importance of winning APSA elections. The resulting victory of the Marxist faction of the Caucus led to a partial withdrawal from APSA politics, the launching of a journal, and a renewed emphasis on organizing local chapters, recruiting graduate students, and working with "community groups." At present the internal life of the APSA has something of a Center-Right tilt, despite the continued presence of a sizable radical cohort. In fact, prominent centrists or neoconservatives such as Seymour Martin Lipset and Aaron Wildavsky have recently served as APSA presidents.

A very different situation prevails among historians, sociologists, and anthropologists. The Organization of American Historians has elected several leftists to its presidency in recent years, including Eugene Genovese in 1978, William Appleman Williams in 1980, Gerda Lerner in 1981, and Leo Litwack in 1986. This year the American Historical Association elected its first woman president, Natalie Zemon Davis, editorial associate of *Radical*

History Review. Writing in the *Nation* (May 24), the historian Jon Wiener has approvingly described the growing gap between the political sensibilities of the Reagan era and the intellectual life of his field. Wiener reports that at the last meeting of the Organization of American Historians in April, "fourteen past and present officers drew up a petition opposing aid to the *contras.* The signers included the current president and two past presidents...." Straining to provide some scholarly justification for this naked excursion into politics, the petition pretended to deplore "President Reagan's distortion of history for political purposes in describing the Nicaraguan *contras,* whose systematic abuse of human rights has been documented by independent observers; as the 'moral equivalent' of the founding fathers..,."

Both the American Sociological Association (ASA) and the American Anthropological Association (AAA) also regularly elect radical scholars to top leadership posts, habitually endorse leftist political positions, and in a variety of other ways consistently display radicalized ideological sensibilities. Recent business meetings of the American Sociological Association, for example, have approved the passage of resolutions submitted by the association's Marxist section condemning American foreign policy and endorsing the "sanctuary" movement. Somewhat more officially, the ASA's elected council has, over the past several years, endorsed motions supporting "gay-rights" legislation, defending *Roe v. Wade,* and calling upon the United States government to respect the "civil liberties and sovereignty" of the people of Central America. (The council did manage briefly to break stride and condemn the "violations of academic rights" in the Soviet Union as well.) Worse yet was the decision in 1984 of the criminology section of the ASA to present its first Latin America Scholar Award to Vilma Nunez de Escoria, vice president of the Nicaraguan Supreme Court and a former member of the Sandinista National Liberation Front, who was then traveling through the United States on a speaking tour organized by a group named United States Out Of Central America. Following the awards presentation, which singled out her work in human rights, she was feted as a guest of honor at a reception hosted by then-ASA president, Kai Erikson.

Yet this pales in comparison with what can go on when anthropologists assemble in national convention. Then, in the words of one participant, "late at night, after the reactionaries [have gone] off exhausted," an atmosphere can develop that would be hard to duplicate at any major gathering in North America outside the bounds of Turtle Bay. A typical cascade of denunciation, the product of the December 5, 1982 meeting, included adoption of the following: a motion urging anthropologists not to undertake work for the CIA or the U.S. military, both described as supporting regimes "engaged in overt repression indigenous peoples.., [and] genocidal policies"; a motion condemning U.S. immigration policy for "excluding people from capitalist regimes and nonwhite peoples in general"; a motion condemning a video game called "Custer's Reverige" for its celebration of "the historical oppression of Native Americans by the U.S. government"; and a motion calling upon the U.S. government to "freeze the development, production, and deployment of nuclear weapons" and "dismantle its existing arsenal" (an amendment to include the Soviet Union, and urging a bilateral and verifiable freeze, was defeated). To make this ideological *Walpurgisnacht* complete there were two resolutions denouncing Israel, the first for "the systematic and deliberate destruction of Palestinian and Lebanese peoples and cultures" (passed after an hour of debate and the defeat of several amendments to broaden the focus of the resolution); and the second for restricting research and suppressing academic freedom in the occupied West Bank (passed without debate).

In reaction to such excesses, a resolution approved in 1984 required motions passed at business meetings to be submitted to the AAA's membership via a mailed ballot. Given the apparent proclivities of most anthropologists, this has proved only a partial remedy. When the 1984 business meeting passed a resolution declaring that "mass opposition and resistance to war preparations must achieve new heights," and calling upon "all its members to take part in diverse events across the country expressing this opposition and resistance," it was approved by 82 percent of the membership bothering to vote. (This year, the referendum procedure is itself under challenge in a referendum.)

It is tempting to dismiss all this as meaningless bombast that simply discredits those associated with it. (The same thing has been said about the resolutions passed by the UN.) But while most sociologists or anthropologists may keep their distance from such antics, it would be unwise to assume that they are unaffected by them. At the very least these maneuvers represent a continuous endorsement of the advocacy style in social science, and, by lending legitimacy to extreme postures, gradually shift the spectrum of respectable opinion further and further to the Left. They also confer some scholarly respectability on the use of vituperative and emotional language, and, even worse, on hack formulations lifted from Soviet propaganda. Finally, they discomfort those who disagree, as constant reiteration works symbolically to redefine membership in the social-science community along ideological rather than professional lines, threatening dissenters with the status of moral pariahs. Thus, though these motions may heat up the deliberations of a good many conferences, their approval inevitably has a chilling effect.

Ortega Y. Gasset remarked more than fifty years ago that "the simple process of preserving our present civilization is supremely complex and demands incalculably subtle powers." There is nothing subtle, however, in the intent of the zealots now so amply represented within the ranks of academe, nor much in their doings that would work to strengthen the foundations of civilized life.

In its traditional liberal vision the university perpetuated the ideals of Western civilization in two separate but related ways. First, it imparted a sense of intellectual method that rejected dogmatic, monistic, and conspiratorial formulations in favor of a broadminded empiricism and a regard for the world's complexity. Second, it conveyed an appreciation for the underlying values of free societies, most notably a respect for the moral worth of the individual and for the ideals of personal liberty and constitutional democracy which emanated from it. As a result the university experience had a dual character, in part a process of intellectual training and in part a process of socialization.

At a deeper level, however, method and values reflected and reinforced one another. Operating within such a system, academics were able to illustrate what was just and admirable about Western civilization simply by adhering to the canons of their own fields of scholarship. Or, taking the other tack, they could promote intellectual openness and tolerance through an honest reading of the West's achievements. A study of ancient Greece was a study of life, not a preachment or conversion; but the highest ideals of that civilization carry their own persuasiveness, and are the precursors of our own.

All this is quite alien to the spirit of what aspires to become the new, radicalized academy. Armed with a variety of totalistic visions and millennial expectations, its partisans have little sympathy either with open discourse or with analytic procedures that fail to guarantee desired conclusions. It is not a coincidence that the epistemological relativism prominent in the early writings of Marx is also a common feature of the theories of contemporary academic radicals, be they feminists, deconstructionists, or Marxists. After all, if one wishes to reach a rather improbable goal without undue let or hindrance, the fewer the methodological constraints the better. As Howard Zinn, professor of history at Boston University once put it, "In a world where justice is maldistributed, there is no such thing as a 'neutral' or representative recapitulation of the facts." In such a view, objective truth is only what the present dictates or what the future requires.

The organizing principle of radical scholarship inheres in its purpose rather than in its methods or theories. And its purpose is unremitting attack on existing cultural traditions and political and economic institutions. Thus, Paul Attewell, in a friendly survey of the work of radical economists, can locate "a major goal of most Left theorizing" in "the *dual accomplishment* of a political-economic analysis and a moral critique in which the economic analysis shows that an 'evil' is systematically and necessarily produced by capitalism" (emphasis in the original). Of course, a scholarship which sets out to prove that which it already knows, and whose underlying conviction is the necessary and systematic relation of the universe of evils to the structure of a free society, is no scholarship at all. What this statement describes is something quite different: a campaign of defamation.

Perhaps the most ominous aspect of this campaign is the use of the classroom for the cultivation of ethnic and class resentments, particularly among minority students entering into higher education for the first time. Until recently the university served as an important means of integrating the future leadership of American society and assimilating the upwardly mobile. A significant part of it now strives to do precisely the reverse, by fostering political estrangement and cultural segmentation. And even where, as is generally the case, the result falls short of instilling hatred, the atmosphere so created sours the country's image for many of those emerging into active citizenship.

At the very least, the rise of adversarial education has deprived many students of an adequate opportunity to be exposed to what is best in their own cultural tradition. (And given the decline of American secondary instruction, colleges are frequently the only place where such material can be absorbed.) In its search for opportunities to investigate the underside of American life, the Left has littered college catalogues with all sorts of marginalia. Some of these novel courses may have limited academic relevance. Unfortunately, however, time spent studying "Chicano Theater" or "Sex and Violence in the American Family" is time lost from the study of classics of political theory or world literature. The result is often a college graduate with as little sense of the deposited wisdom of his civilization as that of a troglodyte who never opened a book.

To an astonishing degree the relative acceptance of radical ideas at our universities has been accompanied by changed ground rules for teaching, scholarship, and peer review. In the process, academic freedom, which is the foundation on which teaching and learning prosper, has been transformed. As a principle it was meant to shield the academy from external pressure and manipulation, but, like most other freedoms, it simultaneously conferred a responsibility, involving a willingness to uphold basic standards of inquiry and to render judgment on the quality of colleagues' ideas.

The zealots who now threaten the academy do so out of the certainty and urgency with which they embrace their favored truths. But milder men also threaten it when they cease to believe in any truths at all, or lack the courage to bring their beliefs to bear on professional decisions. What follows is a careless latitudinarianism that parcels out portions of the academic terrain among every group too large, too vocal, or too assertive to be comfortably ignored, whatever the intellectual merit of its positions. The *reductio ad absurdum* of this appeasing attitude, a kind of ideological affirmative action, is nicely captured in Professor William Van Alstyne's recent complaint at an AAUP meeting that Marxists are underrepresented in college classrooms since, in contrast to the academy, "two-thirds of the globe is persuaded by Marxism writ large."

In the last analysis, it is less the academy's radical minority and more its liberal majority that is at the heart of the problem. Since the mid-1960s a diminished belief in American society has left that majority unable effectively to counter the genuinely impassioned forces of the Left. Accordingly, it is a revival of that robust and clear-sighted liberalism, once so cognizant of extremist dangers in all their forms, which constitutes the essential condition for restoring a healthier campus climate. The future of higher education hinges on how the internal crisis of American liberalism is eventually resolved. □

Notes

1. According to figures provided by the publisher, since 1980 there have been eighty-five college adoptions of Parent's textbook, *Democracy for the Few*. This is a relatively small number compared, say, with Paul Samuelson's textbooks in economics, but it is considered quite respectable by standards within the book publishing industry.
2. See "Terrorizing Children," by Joseph Adelson and Chester E. Finn, Jr., April 1985, and "The Scandal of Peace Education," by Andre Ryerson, June 1986.

2

College Life from 1968 to the Present (The Barzun Perspective)

Introduction*

This is a statement I very much wanted to make. *The American University,* published in 1968, still stands as one of the most lucidly informative statements about the subject ever written. With keen insights Jacques Barzun has described the university and its quintessential features. He demarcates the ancestral, perhaps more congenial, university from the one emerging in his day as teacher and administrator in the 1960s. Presciently he walks the reader through the minefields of sixties "reform," ever hopeful about the future of an institution to which he has devoted his professional life. I greatly admire his vision and his power of analysis. But even Barzun did not fully foresee the extremes that emerged from the noisy radicalism of the 1960s. Even he could not imagine the corrosive influence of an all-embracing orthodoxy on campus.

The American University is essential reading for any scholar who wishes to understand the essence of his role and the nuances of university life. The book is a primer on the atavistic yearning of youthful rabble-rousers. There is a wisdom displayed in these pages that can guide college administrators and embolden presidents. Most evident to me is Jacques Barzun's wonder and excitement

---

*This article used the Barzun book as a launching pad to describe the changes that occurred in higher education since the publication of the *American University* in 1968.

over the teaching and learning process. To read these pages is to understand why former students, now in their fifties and sixties, still wax lyrical when describing his classes, for lyrical they were and lyrical his observations remain. May this book have yet a second and third life; it deserves to be read again and again.

What I propose to do is to give my considered view of the present state of the American university. It is for me a unique opportunity to compare the judgments made by Jacques Barzun through the decades of the forties, fifties, and sixties with subsequent events and performance in higher education.

There is in Barzun's treatment of university life a clear demarcation of an era when interests were simpler and gentler than ours, a less fanatical era, when errors in judgment could be corrected without heroic effort. The university in that less complex era was not saddled with affirmative action policy and redressing the wrongs of the past, nor was it entwined with government interests, refashioning the curriculum in order to satisfy politically active groups, settling community concerns, and conceived of as a problem-solving institution of first resort. How prosaic it now seems to describe the university as a purposeful sanctuary from the "real world."

The president in that innocent period could, as Barzun notes, "deal offhand with seventy or seven hundred people and take care of their infrequent wants, easily knowing what had gone before and what he was doing now, to use or not as a precedent the next time." Now the president is by virtue of his reconstituted role a negotiator who deals with committees, bargaining agents, and legal counsel. His faculty demands are limitless and often put forward discommodiously as "nonnegotiable," a feature of university life first promoted by student radicals. The president's primary role is to maintain campus equilibrium in the face of competing interests, and his success is often determined by an ability to avoid trouble on his watch. It is hardly surprising, therefore, that there aren't any Nicholas Murray Butlers on the campus today.

While Professor Barzun quite appropriately separates the old from the new, the ironic publication date of 1968—the year of the student riots at Columbia University—militates against any analysis of the "post modem" period in university life. This is the era in which the trends Barzun describes became entrenched and a mood of despair and irrationality observed in inchoate form became manifest in curriculum organization and university-wide practices.

While war and depression, government intrusiveness and advanced technology, play a part in changing the face of the university and introducing "a new mode of administration," systemic university change occurred as the society changed. An inability to cope with the vicissitudes of bureaucratic complexity compelled university officials to alter quotidian affairs from a *gemeinschaft* of personal contact and understanding to a *gesellschaft* of contracts and regulation.[1] Mr. Chips was replaced by Perry Mason. The university was caught in the vortex of fundamental social change which it reflected until roughly 1968 and then promoted from 1968 to the present.

This reshaping of the university to accommodate the winds of change is an essential point acknowledged but, due to timing and the rush of events, is only partially explored by Professor Barzun. For most of this century, even going back to the origin of the university at Johns Hopkins and Stanford in the 19th century, purpose and goals were well articulated by the founders. Knowledge was an end worth pursuing. The foundations of knowledge were largely unbound by fashionable trends. And, despite the controversies that occasionally arose over curriculum and academic freedom, the pace of change was slow.

The reason for the slow pace of change until the sixties was the singularly focused purpose of university life, Teaching and research, learning and study, constituted the faculty-student equation. The utopian effort to refashion the society through university reformism was not yet on the horizon; nor was the university yet in thralldom to the adjudication of real and perceived social injustice. Administrators had not yet fallen into a rabbit's hole where symbols were deciphering tools and words were deconstructed like soap bubbles. Not yet had ideas once evaluated on their merit been filtered through the net of race, class, gender, and Third World ideology. Not yet had students' rights been inserted into the Fourteenth Amendment, while *loco parentis* was being abandoned. Not yet did researchers do Washington's bidding in an effort to obtain government subventions for their pet projects. Not yet were many students persuaded that rational discourse itself was little more than a plot to keep them subordinate.

In the "new age" the possibility of economic mobility through a university education has been converted into the right to a university education as part of equal opportunity. The university has become Plato's paradigm for democracy: available to everyone without the necessity of accepting responsibility or meeting prerequisites. In the nineteenth century Charles Eliot, president of Harvard, said that the reason Harvard had so much knowledge was that freshmen bring so much in and seniors take so little out. Today most scholars and SAT scores reflect a different reality in which freshmen know very little, yet think they know a lot, and seniors know a lot about very little and don't know whether to take what they know with them or discard it.

There is, indeed, a college for everyone. But few ask if there should be a college for everyone. With standards reduced to the lowest common denominator, universities have vitiated the pursuit of excellence. One obvious manifestation of this trend is undifferentiated grades. In 1976 I gave up using the dean's list in the college I administered, since it had become little more than a student roster. The pursuit of political objectives in the academy goes on unabated. The Byzantine contortions exhibited by university administrations in an effort to address the representation of blacks, Hispanics, Native Americans, and other designated minorities has forced colleges and universities to reduce admissions decisions to the very considerations of race they allegedly deplore. Hoist by the petard of fairness, justice, and equal opportunity, university leaders are obliged to administer by category, arbitrariness, and inequality. Rather than apply a blind standard of need for financial aid, university administrators are forced to consider race in their calculus in order to satisfy political expectations. It is therefore not unusual for a student with wealthy black parents to be given a scholarship that would be denied to a middle-class white student.

The consequence of such decisions is to drive continual litigation and pit group against group. Ironically, efforts to integrate the campus have led to segregation. With race as a central criterion for all decisions, black students are unjustifiably clannish, demanding, and sometimes permitted to have their own dormitory space and separate eating facilities. At the 1991 Vassar College graduation there was a separate graduation ceremony for black students. Black students wore on their hoods the tri-colors of African liberation (red, green, and black) instead of the Vassar colors. These specially decorated hoods were paid out of general student funds.

In order to accommodate the many interests on campus and the various talents and aptitudes of students, the university has created a metaphorical supermarket of courses. There are courses that are hard and courses that are soft; there are some which pander to race and gender and others bereft of any meaning; there are some with value and others that are translations of "Sesame Street" for immature adolescents. As the university's purpose becomes increasingly ambiguous, catalogues get thicker. Not only is there a college for everyone, now there is a course for everyone. Instead of reading texts that liberate the individual from a narrow, provincial, limited perspective, avatars of a new culture argue for those texts that reinforce the study of what is familiar or what passes for political acceptability.

It is almost a cliché to contend that most college students have not read the great works of Western civilization, or any civilization for that matter, are scientific and math illiterates and cannot construct logical arguments in debate or written statement. It is hardly surprising that, buffeted by the ethos of total egalitarianism and the supermarket of indiscriminate ideas and a radical agenda, most college graduates are "trained in incapacity," to borrow a phrase from Thorstein Veblen. Perplexed by the success of *The Closing of the American Mind,* Professor Allan Bloom asked whether I had an explanation for the book's phenomenal sales. Granting that most people don't read Nietzsche, which comprises the second half of the book, and granting as well that serious philosophy doesn't make the best seller lists, I argued that many parents confounded by the psychobabble their college-educated children employ, and tired of being called bourgeois and philistine, were willing to invest $20 to find out why they were wasting $25,000 a year. Professor Bloom nodded knowingly.

The proliferation of scholarship with specialties now so arcane that the average person cannot possible know what is meant by academic terminology has reduced knowledge to a form of mysticism or revealed truth. A faculty member at the New School for Social Research describes himself as a "post-modem semiotics instructor." After having listened to him lecture, I'm convinced he is a witch doctor enamored with obfuscation of language and meaning. Yet he is not alone. At the risk of exaggeration I have observed two kinds of modem instructors: the Pied Pipers eager for recognition who consider instruction synonymous with sermonizing, and those who are eager to remove themselves from teaching in order to spend their time doing research. The former are frustrated preachers; the latter often opportunists, who see teaching as little more than a means to an end.

As teaching has been downgraded and the curriculum made into a political football, the rhetoric of self-praise employed by academics to describe their craft has risen dramatically. Words like *excellent, profound,* and *life enhancing* are pegged into the vernacular of a university life manipulated by advertising techniques. It's as if adolescents were being told "be all you can be in the university." How, in that case, can parents possibly tell John or Mary "college is not for you?" The college experience has gone from a rite of passage to a right of passage. All the while, the educational experience has been transmogrified into a world rescue experience. Students are now asked to solve problems that even presumptive experts cannot control.

At commencement exercises, university presidents, in an act of collective conceit and deceit, tell assembled family members that this class is prepared to fight hunger, nuclear proliferation, homelessness, environmental contamination, disease, despair, urban decay. There is virtually no limit, it is suggested, to what these youngsters can do. Of course, most students neither believe nor act out such exaggerated rhetoric. It would be a refreshing change if these same presidents were saying, "I can assert that these graduates have read classic texts, can write a coherent paper, make logical judgments, understand the essential principles of science, speak a foreign language, and recognize themes in history." But no, such assertions would be far too commonplace for the by now conventional hyperbole. It is the illusion that counts.

Such illusions have taken universities down a path where every opportunity for a new program is seized. What Professor Barzun calls the "Babel index" is the temptation to do what rewards of money and glory demand. In the face of these blandishments the university is helpless to steer an independent course. It is often defined by the parameters of community involvement and external rewards.

The lure of money and recognition is not only a blandishment for the university as a corporate body; it is also an almost irresistible attraction for the professor. Scarcely a full professor in the Western world is without opportunities to consult, advise, and write for money. Every presidential candidate travels with his coterie of hired academic hands. The compromise an academic makes with a world external to the university has fundamentally altered the expectations, commitment, and loyalty of the professorate. A flight from teaching that has reached epidemic proportions is in large part a function of divided loyalty.

Against this backdrop of divided loyalty and obedience to several masters, there is ambiguity about good teaching and scholarship. Is good teaching necessarily the art of stimulating students? Does it fit into the Procrustean bed established by those expressing a political or social orthodoxy? Is good teaching related to popularity? Is scholarship measured by the number of articles and the stature of the journals in which they are published? Most importantly, who is to judge? In a setting where celebrity status is in the ascendancy, far too often a superficial evaluation is made while the less obvious contribution of well-crafted lectures, concern for students, and careful grading of papers is overlooked. It is, therefore, hardly surprising that the shared bonds of collegiality have retreated before the attractions of money, released time, and recognition.

Foremost on the faculty agenda is tenure—an institution well ensconced in higher education "to make professors independent of thought control." While tenure offers a charter of freedom for the professor, it is an institutional gamble in which the university bets that "the young genius," as Barzun puts it, won't "ripen into a dull old man, who has to be supported for years even when insupportable." The financial vicissitudes in higher education are forcing a careful review of this once sacrosanct institution. But there are other reasons for the reexamination of tenure that Barzun's illuminating analysis of this question could not anticipate.

In the traditional vision, the university perpetuated the idea of Western civilization in two separate but related ways. First, it imparted a sense of intellectual method, which rejected dogmatic, orthodox, and conspiratorial formulations in favor of a broadminded empiricism and a regard for the world's complexity. Second, it conveyed an underlying appreciation for the values of free societies, most notably a respect for the individual and for the ideals of personal liberty and constitutional democracy that emanated from it. As a result, the university experience had a dual character; this was in part a process of intellectual training and in part a process of socialization.

This view of the academy, however, is alien to the spirit of what aspires to become the new, activist vision, protected l)y the same institution of tenure and academic freedom as the traditional version, yet fundamentally at odds with it methodologically and Substantively. Armed with a variety of totalistic visions and millennial expectations, its partisans have little sympathy for open discourse or analytic procedures that fail to guarantee desired conclusions. As Howard Zinn, erstwhile professor of history at Boston University, once put it, "In a world where justice is maldistributed, there is no such thing as a 'neutral' or representative recapitulation of the facts." In such a view, objective truth is only what the present dictates or the future requires.

The organizing principle of the new scholarship inheres in its purpose rather than in its methods or theories. And its purpose is unremitting attack on cultural institutions, as well as political and economic institutions. This is a scholarship that sets out to prove what is already known—in short, the direct antithesis of what scholarship is.

Yet the ally in this systematic campaign to "capture the culture" (to borrow a phrase from Antonio Gramsci) is tenure and academic freedom. The classroom is now frequently employed as the setting for ethnic and class antagonism. Until recently, the university served as an important means of assimilating the upwardly mobile and integrating future leaders of American society. A significant portion of the professorate now strives to do the reverse, fostering political estrangement and cultural segmentation. Tenure and academic freedom in the febrile minds of would-be revolutionaries have been transformed from institutions that militate against external pressure and manipulation into institutions that promote them.

One point where I disagree with Professor Barzun is in his assertion that "The loss of intellectual revelation [among students] is partly due to the improvement of the high school and its adoption of much of the contents of general education. Many colleges today give the freshman the sense of repeating what he has learned." This claim doesn't square with my experience. Not only am I convinced that high schools are not improving, based on my assessment of incoming freshmen, but the number in the highest quintile of SAT scores—as one superficial symptom of the school malaise—has been declining since 1963.

The agitation organized by students during the overheated period from 1967 to 1973 was prompted, in my judgment, by rootlessness. The combination of war, the draft, a desire for social experimentation, spiraling divorce rates promoted activism instead of thought, problem solving instead of evidence gathering, and doing instead of reflecting. The university as a center of learning was converted into the Paris Commune.

As I look back to that period, the high school education that students received did not help matters. It was an era of curriculum experimentation producing a generation out of touch with basic cultural cues and unfamiliar with even the rudimentary facts about government and history. As Chester Finn Jr. and Diane Ravitch have pointed out in *What Do Seventeen Year Olds Know?* the answer, after much testing, is not very much. Thrust into a college setting, in thralldom to a utopian vision, these naive seventeen-year-olds, who do not know that the American Revolution came before the French Revolution, turned into right-thinking revolutionaries. Rather than arriving at opinion through a process of learning, reasoning, and concluding, these products of American high schools made judgments *parti pris,* as if it were in the air they breathe or the coaxial cable that brought them visual images.

Where Jacques Barzun is unquestionably right is in his contention that students are "caught in the mandarin system" that makes a degree indispensable for a professional career. Therefore, students are obliged to endure bad teaching and other manifestations of neglect. In a sense not well understood by student radicals of bygone days and certainly not understood by students today, they are often victimized. Yet this wasn't and rarely is the reason for campus agitation.

The prototypical student radical of the late sixties has been replaced by a different, complacent prototype today, albeit rootlessness is a feature common to both generations. In the past, rootlessness manifested itself as rebellion, now it is manifest as a search for orthodoxy, whether that takes the form of symbols, deconstruction, or the emergence of an obsession with Third World authors. Students, as befits their age and idealism, have been in search of facile answers to complex questions, but it is-or should I say was-the responsibility of faculty members to lead them to a path in which truth is sought rather than slogans. But truth is elusive.

Clearly Professor Barzun has great insight into the evolving student orientation in the sixties and beyond, but perhaps the clearest demonstration of his perspicacity is in his description of university administrations as "above and below." As an administrator for twenty years I understand full well that I work for a faculty and that whatever limited influence I possess stems from my artful use of persuasion. I cannot pull rank since rank as an ascribed state doesn't exist in the increasingly egalitarianized university. I am after all only one member of a team consisting of president, vice presidents, and other deans who in synchronous devotion to a well understood and accepted goal can move the university community along haltingly and who, under normal circumstances, may only debate, consider, review, and disagree.

Today's decanal duties include nourishing a faculty with grant money, foundation support, concessions from the central administration and a filtered assessment of how government regulations and the latest administrative missives influence its work, what Barzun calls "intelligent facilitation." A dean is part mountebank, part manager, part executive, part interpreter, part fundraiser, and part alchemist. He must keep his school intact by orchestrating natural antipathies among faculty members, students, and alumni groups, and he must do so with sufficient good cheer so that confidence in his management is maintained.

Perhaps the most notable shift in higher education is that a professor who once focused on his students and his pension and did almost everything for himself, has been thrust into a setting where as a result of specialization, regulations, and diverse and clashing interests, he is obliged to rely on others, most especially his dean. At bottom, a faculty doesn't want to administer the college, except when it believes the administrative decisions have impinged on the prerogatives of teaching and scholarship. As Barzun wisely notes: "it is his [dean's] business to serve *them* [faculty members], not his likes and dislikes" (emphasis in the original).

For me the most resounding moment of recognition in a book filled with echoes of my past occurred when I read the chapter about the budget. The budget has a mystical air to it. Although prepared with a precision that reifies numbers, it is also a chart of priorities and standards. The budget measures nothing tangible; yet whatever is tangible in the university cannot exist without it. It is a document of compromise, deliberation, and assumptions; it is a distillation of views about the future, yet firmly anchored in the past. It is most assuredly a metaphorical pie in which departments, individual faculty members, and other constituents brandish knives to get their "fair" slice. Amidst the bickering and compromises there is an objective reality composed of debits and credits and the fear of a deficit. The word *education,* however, is rarely mentioned in the budgeting process, and there is a decided tilt toward the retention of those programs already in place. Rarely does anyone apply "zero budgeting" methods, in which each program director is obliged to make a case for his budget each year. Should such a policy be introduced, the university would probably not be the same again; whatever animosity exists among faculties would be exacerbated by a stated justification for their existence. Recognition of this likelihood is what greases the budget-resolution wheel. Most constituents would rather have partial rewards than a Hobbesian world of each against all.

Leading the charge for university budget reform are those who wish to change the university to reflect their political principles. These are the neo-libertarians, who, through a prism of dissatisfaction with the status quo, wish to convert the university into their version of utopia. Utopia, for them, is related to curriculum reform, which often includes eagerness to erase the distinction between teacher and student, authority and constituent. That a university cannot directly serve social ends is a point overwhelmed by the flood tide of political discontent. Even normally sober academics now engage in the hyperbole of some brave new world led by recent college graduates who have the wisdom to solve social problems their elders are unable to remedy. Mercifully, the era of "relevance" has come to an end. But it has been replaced by an age of irrelevance, though not perceived as such, since many academics assert, on the contrary, that they are curing present ills.

It is, of course, customary for university presidents to proclaim that graduates are being prepared to face the demands of modern life. Yet the meaning of these words "prepare for life" is ambiguous. Recently a colleague tried to address this problem by proposing that students should learn problem-solving techniques as undergraduates. When pressed, he had to admit that problem-solving without knowledge was impossible. On another occasion I heard a distinguished scholar refer to the need for student "experience." Again the claim had a spurious ring to it. If experience is the essence of education, then my grandfather quite obviously deserved a Ph.D.

Professor Barzun advances the notion of *preposterism* to make the point that since knowledge is valuable, every intending college teacher shall produce research. The resultant knowledge explosion has had its fallout in every sector of society. There is more work published to little purpose than was ever the case before. And the more that is published, the less we understand about our nation, our individual roles, our principles, our beliefs, and ourselves. So much of this so-called research is produced at the expense of teaching. Professor Barzun contends that the best liberal arts colleges have "a strong grip on solid subject matter and trust to its broadening, deepening and thickening effect." If this claim was once true, it is most certainly less true now. Universities compete for scholars judged mainly by reputation. Despite lip service given to teaching, it is much less valued than research, as both the allocation of chairs and salary determination amply show.

The explosion of research has also trivialized the curriculum through the proliferation of courses, which pay obeisance to what is fashionable; one critic of higher education refers to the course guidebook as the "Chinese menu for dilettantes." What the extensive listing of courses actually represents is the abdication of faculty responsibility. In an atmosphere in which the purpose of higher education has been obscured by a reformist agenda and the curriculum has been turned into a battleground for departmental scrimmage, the number of courses grows in proportion to designated self-interest and the effort to accommodate "new" disciplines. The by-product of this change is an undergraduate program often devoid of commitment to teaching and often lacking any coherent purpose.

The ambiguity in the curriculum of most colleges is deeply embedded in the general ambiguity of what a university should be. Dr. Barzun notes the two oft repeated contradictory messages in higher education: this is a public institution capable of participating in the affairs of state (At NYU we say "a private university in the public service") and this is an elite institution, an ivory tower, if you will whose majesty should not be compromised by the affairs of state. Retaining the dignity of the university, specifically its devotion to research, is increasingly difficult when the desire to merge and blur all roles and all purposes dominates university life.

It is instructive, I believe, that as demands are imposed on universities which they cannot fulfill and do not resist, the rhetoric associated with higher education has changed. Literature describing the institution invariably refers to saving neighborhoods and even saving nations, having world-class athletic programs and world-class laboratories; rarely do these descriptions mention the value of simple exchange between mentor and student that may inspire a thirst for knowledge.

A. N. Whitehead maintains in *Science and the Modern World* that the twentieth-century research university is constructed according to principles of seventeenth-century physics. He argues that the revolutionary physics of our century, with its reconceiving self and world and its integration of fields of study, came too late to be incorporated into a Newtonian structure of mechanical parts separated by function. The "new" university is in fact old at heart, fracturing science and the humanities and reducing truth, goodness, and beauty to mere expressions of subjective judgment. Moral virtue, which was an essential component of education before the Enlightenment, has been relegated to the archaic as professional and technical studies are in the ascendant.

William James's discussion of this "scientific nightmare" did not deter the evolution of the modem university, nor did the emergence of revolutionary ideas in physics and philosophy. These ideas offered a conception of an integrated world of freedom, responsibility, and moral vitality. But the university was already well on its way to a Cartesian world of departments and bureaucracy. Although I may be daydreaming, I'm persuaded that many people outside the academy believe that the university has failed to address the common concern for meaning, for the humane, and for the ethical.

In the present form of the university, each department guards jealously a domain of expert knowledge, a subject-matter base underwritten by professional associations. Hence, willy-nilly, the university has become a gatekeeper for professional power and an academic identity. In trying to assemble disparate parts into a whole, the university community presupposes an experiential sense of the world, a sense contradicted by the very compartmentalization of knowledge the university promotes. Moreover, as technology is increasingly focused and as professionals are increasingly specialized, judgments about the world that emerge from the study of disciplines are construed solely in technical terms, often imperiling a sense of broadly defined human significance.

It is hardly surprising that a new breed of humanities professor has similarly relegated all subject matter to the realm of ideology, on the principle that truth is transitory. Universals are repudiated by this new-age professor, nurtured by an environment that is narrowly specialized. Professionalizing the humanities should be seen as an essential contradiction. It is worth recalling in this context the subtitle of Allan Bloom's *The Closing of the American Mind. It is How Higher Education Has Failed Democracy and Impoverished the Souls of Today's Students.*

The failure of the modem university is, in my opinion, its unwillingness to consider "holistic" thinking that cuts across disciplinary barriers. To conceive of a mind separate from a body is to misunderstand the interdependence of all the elements within the self. At the same time, an obsessive concern with the self, with the ego's interests, has converted much learning into the pursuit of I. I have lost patience with colleagues who start every discussion with the words, "How do you feel about...?" Since the meaning of personal feeling cannot be dissociated from the meaning of the world, the question is ultimately foolish unless clearly related to a reasoned conception of life.

When Wittgenstein engaged Freud in a conversation about psychotherapy, the would-be master of the mind replied that through protracted and undirected talk one can ultimately decipher the mystery of the unconscious. Wittgenstein, however, remained unpersuaded. "Sigmund," he reportedly said, "the reason I believe your assumption is wrong is that talk without limit or purpose ends in futility." It seems to me that Wittgenstein was not only making "point about psychotherapy, but also about education. Pedagogy demands limits and purpose. We cannot study everything or know anything without some idea of what is to be learned.

With cynicism about higher education increasing at a rate slower only than the increase in tuition, it is time to consider the end of the university as we have known it. I should hastily note that I do not welcome this outcome; my observation is little more than a logical extrapolation from what I have seen and experienced since Jacques Barzun wrote the *American University* a quarter of a century ago.

In her book *The Case against College,* Caroline Bird maintains that in calculating the costs and benefits of a college education, middle-class parents should not automatically rule in favor of college for their children. Whether a degree provides the economic rewards widely promised relative to the investment is, however, less significant than the fact that the university is a likely casualty in a changing climate of opinion.

The lockstep high-school-to-college odyssey is in retreat, because the economic conditions in society, the tuition cost in the university, and the politicization of the academy militate against the expectation of business as usual. Tuition costs, as everyone knows, have soared beyond the reach of even of many well-to-do parents. In the past four years, with inflation hovering around 3.5 percent annually, tuition increases at private colleges have averaged 9 percent. The typical salaried parent sending a child to a private college (let us say someone earning $50,000 a year) is in a vise, because it is presumed by admissions officers that the parent is earning enough to pay the tuition tab. But if this parent were to send a son or daughter to, say, Princeton, it would be inviting bankruptcy. After covering tuition, room and board, books, and other expenses totaling more than $25,000, the wage earner would, after paying taxes, be driven into the ranks of the poor.

College presidents routinely descend on Washington with their lobbyists seeking succor for financial problems; and to an extraordinary degree they have been successful. Aid to higher education—*after* the so-called cuts of the Reagan-Bush years—is in the $12 billion range. We are now, however, in the era of budget cutting; the halcyon days of guaranteed assistance, minimally at the inflation rate, are over. The once sacred cow of educational spending is now simply another budget item. If government is no longer a savior, neither are continued tuition increases. Raising tuition expense above inflation only exacerbates market conditions, since the pool of potential applicants for admission is reduced. Scarcely a university administrator in the country fails to lament a condition in which universities price themselves out of a middle-class market. Is it any wonder that admissions standards have eased in most colleges and that the search has begun in earnest for the "new" student, a person older than the typical eighteen-year-old freshman?

Clearly, the demographic character of the nation is affecting college enrollment. The baby boom is a distant memory and the recent baby "boomlet" will not have a profound effect on the percentage of adolescents in the population. In fact, the over-60 population will soon be growing faster than the under-19 population. Thus, the 1960s are not likely to be repeated. We will not see anytime soon—and probably not again—an American population with one out of three people attending a college or university. If anything, the "birth-dearth"—a decline in the number of children per family—is likely to characterize the U.S. population for some time to come. With the present birth rate of 1.8 children per family, there is little doubt that there will not be enough adolescents by the year 2020 to sustain the present number of colleges and universities, unless a larger than characteristic portion of the nation's high school graduates are encouraged and subsidized to attend colleges and the number of colleges is reduced.

Both of these changes are already evident. Many colleges have closed their doors and other such closings are imminent. Some colleges have joined with others in a confederation of necessity. Some have engaged in a systematic reduction of both faculty members and enrolled students; still others, are seeking adult students to replace the diminishing adolescent pool, and yet others dip deeper into the cohort of high-school graduates to secure enrollment.

At Hampshire College, for example, officials argued in 1982 that in order to retain an enrollment of 1200 students they would be obliged to lower admission standards. After an unsatisfactory experiment with marginal students, they switched gears and reduced enrollment from 1200 to 1000—at the same time reducing the faculty by 10 percent. This decision to retrench is typical. If not retrenchment, merger: in 1985 Barrington College of Rhode

Island merged with Gordon College of Massachusetts. When merger isn't the answer, coeducation sometimes is. Vassar College strengthened its precarious financial situation by becoming a coeducational institution. Even one of the last holdouts, Goucher College, a woman's school since its founding in 1885, decided to become coeducational in 1987.

Reinforcing this enrollment trend is the growth of corporate-based alternatives to a college degree, including the conferring of degrees by corporations. One no longer has to go to college for a diploma. I.B.M., to give one illustration, now operates the largest "university" in the world from its Armonk facility. Bell and Howell offers a degree program for its present employees and as a lure for potential employees. Corporations can attract some of the brightest graduates with a promise of free tuition, a secure job, and training appropriate to the workplace. While university officials contend that this kind of corporate education is narrowly specialized and often does not include liberal arts courses, these programs must be seen against a backdrop of increasing cynicism about the value of a liberal arts education and toward what is regarded as its often fraudulent character. Despite the claim that the university is a guardian and custodian of the culture, an assumption shared by Barzun and others, the conflation of fiscal demands and a reduction in university standards is making the corporate B.A. competitive with the conventional college degree.

Very few academics who have thought about the subject would contend that the manner in which college degrees are presently offered will prevail in the next century. Fiber optic technology and the marriage of computer and television permit a high quality, customized, and inexpensive degree accessible at home to everyone. The capital investment in university buildings and equipment, the investment in tenured faculties, and the cost of recruiting students militate against the continuation of the present university system. If the university has gone through two phases in this century—the time of innocence and dominant leaders and the era of bureaucracy—a third phase, dominated by technology, is looming over the near horizon.

If the legitimacy of higher education were not in question, perhaps the tide of technological change could be slowed. But since the 1960s, in fact since the publication of the *American University,* the university as the broker of ideas has been converted into the university as the would-be molder of history. In the process, the authority of the institution has suffered in public word and deed. During the decade from roughly 1964 to 1974, the university was in the center of a political maelstrom which included anti-Vietnam sentiment, a "free speech" movement, and calls for participatory democracy.

As the sanctuary for *all* unpopular opinion, the university was being converted into a hothouse for a succession of fashionable views. Academic freedom became an apparatus for protection from criticism. When opponents disapproved of the propagandizing, the flag of academic freedom was raised along with vague references to McCarthyism.

If the academic responsibility of the past was to nurture youthful minds and provide a context for judgment, however questionable some of the methods may have been, the febrile members of the academic community now see their job as conversion, that is, excoriating "naivete" and exposing the "corrosive" elements in the nation and in the culture—not that this effort has been entirely successful. Students today are like students of the past: skeptical of their professors' views. But despite student skepticism, a conventional wisdom on campus has emerged. Feminism is a given, invariably accepted without question. Affirmative action is part of the academic catechism. Investment in South Africa is verboten. The Strategic Defense Initiative is the wrong policy. Rich people are by definition exploitive. Businessmen are avaricious. These views are not hypotheses subject to analysis. They are incantations accepted without even a nod to rational investigation, as "sensitivity training" and its resultant bureaucracy on many campuses would seem to suggest. Partly as a consequence of this development, there have been a staggering number of federal and state reports about the university in the last ten years, all concluding in one way or another that something is wrong.

William Bennett, the former Secretary of Education, writes in *To Reclaim a Legacy* that the liberal arts have become so "diluted" that college graduates know little of the "culture and civilization of which they are members." A knowledge of American history or European civilization isn't a requisite for graduation from a majority of colleges. Frederick Rudolf, coauthor of *Integrity in the College Curriculum,* points to "the accelerating decline of the undergraduate degree." He contends that in what passes for a college curriculum, almost anything goes." Even those efforts to restore quality to the undergraduate program are often subverted by a university pork barrel in which the retention of one course in French is secured by the like consideration for one in philosophy within the so-called core curriculum.

While administrators invariably claim devotion to high standards, tuition dependency cannot help affect them adversely. The National Education Association, notably charitable to student opinion, notes in a report on colleges that students are "increasingly reluctant to undertake courses of study in colleges that challenge their academic skills." This condition, by the way, is not likely to change in a "buyer's market" unless all universities institute the same requirements—a highly implausible scenario. As an example, Secretary Bennett points out that fewer than half of the nation's colleges demand the study of a foreign language as a degree requirement, compared with 90 percent a scant twenty-five years ago. Professor Rudolf describes higher education as "a supermarket where students are shoppers and professors are merchants."

While the liberal arts have fared badly, career programs have grown in stature and importance. They also pay the university bills. Business and engineering, to cite "hot" fields, often require nothing more than a rudimentary brush with the humanities. At many universities, Master Liberal Arts programs have been introduced for B.A. graduates *without* liberal arts training. These ploys are not altogether the fault of universities. A desire to use higher education as a democratizing instrument placed the university squarely in the middle of an obligation it could not shirk. Many students lacking adequate preparation for college study were "dumped" into the academy with the expectation that in four years small miracles could be performed. However, faculty members trained in a narrow area of specialization and often not equipped with pedagogical skill were poor operatives for the task of remedial teaching.

The answer to this dilemma was a variety of reforms, including undifferentiated grades (pass/fail) that blurred differences in ability and contaminated the meaning of a degree. Between 1963 and 1992 the share of the student population majoring in traditional arts and science disciplines declined precipitously. Philosophy lost 60 percent of its students, and English 72 percent, while psychology, arguably the softest of the social sciences, gained 56 percent. Journalism is the fastest growing undergraduate program, and at NYU it has the highest enrollment of undergraduate students. Of course, part of this trend can be attributed to the economic recession and poor instruction, but some portion of the shift is related to the virtual abandonment of the much-touted goal of excellence.

How serious can the university's mission be when "freshman" is eschewed from the language as an offense to first-year female students; when Crispus Attucks, an obscure mulatto who was inadvertently killed in the Boston Massacre, is exalted as an American hero in history courses, and when "peace studies" are introduced as a discipline in order to decry the existence of nuclear weapons? It is the attention given to such issues and the media coverage of campus turmoil that have altered the once rubber-stamp public support for higher education.

The baby boom of the post war era accelerated public and private spending on colleges and universities to levels grossly out of proportion to any future demographic reality. Higher education was deemed an unqualified good; therefore, the more you have of it, the better it is for the body politic. One cannot travel for more than three miles on the San Diego Freeway without seeing a sign pointing to a community college. That these colleges may be superfluous with the declining pool of adolescents in the nation seems obvious.

What is not so obvious is the continuing misguided faith in education as an anodyne for all that ails us. As evidence from the past three decades illustrates, most of the social reforms imposed on universities in order to relieve perceived social problems had a greater effect on the university than on the social problems themselves. For example, affirmative action policy has had a profound effect on the proliferation of university bureaucrats and on admissions policy, but it has not had any influence on relieving racial tension. Some academics argue, validly I believe, that this policy has exacerbated racial tension.

Many communities with a population over 50,000 considered it a disgrace if the town didn't have a community college. After all, if it's good for the big cities, why shouldn't it be good for the towns and the suburbs? Community status became entangled with the presence of a college. Governor Nelson Rockefeller of New York described the state-supported college system as his greatest accomplishment. He neglected to point out the enormous cost to the taxpayers of the state: $4.5 billion a year, equal to a $17,000 subvention per student. In this era of austerity, taxpayers have a valid reason to voice their concern about the way in which their money is spent. A taxpayer revolt on aid to higher education—public and private—is not yet manifest, but the context for legislative decisions on education has so changed that higher education is not shielded from disapprobation.

Much of the money on campus is being spent on an activity that is increasingly subject to careful scrutiny—research. As the vast majority of Nobel laureates can attest, most researchers have a university appointment. A symbiosis between the university and basic research has evolved over the past half century. It was in large part fostered by government, since this was a relatively inexpensive way for the state to support universities and simultaneously to support research. It saved an enormous investment in government-sponsored research centers. This convenience for government and benefit for the university has been criticized by some academics as obliging the university to do the government's bidding. Recent controversy over the research for the Strategic Defense Initiative demonstrates the point. It seems to me that if one is concerned about securing the autonomy of the curriculum from an assault by ideology, then one should also be concerned about the intrusion of government projects into university life, an intrusion that may jeopardize the independence of researchers.

At this writing, it appears that government is involved in a gradual but perceptible disengagement from university research programs. At the same time, a host of think tanks have been organized to fill the gaps universities have left in basic research. Scientists are as likely to do research through Bell Laboratories as they are at a university. It can also be shown that the majority of college and university facilities are not used for serious research. A recent National Science Foundation report, after reviewing faculty contributions, indicates that only about fifty universities constitute serious science-research centers. Perhaps if the paucity of research at most colleges were recognized, the transition to alternative research facilities and the corresponding budget retrenchment would not seem so formidable.

Professors are in a "declining industry" where salaries have not kept pace with the level of inflation. As a result, many moonlight in order to keep pace. The moonlighting usually takes the form of consulting, which diminishes loyalty to the university and dedication to teaching, particularly the teaching of general undergraduate courses. In report after report on university instruction, whether from the National Endowment for the Humanities or the Carnegie Council on Teaching, reference is made to unsatisfactory college teaching. But where will future teachers come from when the liberal arts have fallen from grace, when serious scholarship isn't encouraged and only rarely found, and when salaries cannot compete with those in comparable fields? The college classroom may once have been the arena for vigorous intellectual discourse, but a report of student complacency in the *Chronicle of Higher Education* indicates that this condition is no longer general. In most student polls, college undergraduates can rarely name one professor who inspired them. Where, for a contemporary generation of students, is the inspiration that students at Columbia enjoyed in the period from 1940 to 1970, when they were taught by Jacques Barzun, Lionel Trilling, and Mark Van Doren?

To an extraordinary degree, college education has become, in the bad sense of the word, personal—too intensely personal, another example of solipsism in our society. It is no coincidence that Mr. Bennett points out how frequently success in school is not related to success outside of school and how academic subjects tend to be "of limited consequence in the real world." If he is right, or even partially right, then the university's legitimacy has ceased to exist. A National Institute of Education report concludes with the plea that "all bachelor's degree recipients should have at least two years of liberal education." If they are not getting it, what are they getting? Visibly, young people are scrambling to get jobs, which they think requires only training, not education. At a time when colleges are trying to lure students, the wise offer of an education is not likely to find many takers.

James Fallows noted in an *Atlantic* magazine article entitled "The Case against Credentialism" that "What is rewarded is excellence in school, which is related to excellence on the job only indirectly and sometimes not at all." If college work has so little application to employment, why should parents invest thousands of dollars in it? And if the argument for higher education is not utilitarian (which it is only indirectly) then a case must be made for learning as the edification of soul and character. Yet even the remaining ardent defenders of the university are incapable of making this claim effectively. What we are left with is college as an adolescent rite of passage that provides a remote chance youngsters will discover an area of vocational interest that may prove to have a lasting effect on their lives.

Thirty years ago the university was placed on a pedestal as the place where "the whole man" was developed (it was a time when the word *man* still had its full, genderless meaning of "human being"). So confident was this assertion that, so far as I know, very few of my classmates questioned that claim. The university could be exalted because it stood for something worthy and intelligible. That is no longer true. I could argue that the fate of the university is not related to the future of education; the two aren't necessarily synonymous. But reflecting on what I have noted in these pages and the observations skillfully developed by Professor Barzun, I am convinced that we are entering a new phase in the evolution of the university. It is already the case that learning and research are being fostered elsewhere, chiefly by business corporations acting in self-defense against ill-prepared college graduates. Once parents are persuaded that this less costly alternative can confer the same advantages as the elite institutions, the university we have recently known will be obsolete.

There is much to be lamented about the passing even of the university in its most recent incarnation. At its best, the university can promote the exchange of ideas and develop an appreciation of our common humanity. It can usher in moments of enlightenment that for young minds can be intoxicating. It can inspire vocations and arouse devotion to public service. There must be dozens of men and women today so inspired by the Barzun-Trilling seminars at Columbia decades ago that they decided to follow the path of their mentors into teaching. If the university is destined for decline and death, as I have suggested, the present moment is not one for rejoicing. □

Note

1.   This terminology is borrowed from Ferdinand Tönnies, *Gemeinschaft lund Gesell-schafl* (tr., *Community and Society*).

3

Decline and Revival

This series of pieces from various publications outlines the decline and strategy for revival in academic life. The first article was the very first piece published in *Academic Questions*, the publication of the National Association of Scholars.

A Call to the Academy
"From the Editor," *Academic Questions,* Winter 1987-88

Most professors on American campuses give lip service to the principle of free exchange of ideas on the campus. But something has changed at American colleges and universities. The defense of academic freedom, on which there was consensus and on which the foundation of liberal thought rests, has become a defense for intolerant positions and those hostile to free inquiry. While ideologues do not dominate academic institutions, they have been catapulted into prominence through the *protective* embrace of academic freedom itself and, more importantly, through the abdication of responsibility by defenders of the liberal faith. To attack the ideologues is to be seen as culpable of the very intolerance they practice. *Moreover,* the ideologues, having mastered the cues in the Zeitgeist, have arrogated to themselves the moral high ground.

The mere criticism of their views evokes a storm of censure. After all, they believe themselves to be in the vanguard of reform. To oppose their views is to place oneself outside fashionable opinion. Even the condemnation is pegged into the vernacular of the times.

To object to a feminist position is *ipso facto* evidence of "sexism"; to challenge democratization of rights is proof of "classism"; to contest homosexuality as another form of normalcy is to be labeled "homophobic"; to pronounce the Church's position on abortion a legitimate one is tantamount to "moral backwardness."

Ideological orthodoxy has insinuated itself into the Academy as more than personal opinion. The liberal arts disciplines themselves have been infected by what David Hume once described as "the contagion of opinion." Subjectivism is the reigning deity in the academy. Its influence is manifest in structuralism, semiotics, deconstruction, social history, to cite a few examples. The text has meaning only to the extent new age interpreters give it meaning. As a consequence, the interpreters are the sole decoders of the intellectual tradition, the contemporary priests who possess the power to determine what is truthful. The collaborative search for truth involving faculty members and students has retreated before manipulators shaping the past to serve the present.

While the traditional liberal vision of the university promoted the ideals of Western civilization through a broadminded empiricism and a respect for the world's complexity, the new vision-if it may be called that-relies on dogmatism, conspiracies, relativism, and notions of society that challenge the pillars of liberty and constitutional democracy. As a consequence, what is admirable about Western civilization has been obscured and the requisite canons of scholarship altered to accommodate the radical spirit. That spirit in its undiluted form is unremitting criticism. The locus for its campaign is the classroom, where class and ethnic antipathies are often cultivated and where political estrangement is usually the result. This adversarial education has deprived students of exposure to, much less understanding of, their own culture. They are contemporary soul searchers filled with indignation, but ignorant of the place in which they reside.

As adversary culture has spread to the Academy, the ground rules for teaching and research, promotion and tenure have changed. The university alters its shape and purpose to accommodate every new theme. All one has to do to get attention is organize, complain, petition, and disrupt. Late-sixties student demonstrations are still with us under the auspices of university participatory democracy. Now everyone has a voice in the affairs of the academy. Lest rhetorical flourishes damage the nuance in this argument, it should be noted that the radicals, despite their influence, are less dangerous to the campus atmosphere than the liberal majority that has manifestly surrendered to the pressures of vocal opinion.

Who then will defend the university's best traditions? Will they wither and die through incessant attack and inattention by the majority? Will there be a spontaneous resurgence of responsible academic opinion asserting itself for the restoration of the Academy? The jury is out on these questions. However, the trial continues for everyone associated with higher education.

The National Association of Scholars is an organization devoted to challenging ideological cant of the left or right that prohibits the pursuit of truth. Its instrument for the dissemination of academic opinion is *Academic Questions,* a monthly journal now published as a quarterly periodical. Those of us associated with this publication recognize it as an effort to ask the right questions about higher education. More importantly, it is a beam of light shining over our campuses during these dark hours in the hope that kindred spirits will join our effort to revive the best in the academic tradition. In 1937, with European war clouds on the horizon, George Orwell said, "It is the first duty of intelligent men to restate the obvious." We consider it our duty as responsible men and women in the academy, recognizing the intellectual drift in our age, to restate and assert those principles on which our profession and our institutions depend. □

The Decline of American Universities

For those curious about the vagaries of higher education—which include the total surrender to a radical orthodoxy—recent events provide sufficient graphic evidence to confirm my suspicion.

The stories emanating from American universities make Stephen King's characters seem tame. It appears as if universities are at war with tradition, bourgeois values, normative behavior, and religion. This walk on the wild side is the embodiment of higher education today.

Recently Mr. Robert Swope, a senior at Georgetown University, was fired from his position as columnist for *The Hoya*—the student newspaper—after he wrote a scathing critique of a student production of the *The Vagina Monologues*, a play about violence and a woman's sexuality.

His article entitled the "Little Coochi Snorcher That Could" set off a firestorm of vituperation from faculty members and students alike. His review was described as "divisive," "inflammatory," "misguided," and "hateful." What could possibly bring the campus to this level of high dungeon?

Mr. Swope described for his readers the "snorcher" scene in which a thirteen-year-old girl who, after being given an alcoholic drink, engages in a sexual experience with a twenty-four-year-old woman. The columnist noted that the mostly female audience laughed throughout the encounter.

"If a 24 year old man had gotten her liquored up and then has sex with her, rational people....would consider that rape," he wrote. Moreover, he criticized the Roman Catholic university for allowing the play to be performed.

For this infraction against political correctness, Swope has been vilified on campus. The newspaper's editor-in-chief, David Wong, relieved him of his duties because, as he noted, Swope "had shown disrespect toward the opinion editor and the newspaper."

Of course Swope showed disrespect; his article was censored because it was inconsistent with the radical orthodoxy on campus. It violated the not so hidden code of acceptable standards in student journalism.

Perhaps what is most interesting is that Swope was criticized for upholding traditional morality and the Catholic point of view at a Catholic institution. Even the vice dean of the college weighed in with the reflexive refrain for academic freedom on campus and her distaste for intolerance.

Needless to say, intolerance is a one-way street. Swope is intolerant for raising any question about lesbian pedophiles; but the editors of *The Hoya* are not intolerant for censoring the expression of a position they don't share.

Even if a private university has the right to perform perverse and questionable plays on campus—leaving the issue of taste aside for a moment—what right does it have to censor views it considers objectionable? Every self-respecting liberal who values the free exchange of ideas in a university should find the Swope firing appalling.

Many women's studies programs, like the one at Georgetown that sponsored *The Vagina Monologues*, have become propaganda mills for a lesbian agenda. Any resemblance to serious scholarship is usually coincidental.

It would seem to me that Mr. Swope committed a public service in pointing out the foolishness in this play. He was right to condemn those who laugh at rape. And if he didn't criticize the women's studies program, he should have.

If university officials criticize anyone it should be the editor of the student newspaper who exercised his authority thoughtlessly, even though his decision was uniformly commended. Irreverence, if indeed that is how one interprets Swope's words, is not justification for quashing free speech.

That this is the standard for discourse at a Catholic university is quite remarkable. If there is any outcry over this issue it should be the voice of sensible opinion enraged at the myrmidons of radical culture.

Where events like those at Georgetown are taking this society is already clear. *Soi disant* radicals are guarding their victory over university culture. They will not tolerate criticism and they will not permit opposition from either the faculty or the student body. In any other context Swope's critique would have been described as logical and unobjectionable, but in the Georgetown hot house it is beyond the pale.

Years ago, when another Georgetown student wrote about the quota system for admission to Georgetown Law School, he was excoriated in the student press and by the administration. While a generalization isn't derived from a sample of two, it is possible that those who criticize activities on the Georgetown campus are deserving of acclaim rather than condemnation.

Perhaps the Pope should say anyone willing to challenge anti-Catholic activity at a Catholic university is a candidate for beatitude. It sure takes more courage to challenge the radical orthodoxy than to embrace it.

The once idyllic setting at universities where the free exchange of opinion was promoted is over, a casualty of political correctness.

At a recent SUNY Albany student picnic to honor Jackie Robinson's breaking of the major league baseball color barrier in 1947, campus fury erupted. A bizarre debate emerged when forty students at the university objected to the event being called a "picnic"—a term these students incorrectly alleged emanated from racial lynchings (actually the word is derived from the French term *piquenique*, a social event where attendees bring the food).

Despite the wrongfully placed angst, SUNY Albany student leaders forbade the occasion from being publicized as a picnic. But the problem did not end there.

When the organizers considered calling the event an "outing," a gay student leader objected, noting the term's use to describe the public attribution of homosexuality. Eventually the event was publicized without a title.

SUNY Albany's Student Assembly Affirmative Action Director Zuheer Mustafa told the *Albany Times Union*, "My job is to make sure people from underrepresented groups are heard. Whether the claims are true or not, the point is a word offended."

Now this is a curious standard. Presumably, if a word offends—whether or not the word is offensive—there is an obligation to prevent its use. I am reminded of a recent incident in which the word "niggardly" could not be employed because it offended black students who mistook it as an insult.

Self appointed campus police are sensitized to any offense even when none is intended. What is emerging are affirmative action administrators whose job it is to ferret out insults—intended or not—to designated minorities.

America's campus Red Guard don't force perpetrators of language infractions to wear pointy hats, they just bring the "guilty" up on charges. Insensitivity being the one infraction for which there isn't any defense.

Try calling a female student a "girl" or a well-built male a "stud" and the campus police will descend. In order to stay on the straight and narrow students require orientation sessions that prescribe existentially acceptable speech.

Use of the correct terminology of course doesn't guarantee acceptance. Terms change. Who would have guessed that "picnic" would offend a group on campus?

There was a time when colleges issued a behavioral guide to students. Alcoholism was discouraged. At the moment almost any behavior is tolerated, but colleges impose a form of thought control. Certain words cannot be used.

Moreover, anyone offended by a statement is *ipso facto* the judge and jury of the person who made the statement. Therefore, ordinary rules of fair play are meaningless. The explanation that "I didn't mean to offend anyone" no longer applies. If someone is offended, you are culpable—evidence is irrelevant.

Social interaction is best engaged in with either an attorney or a member of the Red Guard who enforces prevailing campus norms. "Would you like to go out?" is not a question a young man may ask a female student. Like President Bill Clinton, the semiotician, the female will ask what do you mean by "like"? "What is the intent of 'go out'?" The young man who cannot answer these questions satisfactorily could be in hot water.

Seduction is a nonexistent campus phenomenon; it has been transmogrified into rape even when both parties consent. The reason for this is the implicit power one party may have over the other, even if unstated.

"No" once meant "maybe" and "maybe" meant "yes." Now of course words mean only what the interpreters say they mean. "I may have agreed, but in retrospect I disagree" is a position welcome among post-modern dissemblers who determine justice on campus.

How then does one engage in discussion on campus today? The answer is very carefully. The wise student is he who keeps his mouth shut.

This is a curious time to be a student. Understanding cues on campus is critical. Knowing what to say and how to express it becomes the litmus test for social success and even academic success.

I know a student who failed a composition because he refused to write "he or she" throughout the paper. One can't trifle with the campus Red Guard.

This Spring, don't ask fellow students to join you at a picnic. Don't ask a young lady out. And under no circumstances should you say anything that might offend someone on campus.

Each year the estimable Intercollegiate Studies Institute (ISI) bestows its annual "Polly" award for the most egregious act of political correctness on an American college campus.

This year's "award" was given to San Diego State University graduate teaching program, which has a requirement for each student to recite aloud "I am gay" and then describe how it feels to be homosexual, whether he is homosexual or not.

While this act may be egregious, it is not unusual. Diversity training is now incorporated into the orientation at dozens of colleges. Of course, by diversity I'm referring exclusively to a left-wing agenda that emphasizes race, class, gender, and sexual preference. Everything else is written out of the script.

For example, now that Mumia Abu-Jamal—the convicted cop killer—has been asked to speak at Antioch College during commencement, I wonder if a college in the US would consider having Maureen Faulkner—the widow of the officer killed by Abu-Jamal—address its graduating class.

I wonder as well whether there is a college that would engage in a serious open, forum on IQ heritability by inviting Arthur Jensen, Charles Murray, and other advocates of nature over nurture as a determinant of intelligence.

I wonder whether Christian fundamentalists can be considered aggrieved parties at any university where their rights are systematically denied.

I wonder if *non*-chemically free dorms would enforce the law by restricting marijuana use on campus.

Is there a campus that would give pro-life organizations an equal opportunity to express their views?

Do campus speech codes include a prohibition against anti-

Catholic diatribes? If not, why?

Who has received more honorary degrees, Bill Cosby or Thomas Sowell? Since the answer is Cosby and he hasn't engaged in significant scholarship, doesn't anyone want to know why this is the case?

Now that most colleges have an office for homosexual and transsexual complaints and concerns, why isn't there an office for heterosexual complaints and concerns?

Why do Economics Departments consistently exclude the Austrian School of Economics that emphasizes the free market?

Why do affirmative action decisions rely exclusively on blacks and Hispanics and exclude Asians?

Why is modesty on campus routinely treated as freakish?

If segregation is a violation of the 1964 Civil Rights Act, why are dorms regularly segregated by race?

Perhaps, most significantly, if a university education is advertised as a broadening experience in which the free exchange of ideas is encouraged, why are only certain themes permitted?

There you have it. The university case for tolerance is brokered for only selective cases. Diversity is a misnomer since it has been transmogrified into its Orwellian opposite, indoctrination.

For parents the operating principle should be caveat emptor. Be aware of the false claims in college guidebooks and beware of an orientation program that has moved from behavioral standards to thought control.

In a nation that prides itself on First Amendment rights and academic freedom on campus, it is indeed remarkable that the current censorship continues at colleges and universities largely unabated and rarely commented on.

Should a faculty member—even a tenured faculty member—publicly espouse views different from the prevailing orthodoxy on campus, he will most likely face the chastening effect of exclusion and rejection. Young faculty members usually learn that the road to success is dependent on getting along and going along.

I can only imagine what would happen if a faculty member said publicly that homosexual acts are inconsistent with his religious beliefs and that his First Amendment privileges were being denied in the enforcement of homosexual rights and the subversion of his criticism.

Suppose a member of the English department said that it is far more advisable for educated students to read Shakespeare rather than Toni Morrison.   Suppose a faculty member argued that *Cider House Rules* is an abomination since it glorifies abortion. The response would be swift and firm. Demonstrations would be planned and the "guilty" parties would be targeted. This is what we now call higher education.

It is remarkable that this condition is not an April Fool's Day trick, but rather an experienced academic's opinion of what university life has become. Before you dismiss my concerns as the lamentations of a disgruntled scholar, apply the "test." Ask any of the questions cited above and see what kind of response you get on campus. Free speech, you'll find, is very costly.□

The Silent Revolution in Higher Education
"Point of View," *Academic Questions*, 2008
*With Mark Draper**

There is a silent revolution going on in higher education that in time will change the face of the academy. This is not a revolution in curriculum, albeit that is probably necessary. Nor is it a revolution in requirements, albeit that, too, would be desirable. The revolution we refer to is in the delivery system, i.e., the way information is conveyed and the manner in which students learn.

Amazing new technologies already under development in American labs are about to transform learning in profound ways. Rapid advancements will produce powerful new learning environments and experiences using such new tools as simulation, visualization tools, virtual environments, personal intelligent tutors, vast digital libraries, and interactive museums—learning and collaboration unbounded by geography.

Emergent technologies could help students of all ages reach their goals by teaching individuals precisely what they need to know in

*Mark Draper is vice-provost of Grantham University.

the way they learn best and at their own pace. Students will be able to learn faster and better than is now the case. They'll reach much higher levels of achievement, and at a drastically lower cost than even the relatively low tuition of public institutions of learning.

The first milestone will soon be reached: twice the learning in half the time at one-tenth the cost. Futurists like Thomas Frey predict that the speed of learning will increase tenfold, with the possibility that the equivalent of our current K–12 education system will be compressed into as little as one year.

This appears a less exaggerated claim when one considers the inefficiency of the present system. At the moment, higher education generally fails to exploit the amazing power of the new educational technology. Computers have now been in classrooms for decades, yet almost none of the opportunities they provide for new approaches to learning and teaching have been realized.

If higher education had exploited the new technology to the fullest, everyone on the planet would already have access to a top-quality college education for pennies a day acquired in less than half the traditional four years. Instead, academics in most instances talk about the value of the machine, but fail to harness the educational value of the computer over the tried and tired method of the lecture.

As Graham Gibbs points out in "Twenty Terrible Reasons for Lecturing," the shortcomings of lecturing are well known.[1] These shortcomings are addressed as well in such works as Donald Bligh's *What's the Use of Lectures?*[2] These authors demonstrate that reliance on lecturing to teach is a poor use of time and energy for both student and teacher. The dominance of the lecture deprives students of rich and rewarding educational experiences available through technology-enhanced instruction. Overwhelming evidence demonstrates that while the lecture is not woefully inadequate—even the worst lecturer probably teaches something—whatever course objectives it does achieve can be surpassed and in a more involving, interesting, and entertaining way.

Survey after survey shows that students find hour-long lectures boring. Lancelot Macmanaway found that eight in ten students reported that the longest they could stay focused on a lecture was twenty to thirty minutes.[3] This observation fits with the evidence from J.O. Johnston and Paul Calhoun's 1969 study that found that students remember less from the middle of a lecture than from its beginning and end.[4] James Trenaman found students absorb significantly less after fifteen minutes, and after a half-hour either cease to learn more or start to forget material learned earlier.[5]

Most students are not skilled note takers and few make good use of notes they do take. A study by James Hartley and Alan Cameron notes that while all students studied said that they intended to go over their lecture notes, nine out of ten never even look at them again.[6] In short, the evidence is clear and compelling that the traditional lecture format has major limitations as a teaching method.

Unfortunately, habits obstruct change. Professors distrust innovation and cling to their existing processes and techniques. This is a natural and necessary phenomenon. We need fairly robust notions about teaching when we stand up in front of students or we would not be able to cope with what, after all, is a fairly difficult task.

We also distrust students. We do not trust them to work independently or find out for themselves, and we feel more secure when they are sitting in front of us doing exactly what we prescribe. Lecturing meets our needs better than those of our students.

By contrast, educational technology presents a new and enhanced form of "learning by doing." Learning does not take place in a classroom isolated from real world job requirements, but in a simulated work environment that provides a low stress, smooth transition into real world work. Learning and doing are essentially indistinguishable.

It seems to us inevitable that more of this approach is going to happen. Fledgling surgeons will interact with robotic technology honing their skills to perfection in hundreds of simulated operations identical to the real thing but with no patient risk. New drivers will learn the consequences of poor driving by experiencing dozens of injury-free automobile accidents. But as impressive as are the richer and real learning experience that technology provides, probably its greatest importance is the near elimination of the cost of education.

We believe that it is essentially inevitable that the very best of knowledge management, learning theory, technology, and curriculum will be synthesized into a highly automated teaching program linked to a robust online community of learners and teachers to provide a world-class, dirt-cheap college education. The key significance of such a "B.A. in a Box" is that it reduces the marginal cost of each additional student to near zero. This means that high-quality instruction can be provided at a cost that anyone on the planet can afford. We are not arguing that you can push the perfect college experience through a wire. But we can assert confidently that the actual knowledge imparted will be at least equivalent to what a good student learns in four years at an excellent liberal arts school. We are also sure that the graduate will have writing and thinking skills superior to that of the average college graduate today, along with a well thought out master philosophy of life.

In our judgment, deployment of educational technologies for learning will change everything in the academy. It will also have profound effects on America's competitiveness, job opportunities, and standard of living, as well as the fitness of our citizens to restrain the power of government. With rapid technological change and growing competition around the world, a highly-skilled, constantly-learning workforce is more vital to our nation than ever before. The growing centralization of government power makes it ever more critical that we have an educated citizenry who can understand complex issues, detect manipulation by demagogues, and grab hold of the levers of power.

It is instructive that despite the protests of professors desperate to hang onto anachronistic methods, technology works. In Indiana, the Buddy System gave students at eighty schools networked computers. During its first ten years, researchers found that this project had the impact of adding a free month of instruction to the school year without keeping the school doors open a single extra hour. And it cost only as much as keeping the schools open one extra day. Incidentally, these results were true for both urban and rural students—for those from high- and low-income families alike.

It is a cliché to argue that we are experiencing a fierce pace of change in an increasingly global economy. But it is also true. The challenge for schools was stated quite clearly by Jack Welch, former CEO of General Electric, when he said. "If the rate of change inside an institution is less than the rate of change outside, the end is in sight."[7]

Schools that ignore the trends shaping tomorrow will cease to be relevant in the lives of their students, and will disappear, though perhaps not so quickly as one would hope. We must transform all formal institutions of learning, from pre-K through college, to insure that we are preparing students for their future, not for our past.

We believe a synthesis of the best thoughts of the best minds of the past and the best of emerging technology will actually make it possible for people to literally create and successfully sustain their own realities, to choose the cards they want rather than waiting to see what the dealer hands out.

The age of electronically customized education is just over the horizon. We see it now; the revolution is here. □

Propaganda Exercises at American Universities

For middle class parents who spend a king's ransom to send their children off to college there is the expectation that their offspring will receive an education in science, math, the humanities and social sciences. This rite of passage is not merely an expensive dalliance, it is regarded as a union card for success. After all, the education pundits are always saying a college degree pays for itself in increased earnings.

What these parents don't know or rarely realize is that universities have become reeducation centers on the model of the old communist institutions that manipulated opinion for "higher" purposes. Let me cite one example that makes this point in an unadorned way.

Professor Richard Rorty, the much acclaimed philosopher who passed this mortal coil, argued that professors in the university ought "to arrange things so that students who enter as bigoted, homophobic religious fundamentalists will leave college with views more like our own." Rorty noted further that students are fortunate to find themselves under the control "of people like me, and to have escaped the grip of their frightening, vicious dangerous parents." Indeed, parents who send their children to college should recognize that as professors "we are going to go right on trying to discredit you in the eyes of your children, trying to strip your fundamentalist religious community of dignity, trying to make your views seem silly rather than discussable."

These were not comments made at Marxist Leninist University or by the Red Guard. Nor was this the ranting of a deranged atheist opposed to the Commandment that says "honor your father and mother." These views are those of a greatly respected senior professor whose positions not only influenced his colleagues but, to a degree, embody their sentiments.

Rather than teach, the prevailing pedagogical assumption is that you should preach. Indoctrination has become the university calling card. Since students enter the halls of the Academy having been "brainwashed" by parents and religious leaders, professors have arrogated to themselves the role of oracles who can decipher moral conundrums with ideological precision.

Is it any wonder that in the hothouse of political correctness we call the university, designated subgroups have privileged status, but evangelicals are routinely ostracized? Is it any wonder that religious observance is routinely derided, while secularism is embraced with religious fervor?

At one point in the history of the university, educate was a reflexive verb. You educated yourself through exposure to great books, scientific analysis and logical exegesis. In the Rorty age, students do not have this privilege. Now they are obliged to be brow beaten into submission, mere clay in the hands of ambitious professors who are intent in shaping students beliefs.

At one point universities were committed to the transmission of knowledge from one generation to the next. That idea is also anachronistic. Now each generation confronts ideas as if existentialists resistant to a past and often loyal to the musings of teacher/preacher pronouncements.

Unfortunately most parents who pay the tuition do not have the foggiest idea of what it is they are indirectly promoting. What they see with rose colored glasses is a son or daughter closing a chapter in their lives and entering the workforce. They rarely consider what the university experience means or the extent to which their own bourgeois and religious beliefs are under assault in our colleges and universities.

Without knowing it, Professor Rorty has actually performed a service. He said what many professors think and what may students experience. Lamentably parents have not yet made the connection. But that day may be coming. And when it does, the university will have a hard time defending itself.

Let me offer an illustration that hits rights at home.

In order to fulfill the requirements for a major in history at Northwestern University, my daughter took a course called "The Cold War At Home." As one might imagine in the hothouse of the college system, left wing views predominate. The students read Ellen Shrecker, not Ronald Radosh. Joseph McCarthy has been transmogrified into Adolf Hitler. And victimology stands as the overarching theme of the course.

Communists in the United States are merely benign civil rights advocates and union supporters. The word espionage never once crossed the lips of the instructor.

An extraordinary amount of time and energy has been devoted to the "lavender persecution"—harm imposed on gay Americans. Presumably, this group was more adversely affected by McCarthy's allegations than others.

Despite the recent scholarship on the period such as Allen Weinstein's well researched book on Alger Hiss or Stanton Evans' biography of Senator McCarthy, views that do not fit the prevailing orthodoxy aren't entertained. Pounded into students is the view that America engaged in "totalitarian practices" not unlike the Soviet enemy we decried.

Although the course is entitled the Cold War at Home, you might think the instructor would be inclined to ask who the enemy is, why was the Soviet Union an enemy and what tactics did this nation employ against us. But these issues are not addressed.

Class session after class session was devoted to the drum beat of criticism. I asked my daughter if she read anything about Gus Hall and the American Communist Party or if she ever heard of I.F. Stone or if any time was devoted to the Venona tapes. She looked at me perplexed.

There is only one theme: the U.S. government was wrong; there wasn't any justification for harassing communists and Edward R. Murrow and Victor Navasky are the real heroes in this period.

Needless to say the historical story of that time is nuanced. McCarthy was over the top, but communists of the Alger Hiss variety did insinuate themselves into key positions in the State Department. Not every communist in the U.S. was a threat to national security, but many were and some gave military secrets to the Soviet Union.

Victor Navasky attacked Elia Kazan for naming names in Hollywood, but as Kazan saw it, he was protecting artistic freedom from communist handlers who wanted to approve every line in a film script.

Looking back, it is not so easy to describe heroes and villains, unless, of course, the instructor responds reflexively to the standard left wing agenda.

Here is the rub. I don't mind having my daughter exposed to the jejune interpretation of Navasky apologists. What I do mind is the lack of balance – the unwillingness to consider another point of view.

When I suggested that she should write her final paper on the role of anti communist liberals such as Sidney Hook, Irving Kristol, Stephen Spender, Midge Decter, among others, my daughter said "my instructor doesn't admire these people and I don't want to jeopardize a good grade by writing about them." So much for open discussion.

Of course, the condition I described is not atypical. Courses in the soft disciplines have become propagandistic exercises as instructors have arrogated to themselves the role of moral arbiters. Invariably the United States is wrong; our historical role in the Cold War malevolent and civil liberties were put at risk by demagogic politicians.

I can only wonder what historical scholarship will look like in a generation as my daughter's brain washed cohorts enter the ranks of the professoriate. □

Adding Competition to the Ivory Tower

For most of this century, even going back to the origin of the university at John Hopkins and Stanford in the 19th century, purpose and goals were well articulated by founders. Knowledge was an end worth pursuing. The foundations of knowledge were largely unfettered by fashionable trends. And, despite the controversies that occasionally arose over curriculum and academic freedom, the pace of change was slow.

The reason for the slow pace of change until the sixties was the singularly focused purpose of university life. Teaching and research, learning and study constituted the faculty-student equation. The utopian effort to refashion the society through university reformism was not yet in thralldom to the adjudication of real and perceived social injustice. Administrators had not yet fallen into a rabbit's hole where symbols were deciphering tools and words were deconstructed like soap bubbles.

Since the sixties, however, colleges and universities have lost sight of their earlier mission and have become institutions at once inefficient and, to some degree, irrelevant. As a consequence, there is probably no area of American economic life in which the opportunities for profitable investment are greater than they are in higher education. This is true for several reasons:

1. It is an immense industry accounting every year for expenditures of more than fifty-three billion dollars, with over fourteen million student "customers" served by it annually.
2. Its cost are hugely inflated, a practice encouraged by heavy direct and indirect government subsidy, an immense amount of organizational inefficiency and inertia deriving from its not for profit status, a consequent inability to make maximum use of the new information technologies, and internal conflicts between its research and teaching functions.
3. A set of products especially with respect to undergraduate education that have become steadily degraded in quality and

steadily less individualized in design, an anomalous circumstance in light of its high cost and differentiated demand.
4. A pervasive "politically correct" outlook, alienated from traditional American values and repellant to a large and growing segment of the American population.

Why, in light of these facts, has the higher education market not been invaded by superior and differentiated alternative products? There are several reasons, but the most important one is the not-for-profit character of the business, which at this point is largely a function of its long history and very calcified habits of mind this history has produced. The not-for-profit character of American higher education cuts it off from the extensive pools of investment capital that would be quickly deployed to transform any other market in which a similar situation prevailed. What exists instead is a process of capital formation inherently unresponsive to demand, dominated by income generated through government subsidy, historically accumulated endowments, and a system of charitable giving governed by sentiment rather than market opportunities.

What characteristics then should a for-profit college have in order to break into the higher education marketplace? First, it should have a clear commitment to the highest educational standard. Put more provocatively it should be self-consciously elitist, trumpeting its challenge to the hollow, mushy egalitarianism that now constitutes the zeitgeist even at so-called prestige institutions.

Second, the curriculum would do what almost all others today strenuously avoid: that is, take the institutions of freedom seriously and devote extended space to their study in depth. Likewise, it would unapologetically affirm the existence of cultural excellence, both literary and artistic, and promise its students a sustained and systematic exposure to it.

Third, its faculty should be well paid but not tenured, allowing it to discharge the non-productive and rearrange programming as patterns of demand change. The faculty should have no formal share in the governance of the institutions allowing its executives to make decisions and changes expeditiously and as needed. And the faculty should not be expected or paid to do research but only to teach. In the public and not-for-profit institutions—especially within the prestige strata—most faculty time is spent on research, vastly inflating the expense of the instruction delivered.

Fourth, the curriculum should be largely prescribed, with comparatively few electives, again in marked contrast to the enormous range of free electives typical elsewhere. This would translate into maximum use of class space and instructional time and optimal teacher-student ratios.

Fifth, there should be little administrative overhead. The relatively streamlined structure of the system and its efficient governance procedures will hold down the number of decision-making levels the college need contain.

Sixth, the college's placement services should develop close connections with the industries likely to hire its students. Instead of the internships in government, "public interest groups" and community organizations, favored by conventional colleges and university, the institution could develop business internships and apprenticeship programs for its students.

Seventh, the college should have a physical plant strictly limited to its needs as an educational institution. Sports, theater, recreational complexes, sprawling acreage, and other costly frills should be omitted from its design.

Eighth, unencumbered by faculty vested interests and outworn habits, the college should make very aggressive and innovative use of the new information technologies. This will allow virtually all purely lecture presentations and a significant amount of student/faculty and student/student interaction to be delivered at the student's home or place of work, and at times convenient to the student.

With public institutions facing retrenchment and private universities rapidly pricing themselves out of a middle-class market, notwithstanding discounts in the form of financial aid, the moment is propitious for a for-profit alternative. The only impediment to this prospect is the well-entrenched interests in higher education that do not want it to occur. Fortunately, the marketplace may not give them any choice. □

Scots vs. English in a Pedagogical Battle

I recently came across an educational distinction that in some ways illustrates the present dilemma in the academy. In the nineteenth century, Scotland and England each had its own view of pedagogy. The English opted for the concrete, for the education of facts; the Scots selected an education predicated on speculation.

The strength of the English pedagogy was its emphasis on a knowledge of foreign language, computational skills and the physical sciences. A bias in the English mind confined training to the ascertainable and concrete. In Scotland the contrast was stark. There, class time was taken up with hypothetical considerations.

In its extreme, the fault of the Scottish system was that it produced vacuous lectures, an ignorance of exact pursuits and the use of diffusive, vague words—a form of nineteenth-century semiotics. Similarly, the English system in its extreme form produced a prickly, factually based knowledge system incapable of generalization or imaginative flight.

Scottish academics would invariably say of their colleagues to the south that they could not engage in speculative debate or cultivate habits of independent and original thought. English scholars would respond glibly that their colleagues to the north speculated in dubious metaphysics and a belief that one can know everything, or, at the very least, purport to know everything.

It seems to me that this pedagogical excursion into the past has its application for the present. Hardheaded Scholars—an endangered species if ever there was one—are like their English predecessors relying on empirically-based knowledge. The theorists, presently in the ascendancy, are like the Scots of yesteryear reducing knowledge to abstractions and engaging in extraordinary forays into the preternatural.

Looking back, it should be apparent that empiricism informs theory. Presumably the building blocks of speculation are ascertainable conditions. In fact, I am confident that on this matter—leaving aside the extremes of each pedagogical school—there is general agreement. The difference of opinion emerges from an assessment of the present state of pedagogy and what academics should do about it.

At the moment, I am clearly on the English side of the pedagogical divide because I am persuaded that basic factual knowledge has been a casualty of abstract speculation. I have observed conversations about revolution and its attendant theories by students who have not read Edmund Burke, do not know whether the French Revolution came before or after the American Revolution, and are not clear about the century in which the French Revolution occurred.

I have encountered debates in prestigious colleges about US reliance on oil as an energy source by students who do not understand the laws of supply and demand, the conservation of energy as a physical principle or the meaning of "energy alternatives."

As almost any instructor will assert the "basics"—the ideas, chronology, skills, formulae—that undergird a knowledge base are often lacking among contemporary students. Therefore, the deployment of theory for students without the building blocks of knowledge is tantamount to constructing an edifice on quicksand. Leaving aside the dubious nature of much theory, how are students going to deconstruct what they have not imbibed in constructive form? How can Derrida's notions of meaning, or lack thereof, be applied to Shakespeare when Shakespeare hasn't been read?

Even if one assumes the validity of theoretical excursions, the intellectual journey must be conducted on some rails with a track bed that provides solidity. At the risk of sounding like an inveterate skeptic, much of what is taught makes faulty assumptions about what is already known. The consequence of this pedagogical error is that what passes for teaching is like deciphering soap bubbles.

My position on this matter is based on what I observe rather than a prejudice against speculation. If I were a scholar in the nineteenth century, I might have been inclined to side with the Scots since they often make valid assumptions about prior student knowledge. That is rarely the case now.

Recently I gave an address about post-World War II politics to a group of American history majors. When I discussed the role of Wallace in the 1948 election, a student raised her hand and asked if George Wallace were running for president that year. I explained that there was a Henry unrelated to George who was the erstwhile Secretary of Agriculture, vice president, and a key figure in the '48 election. While I was surprised that a history major would be unaware of Henry Wallace, I was discouraged by what followed. During the same lecture I made language references to "Achilles' heel," "Alice's rabbit hole," and "Prometheus tethered to a rock" all in the interest of providing texture for my theme. To my amazement, however, these phrases created confusion rather than illumination. As one student noted, "I think your lecture was interesting, but I was confused by the literary references."

Needless to say, generalizations aren't made on a sample of one. But I have heard similar lamentations from colleagues across the country. Because the abstract is so widely used and based on will-of-the-wisp content, theory has become the enemy of information. This, it seems to me, is the tragedy of modern pedagogy. The Scots are divorced from the Brits and don't seem to care about reconciliation.

As long as that is the case, university instructors will be engaged in an enterprise often bankrupt in meaning, and removed from the constraints of reality until the nineteenth-century British pedagogical sensibility is recaptured and wedded to the Scottish paradigm, much of what is called higher education should be relabeled empty speculation.

Additional Evidence of the Zany on College Campuses

In university life circa 1996 the bizarre has become the commonplace. If you want to anticipate the next social craze, consider practices on campus today.

Recently two memos crossed my desk from well-known universities, one public and one private. Each in their way demonstrates how far campus sentiment has veered from the position of mister and missus America.

In one instance, the president issued a letter to all faculty members telling them that as a result of newly adopted Sexual Harassment Policy and Procedures, they are required to attend "a prevention training program." To make sure this matter would not be ignored, a postage-paid response card accompanied the letter so that the date of attendance would be selected.

In the second missive, a Vice President for Student Affairs sent a memo announcing the appointment of a coordinator for "Gay, Lesbian, Bisexual, Transgender Student Services." As coordinator, this person is expected "to oversee programs and services including special events, workshops, newsletters and support groups, as well as serve as liaison to the University community for gay, lesbian; bisexual and transgender students."

Suppose a faculty member objects to compulsory attendance at a sexual harassment policy group, arguing that he or she has not harassed anyone of the opposite sex, acts appropriately to students and colleagues, and doesn't need training in civility, even in this litigious era. Presumably, this would be an act of defiance punishable by dismissal, assuming the faculty member isn't tenured. Moreover, such a requirement smacks of the Chinese Cultural Revolution in which innocent parties are deemed guilty by decree and all must be subject to reeducation. If you don't share the prevailing view of the administration acting as the Red Guard, one can, at the very least, be stigmatized through the power of groupthink.

So influential on campus have homosexuals become that they require their own coordinator. Keep in mind we are discussing a student population of seventeen- and eighteen-year-olds inveterately confused about their sexuality. This homosexual coordinator, who will of course be a homosexual, will oversee university programs including support groups for those unsure about their homosexual leanings. Will such support be granted to those who express misgivings about homosexual leanings? And if a coordinator is needed for homosexuals why isn't there a coordinator for heterosexuals, alas, why not a coordinator for sexual abstinence? I can hear the guffaws now.

In both instances decisions have been made based on the acceptance of a world view. Case one deals with the feminist position that males invariably harass females and something should be done about it, especially sensitivity training incorporating the feminist perspective. Case two deals with a homosexual worldview predicated on the idea that a homosexuality is another civil rights category and must be accepted on its own terms, which translates into special terms. Why exactly do homosexuals need their own liaison to the university community? Don't homosexuals talk to other people or do they only define themselves through their sexual behavior?

Since the presumption behind university life is pedagogical curiosity, it is odd—to say the least—that students cannot weigh the evidence and consider their own judgment on feminism and homosexuality. As these two examples suggest—many others can be cited—university officials tell students what they should think. Instead of parietals of a bygone era that enforced a curfew and the manner of fraternization, the university has moved to regulation enforcing conformity on controversial social questions.

Hasn't anyone considered the position of a devout religious person who considers homosexuality sacrilegious and wishes to maintain that judgment on campus? Isn't it a violation of his First Amendment rights to tell him how he must think? And where is the coordinator for those religious groups that find themselves uncomfortable with the enforced social code on campus? Don't they need programs and services to cope with psychological discomfort?

The one-sidedness, indeed the zaniness, of these proposals stand as vivid testimonials to the emerging moral bankruptcy on campus. For most colleges and universities today, they are not slouching to Gomorrah, as Judge Bork indicates, they are already there. □

Bait and Switch in Academe
Forbes, June 5, 1995

For generations it was agreed what a university was supposed to do. Teaching, learning, and study constituted the faculty-student equation. Not until the 1960s did the universities decide that they were anointed to remake American society.

Since then, they have become, to a large degree, institutions for brainwashing students. They have pulled a bait and switch, promising one thing but delivering another. This creates a remarkable business opportunity.

Higher education is an immense market, $53 billion dollars a year in private institutions alone. Its inefficiency is encouraged by government subsidy and inertia.

While college costs have risen much faster than inflation, contact between teachers and students has dwindled steadily. The time is ripe for private capital to step in. Don't buy pious sentiments about higher education being too lofty to submit to the disciplines of profit making. I have spent much of my life within ivy-covered walls, and I assure you that most institutions are run for the benefit of faculty and administrators, not students. In business the customer usually comes first. In higher education the consumer is rarely even considered.

A few years ago Milton Friedman told *Forbes* that a profit making university could deliver a quality education for $10,000 a year and still make a profit. It's time to test the notion. Could private enterprise bring efficiency without compromising standards? It would have to in order to attract top students. A private university should be elitist, eliminating the mushy egalitarianism that is now the zeitgeist at prestige institutions—a zeitgeist that says "looking like America" is more important than academic ability.

The for-profit curriculum would do what almost all others today strenuously avoid: take the institutions of freedom seriously and study them in depth. It would not dredge up obscure writers and revisionist history to maintain a fiction that all societies and all cultures are equally exalted. It would unapologetically affirm cultural excellence and give its students sustained exposure to it. Gender, guerrilla warfare, and "oppression" studies could be left to the not-for-profit universities.

A private university would pay top salaries but not provide tenure. For "publish or perish," it would substitute "teach well or perish." The faculty should have no role in the governance of the institutions. Executives would make decisions and changes.

Private colleges could tap private capital, where the not-for-profits must beg for money. Perhaps most important of all, the private faculty should not be expected or paid to do research, much of which is worthless anyhow.

Cost savings could be achieved without compromising quality in other ways. The curriculum should offer comparatively few electives. This would allow maximum use of class space and instructional time, and optimal teacher-student ratios. It would guarantee that its diploma would stamp the holder as truly educated, not someone who had breezed through political indoctrination courses.

Huge savings could be made in physical plant. Eliminating stadiums, recreational complexes, and other distractions, or paying for them separately, might take some of the "fun" out of going to college. But it would save tons of money. Unencumbered by vested interests and outworn habits, the privately-owned college would make aggressive use of the new information technologies. Luddite professors and administrator tend to resist technology.

What about the regulatory barriers to for-profit colleges? Right now, the accrediting agencies are controlled by the same people who run the colleges. There are several ways around this. A profit making institution could deliver services through accredited not-for-profit institutions as a subcontractor, thus enabling the not-for-profits to extend their range of courses without incurring heavy expense. In time, with the change in political mood, the present stranglehold on accreditation will be loosened, but ultimately, reputation is the best form of accreditation.

Seventy years ago Henry Ford demanded that his consumers buy what he wanted them to have. His stubbornness nearly sank Ford. Ford's policy had at least this advantage: The Model T was cheap. Modern higher education's Model T is not. It is time for private industry to show how to make a quality product at a lower price.□

Higher Education: A Fog of Misunderstanding
The Jewish Herald, April 19, 1991

It is virtually axiomatic in higher education that more money spent on the educational enterprise yields better results than has been the case heretofore. Exactly what "better remits" may mean has never been clarified to my satisfaction, albeit the nexus between money and quality education is rarely subject to challenge. The word most deplored by academics and administrators is "retrenchment," a word that inspires fear and loathing.

While it is naive to assume that current educational enterprises can continue without money, there is something quizzical about the assertion that money on one side of the academic equation yields comparable results on the other. After years of constructing budgets, I have found very little evidence to support the claim that money buys sound education. In fact, at the risk of facing an *auto-da-fe* organized by my colleagues, I would argue that retrenchment has its virtues.

Very often, a college faculty forced to cut its budget must consider what is truly indispensable in the curriculum. In my opinion this is a much-needed exercise. In the flush period for higher education spending, new programs and courses were added without much debate. Where here was a strong facility inclination, new programs easily found their way into the academic program. These additions were not merely a reflection of a latitudinarian view of educational appropriateness; they were accepted because here was very little consideration of the financial implications of new courses. As a consequence a carefully crafted, philosophically rationalized curriculum caved in to an academic smorgasbord, what some analysts have called the "academic supermarket."

There is a dubious link between scholarship and such fashionable courses as peace studies, feminist literature, social activism, consciousness raising, semiotics, and a host of other trendy ideas. But since the argument could be made that these courses fall into the realm of "curriculum enrichment," and since taxpayers and unwary parents are often bewildered by the financial consequences of these academic experiments, there was relatively little resistance to the rise in spending and the creation of new courses. This exercise, it turns out, is the academic equivalent of "tax and spend." What has happened recently, however, is that he financial well has run dry, and even sacred cows like education have come under careful scrutiny.

In a recent book, entitled *The National Review College Guide,* edited by Charles Sykes and Brad Miner, there is a listing of this nation's "fifty best liberal arts colleges," according to the opinion of the editors. While one might quibble about the selections, there are several obvious points that one can make about their choices. Most of the schools are small without large endowments; Columbia College is one notable exception. All are private institutions unable to count on the beneficence of annual government subventions. And all of these colleges have a well-developed philosophy of education, manifest in a clearly defined curriculum.

Conspicuously avoided in these colleges is the Chinese menu approach to education. These institutions know what is worth teaching and scrupulously resist the idea of having undergraduates determine their own programs. Rarely have I encountered a seventeen-year-old who, upon entering the academy, has a firm grasp of what to read and study. The philosophy of the curriculum is a reflection of the collected wisdom of the faculty. Where there isn't any clear idea of what the faculty intends to achieve through a curriculum plan, you have either a faculty without wisdom or a faculty that has abdicated one of its fundamental responsibilities.

Retrenchment also has the virtue of capturing, faculty attention, somewhat akin to a hangman's noose. As Robert Iosue, president at York College, has pointed out most persuasively, faculty members aren't very productive—assuming that productivity is related to the number of teaching hours in a week. In the 1960s and 1970s it became customary for faculty members to teach between eight and twelve hours a week. Before that period, teaching involved somewhere between sixteen and twenty hours a week. If one were to assume to add the time for preparation of lectures, grading of papers and office hours, the typical professor today works a twenty hour week. The defense of this limited work schedule is that scholars are using their time to explore the frontiers of knowledge. Yet as most surveys indicate, a small percentage of faculty members engage in research and writing; an even smaller number publish.

It, therefore, may be fair to suggest that budgetary reductions can encourage an interest in teaching, an interest that has atrophied in the face of so few demands on the faculty work schedule. Moreover, a resurgent interest in teaching may have some effect on students even though the relationship between teaching and learning is often ambiguous. It is instructive that in the last eight years New York State has increased educational spending by 102 percent in real terms, i.e., after accounting for inflation. During this same period, median SAT scores of our students declined by seven points.

While the spending-achievement relationship is wrapped in a fog of misapprehension, there isn't any reason to assume that educational cuts will adversely affect institutions of higher learning. By focusing the attention of those faculty members now accustomed to peripheral concerns and routine spending increases, such cuts may have the unintended effect of improving the very condition of learning and teaching, about which an intelligent public is justifiably upset.□

Achievements of Ancestors Proves Higher Education Isn't Only Road to Success
New York Tribune, December 15, 1987

If one wants to compile a catalog of inanities, the easiest way to do so is record the public statements of university presidents. There are many examples I could cite, but I don't think any are quite "up to the level" of the recent remarks of Evelyn Handler, President of Brandeis University. Writing in *The New York Times* (11/26/87) about a "Career Beginnings Program," Handler noted, "Higher, education has been shown to be the only truly significant way to provide lasting changes in the lives of disadvantaged people."

Even if one cuts through the hyperbole, the fog of illogic remains. Where is it shown that higher education is the only truly significant way to provide lasting changes for the disadvantaged? What is meant by "truly significant?" How does one determine "lasting change?" In fact, is there any evidence that Handler has discussed her claim with a representative sample of disadvantaged people?

Surely Handler is, one of the new-age scholars who make assertions that can neither be proved nor defended. Presumably it really doesn't make any difference, since her heart is in the right place. Where her head may be, is a somewhat different matter.

Since one can assume that Handler rarely leaves her redoubt at Brandeis—why else should she make so silly a claim?—it is unlikely she met people like my grandparents and parents who did not have the benefit of a higher education. They were also as poor as church mice, albeit fifty years ago no one called them disadvantaged.

Yet they managed to make their mark on our society without going to college. They raised law-abiding, hardworking children who pay their taxes and try to bring up decent kids of their own. However, only the third generation went to college. Most of those youngsters who did and do go to college speak a language their grandparents don't understand, rely on clichés imbibed in classes on semiotics and deconstructionism, and, in most respects, know less about how the world works than their uneducated ancestors.

This is the rarely mentioned lesson higher education has given the disadvantaged. Now to balance the scales: It is only fair to say that many disadvantaged people have benefited from higher education. I can attest to that claim. But there are millions of people who made their way into the upper reaches of our culture without higher education's advantages. Moreover, it is reasonable that many people will continue to be served as well by the blandishments of a free enterprise system as they are by the halls of ivy.

Why must one argue that only higher education can have a truly significant effect on the disadvantaged? A black millionaire who did not have the benefit of a college degree once said, "I don't have a Ph.D.; I have five Ph.D.'s. They are on my staff—Bill, Tom, Charlie, John, and Bob." Another multimillionaire, who also happens to be black, made ostensibly the same point by saying, "I prefer to say 'I is rich' than 'I am poor.'" My uncle Hymie, the consummate traveling salesman, argued, "Everything you'll ever want to learn can be discovered traveling on the highways and byways of this country." Would Handler deny the wisdom in these claims?

Many immigrants who arrive in this land dirt poor find a way to enter our colleges and universities to learn and ultimately prosper. But there are many others who open luncheonettes and fruit stands, some who work on a lathe or sell Bibles, and yet others who join the civil service or the military service without the chance or the desire to enter US colleges. Are their experiences to be written off as insignificant and ephemeral?

An orthodoxy has emerged on US campuses as pernicious in its way as the monolithic belief in radical politics. It is the assumption that the so-called disadvantaged can't get ahead in this society without a college degree. As one might guess, the proponents of this view are academics themselves. Yet the entire history of this nation calls this view into question. There are many roads to success in the United States. Higher education merely represents one of them. There are writers, businessmen, television personalities, heroes, stars, athletes, and actors who have risen like hot air balloons into the stratosphere of national recognition without a college degree and, in many instances, without setting foot on a campus.

Surely these many roads should remain open. It is not appropriate to put up a tollbooth or some other barrier on any road to success in this land of the free. Nor is it appropriate to describe only one way to help the poor. We haven't exhausted the many paths out of poverty in this nation, despite what well-meaning (but incredibly naive) academics proclaim. Perhaps its time for average people to reclaim their legacy from the archives of universities that have largely rewritten our history using erroneous assumptions and misguided notions about how poor people get ahead. □

The Illegitimate College Degree

If events in the late 1960s had a legacy, it was the uprooting of assumptions on which academe depended for 100 years. By suggesting there is no common body of knowledge that should be learned, by rejecting the implicit socializing function of university life, and by avoiding competition as a way of engendering excellence, reformers have dramatically changed higher education.

Area distribution requirements have been abandoned at most major universities to be replaced by a free-floating curriculum. Parietals and any other imposed standards of behavior have surrendered to the onslaught of moral relativism. And grades have lost their legitimacy.

Yet even with these changes, the direction of university reforms remains unclear. Few educators have a reasonable idea of what the BA constitutes. At a recent conference someone asked the chairperson, "What is a BA?" He replied, "Oh, it's 120 credits." But the questioner, still understandably dissatisfied, asked, "But what is a credit?" The chairperson unhesitatingly said, "At my college it's $95."

Before 1960, most colleges had a view of the degree that included the accumulation of credit, the satisfaction of a major requirement, the completion of a project or dissertation, and an oral exam or its equivalent. A degree meant something. The degree had common coinage.

Surely there were good reasons for challenging degree standards. However, the only thing one can be sure of at the moment is the variation in standards. At many non-traditional colleges work, internships, travel, and independent study are equated with courses. Surely these experiences can be as notable, if not more notable, than most courses, but how does one know?

For example, 10 years in the police department as sergeant qualifies a student for 60 credits. The assumption is that something had to be learned in that time and in order to achieve that rank. Obviously, the assumption is debatable; but even when the practice is conducted scrupulously; it challenges the meaning of a degree.

Academic credit has meaning because it is linked to a classroom experience. To give credit for experiences unrelated to a class—regardless of how worthy—may be appropriate but invariably confusing.

For example, my father worked as a salesman for thirty-five years. He was adept at selling anything. However, whenever I gave him some literature on advertising he would say, "I wonder if this author ever tried to sell something to Morris." (Morris was notorious for rejecting any overtures from salesmen.) Now if my father applied for academic credit for work experience how could a fair judgment be made? He obviously knew he was successful at selling, and he would have been the first to admit ignorance of the literature in this field. To grant him credit on the basis of his experience is to suggest that all employees in a similar circumstance are worthy of credit. To reject credit is to apply the standard of the classroom: mastery of a body of literature. But isn't that knowledge supposedly related to performance at some point? And wasn't his performance what business instructors are trying to instill in their students? There are no easy answers.

When seventeen-year-olds announce to parents that they prefer to work rather than attend a university, they are reflecting the spirit of confusion that characterizes the BA degree. When employers bark disdainfully at potential employees with college degrees and no skills, they reveal a prejudice about the BA degree. And when graduate admissions officers smirk when looking at a transcript, the expression is usually a response to the ambiguous description of a degree. These people want a degree with meaning, indeed, with legitimacy.

Lest this be interpreted as a conventional denunciation of experimental programs for vitiating degree requirements, that is far from the mark. Universities need experimentation; they also need clear standards and degrees that have a widely accepted meaning. □

Notes

1. Graham Gibbs, "Twenty Terrible Reasons for Lecturing," SCEDSIP Occasional Paper No. 8 (Birmingham: SCED Publications, December 1981).
2. Donald A. Bligh, *What's the Use of Lectures?* (San Francisco: Jossey-Bass, 2000).
3. Lancelot A. Macmanaway, "Teaching Methods in Higher Education—Innovation and Research," *Universities Quarterly* 24, no. 3 (June 1970): 321–29.
4. J. O. Johnston and Paul Calhoun, "The Serial Position Effect in Lecture Material," T A P *Journal of Educational Research* 62, no. 6 (1969): 255–58.
5. James Trenaman, cited in John McLeish, *The Lecture Method*, Cambridge Monographs on Teaching Methods, no. 1 (Cambridge Institute of Education, 1968).
6. James Hartley and Alan Cameron, "Some Observations on the Efficiency of Lecturing," *Educational Review* 20, no. 1 (1967): 30–37.
7. Jack Welch, quoted in David D. Thornburg, "Reading the Future: Here's What's On Hand for Technology and Education," *Electronic School Online*, June 1998, http://www.electronic-school.com/0698f1.html (accessed February 15, 2008).

4

Experiments in the Academy

In 1972 I established an experimental college at NYU. The word experimental was and remains ambiguous. I argued at the time that students should be conversant with a traditional list of classic texts, but the delivery of instruction may be unorthodox, i.e. the new technologies, tutorial, cross college registration. However, as the enclosed pieces suggest I was in a "small" university overwhelmed by the fervent belief the academy should be transformed along the lines of the prevailing radical agenda.

University Without Walls: Reform or Rip-Off?
Experimental Colleges, September 16, 1972

Student pressures for change—and the academic reform move-ment—have forced university administrators of every persuasion to adopt "experimental programs." In fact, many educators have turned around Lord Falkland's dictum, "When it is not necessary to change, it is necessary not to change" by bringing about change whether it's needed or not.

And so it goes. After having served a one-year term as New York University's campus ombudsman, I was appointed last year to preside over the birth of an experimental college program—a University Without Walls. After all, if the university *ombatman* (the title students gave me) could mediate student complaint, why couldn't he initiate solutions? Where I had once been Solomon, I was now prepared to become Moses. All I had to do—or so I thought—was discover what constituted a sound experimental program, modify it to accommodate NYU's unique character, and accept the plaudits. However, after eight months, after a dozen trips across the nation to look at experimental programs at seventeen colleges, after having the dubious distinction of getting air sick over Pinkeyville, Illinois (on an Air Illinois "mosquito" in my effort to reach Southern Illinois University), I am still perplexed about what an experimental program is and what standards ought to apply.

It is one thing to announce an experiment and quite another, I learned, to implement a program that is truly experimental. In the name of experimentation some very conventional approaches have been pursued. (That, by the way, is understandable; there are just so many "unique" educational options available. When Hampshire College was organized as an experimental institution two years ago, the only alternatives to the lecture system were predictably conventional: work-study seminars, student-initiated courses, tutorials, and independent study.) In fact, aside from modest structural reforms within universities, the only "actual" experiments I have observed are those educational projects conducted outside the confines of the campus. The gospel of Chairman Mao is inexorable: Students must get out "there" away from the cloistered, scholarly elite and close to the common man.

Modest initial attempts to escape the boundaries of the classroom—junior year abroad, work-study programs, and correspondence courses—have paved the way for far more ambitious ventures (*SR,* July 17, 1971). New York's Empire State College, for example, offers students the opportunity to study at a variety of on- and off-campus institutions but has no campus of its own. Projects such as Britain's Open University (*SR,* April 29) have abandoned the classroom altogether in favor of TV, radio, and kits of learning materials. Floating colleges aboard ships and traveling colleges that employ a variety of vehicles seek a global curriculum. The New York State Education Department's Regents External Degree Program awards the baccalaureate to anyone who can pass a series of proficiency exams.

Of all these projects, perhaps the most interesting is UWW, the University Without Walls, a consortium of twenty-one institutions. Organized in 1970 with seed money from the US Office of Education and a supplemental grant from the Ford Foundation, UWW will enroll about 3,500 students this year. A dozen students have already received degrees from participating colleges. The consortium, called the Union for Experimenting Colleges and Universities, offers a "Union- UWW" degree.

University Without Walls is built, if that is the word, on student "internships." In theory, the students construct their own study plans and establish their own community contacts. For example, a candidate for a journalism degree at Skidmore's UWW is doing editorial work for a community newspaper. A second student, an anthropology major at the Berkeley UWW extension of West-minster College, has been living with the Hopi Indians, studying their religion, family customs, and ties to the outside world. A third student worked with a lawyer to establish a community co-op designed to investigate deferred-payment plans and to protect the consumer from unfair interest rates. Primarily because of his experience in the field, this student has been accepted at North-western University Law School.

UWW students can also take courses, theoretically, at any col-lege the UWW consortium. But tuition varies so greatly participat-ing institutions (from $3,400 at Antioch to $300 at the University of Massachusetts) that transfers are granted in only rare cases. In fact, while University Without Walls was designed in a coopera-tive spirit, individual programs tend to be idiosyncratic. A typical student program—to the extent that there is one—includes course work, internship, and independent study. However, the proportion of each varies dramatically from one institution to the next, and at some UWW colleges students plan virtually any combination they want.

At almost all participating institutions UWW faculty members are "adjunct professors," hired on a part-time basis; they are often non-degree holders engaged in business, the professions, or the arts. Presumably, these "mentors" guide student plans and super-vise student activities. But, like most other projects, this experiment is as good or as bad as the experimenters. In some cases, students are given *carte blanche,* usually accompanied by little assistance or evaluation. As long as the student wants to do "'it,'" whatever "it" is becomes worthy of his efforts.

For example, at one eastern college, well known for its experimental bent, a student recently obtained a degree for bee keeping. Her father, a beekeeper, was her mentor. According to her own description, "This study included a minimum of courses or exams; it meant staying at home and giving Dad a hand." At another UWW institution, a black student contended that he should obtain a degree for the same thing he had been doing all his life: "Working in the ghetto." The difference now, of course, is that his activities are being endorsed by the university. Another student at a West Coast college described his internship as "hanging out with the guys." He means the guys in a drug-detoxification program that he entered one year before starting his college "education" and that he continued for credit after enrolling in UWW. In still another instance, a student was receiving eight academic credits a semester for waiting on tables. He contended that this was a "great deal" and added: "I can make 250 bucks a week and complete my degree in maybe five years'"

Despite the rhetorical claim that getting out in the real world is the most direct route to a good education, field activity does not always achieve its intended goal. Some students are deployed solely as a cheap source of labor. In one project I know of, students took jobs as hospital attendants during a labor dispute and became unwitting union busters, to their later dismay. Other students, captured by the enticement of campaign promises, are exploited for political reasons: A whole generation of students can now lick stamps and distribute pamphlets in their sleep. Other students may not "learn" anything from even the most extraordinary experience. After all, as George Bernard Shaw said. "You can take an ass around the world and it won't become a horse."

UWW allows some university programs that have little quality but lots of gravitational pull on students. The bandwagon effect in higher education should not be underestimated; college presidents like the idea of saying, "Look at us—we're experimental." Students, in their turn—particularly marginal students—sometimes view experimental programs as a way of getting a degree that would not ordinarily be available to them. I can't possibly recount the number of times I've heard UWW students say, "Man, this is the way to get an education; it's easy." Harold Hodgkinson, a discerning analyst of trends in higher education considered these factors and others and came to the inevitable conclusion that the University Without Walls is a benevolent rip-off.

It is a situation reminiscent of the Wizard of Oz. Just when the Wizard is revealed as a fraud, he attempts to redeem himself by telling the Scarecrow: "Don't worry about not having a brain. I know many people at institutions of higher learning who do not have one either. But they have one thing you do not: a degree. So, by the authority invested in me, I hereby confer upon you a doctorate in thinkology."

Besides such serious questions about the educational validity of its experimental programs, the idea of the University Without Walls opens a Pandora's Box of procedural nightmares. For example, if the university is attempting to combine scholarship with community service, it seems sensible to offer credit for "life experience" that involves community activity—and all UWW programs do so. They credit, however, the life experience only of those persons formally enrolled in the program. Don't other people have "life experiences" that are equally deserving? To give points to enrollees alone subjects one to the legitimate charge of elitism. And the problem does not end there. If "retroactive credit for life experience" is granted, is it not conceivable that some (enrolled) students will qualify for a degree without having had any college courses whatsoever?

UWW directors at all institutions are now grappling with these questions. The founder of University Without Walls, Sam Baskin, admits that establishing criteria for evaluating life experience "is a very knotty problem. In some places it's still probably kind of shaky. But all UWW institutions are searching for ways to work through this. After all, it's a brand new program, and we're very optimistic."

Life-experience credits can be confusing for students as well as for UWW directors. When we sent out a brochure advertising the new University Without Walls at NYU, begun this fall, we stated that credit for life experience would be granted. Among the replies were these:

"I am an actress, singer, and pianist, and would like academic credit for the work (Broadway, Off-Broadway, E.L.T. stock, television)…and study…I have done. P.S. I am also an' excellent cook."

"What is the responsibility of an educator? To my mind, it is above that of paperwork or tuition and should encourage creativity which adds to the progress of the world…I have earned my music degrees in blood, sweat, tears—and expense…Have I earned my diploma in music? Please send it to me by return mail."

Several institutions avoid the procedural morass simply by supporting all student claims. In one northeastern UWW project, the director's function is to identify "soft touches" (his term) on the faculty who will give students retroactive credit "without the usual hassle." I sat in on a credit-review session in which a young man who claimed to be teaching swimming in a community club was granted six credits of advanced standing in physical education. He presented no corroboration, took no swimming test, and was asked only one serious question ("How long have you been doing it?"). In another case, a student received advanced standing in sociology for having lived in a ghetto all her life. No paper describing her experience was submitted and no examination was required. "My experience is worth more than all the theories in those textbooks," she said, and she was granted eight credits.

Such incidents are certainly not representative. But the very fact that they exist and are generally well known (and often exaggerated) in academic circles adds to the cynicism that surrounds the issue of credit for life experience.

Despite these difficulties, some fifty colleges are applying to join the present twenty-one in the UWW consortium. Many are eager to hop aboard because of the exciting opportunities that the program, at its best, does offer. But it would be naive to underestimate the enormous potential for cost saving and revenue generation that is also inherent in the project. The *First Report of the University Without Walls,* 1972, contends that savings can be realized several ways: "student use of non classroom resources, such as internships and field experiences; [use of] adjunct faculty members...who often serve without pay"; redefining the teaching role as a tutorial and advisement function with a "large number of advisees"; and reducing construction and maintenance costs in major facilities since learning "activities are conducted in the surrounding community...."

The usual cost cited for educating one undergraduate in a conventional liberal *arts* program is between $2,500 and $3,000 a year, only part of which is covered by tuition. In University Without Walls the average cost is between $1,500 and $2,000; often it runs much lower. One reason is that UWW depends on the existence of institutions that it does not directly support. For example, UWW students utilize many university facilities, such as libraries, administrative services, and academic courses to which UWW does not contribute. They also take advantage of community organizations (public libraries, social-service agencies) and courses offered at other institutions—including other universities. Not only must one ask who pays for these services, but also what kind of permanent commitment can be expected from the "regular" (part-time) faculty that may receive no remuneration.

In fact, the University Without Walls calls into, question the fundamental assumption on which universities have been established: the need for resident experts in academic disciplines. Traditionally, universities have been judged by the number of academic luminaries they can attract. At University Without Walls that question is irrelevant. Students can usually select their own mentors a practice that conceivably could erode the educational quality UWW promises to retain. But if an institution can actually maintain its standards and simultaneously reduce the major item in its budget—faculty salaries—the millennium for the university president will have been achieved.

For some universities, particularly the private ones, the issue is not so much cutting costs as increasing revenue. On this score UWW has a special appeal. It is capable of attracting students who would not ordinarily apply for admission to conventional undergraduate programs. Thus, the university can increase its tuition revenue (about $2,700 at New York University an average for private universities) at minimal cost. At NYU only seven of the almost 200 applicants to the University Without Walls had applied to other divisions of the university.

There's more to this, of course, than just the money tree. The UWW is educationally exciting because applicants represent a range in. age and experience that is rarely found in other programs. In NYU's this year are an actress appearing in the film *Fiddler on the Roof;* a seventy-eight-year-old woman who is president of the Senior Citizens' Association; the author of a Book-of-the-Month Club selection; an assistant to the scientist who decoded the porpoises' language; a dancer with the Martha Graham Company; the editor of *National Enquirer;* a corporation president whose daughter will be enrolled at another undergraduate division; a first violinist with the New York Philharmonic; the director of Encounter, Inc. (a drug rehabilitation center); and the editor of a newspaper in New Jersey. As Peter Drucker so aptly put it, "Learning is not reserved for those who are too old to play and too young to work."

It's a happy situation then that the composition of UWW's student logs becomes a graphic selling point to foundations in the incessant academic search for grant money. With traditional sources for undergraduate programs drying up, it is now important to do something "really different" to attract new funds. University Without Walls does this in a way that is often envied by traditional academic projects. In some cases, UWW no doubt deserves its special status and unique ability to fly the experimental flag in search of grants. In other cases, it's just another part of the grand rip-off: Raise tuition revenue, cut costs, and at the same time attract new money to support the experiment. Quality becomes a secondary consideration.

Generally speaking, University Without Walls is a mixed bag: It is not the panacea that some administrators and students believe it to be, and it is probably not the wedge that will open the way to a lowering of the standards of traditional, and at the moment defensive, academics. And, willy-nilly, it is a project that brings to the surface the central issues in higher education. For instance, it demonstrably challenges the nature and meaning of the faculty and its legitimacy as the sole purveyor of knowledge. It asks: If community residents have an integral part in planning student programs, why have professors at all? And if one wants an education from his peers, why attend a university? If one knows as much as his professors, why attend class? And if one does not recognize a community of scholars, why work for the degrees it confers? University Without Walls may try to be a halfway house between the halls of Ivy and the schoolless society, but it can't have it both ways. Either it merges with the community, or it actively attempts to retain the traditions of academia. I have no hesitation in suggesting that it opt for the latter.

This conclusion does not mean the abandonment of experimentation, but it does mean having experiments conform to accepted academic standards. For example, it may indeed be appropriate to offer credit for life experience. After all, work and travel can be learning exercises equivalent to any conventional course. But some consideration must be given to who monitors these experiences, what quality controls apply, and how you distinguish among experiences. From what I have seen, the answers are not yet available and the questions are asked too seldom.

One notable exception is the University Without Walls at Chicago State, which might well serve as a model for other programs. At Chicago State students are offered a program that combines course work and internship in a sensible manner that permits frequent supervisory discussions and the scaling of self-directed learning to student experience and ability. What sets this program apart from others is Its built-in controls and the general good sense of its administrators. Controls are engineered through the idea of faculty-student contracts—an innovation that is being applied in many experimental programs, but with varying degrees of success. The contract obliges students to plan a series of specific activities that can be reviewed and ultimately monitored by a faculty member. It is also a firm agreement that cannot be violated with impunity. And it establishes a standard of judgment and a framework in which to consider appropriate academic activities. For example, at Chicago State only those community institutions that have research activity associated with them are recognized as appropriately educational.

Clearly, that kind of restraint on student choice does not ensure responsible action-obviously nothing could—but it is one way to experiment without violating conventional academic proprieties. And it is adherence to these proprieties that largely accounts for the success of its particular program.

If University Without Walls fails to provide structure as well as openness, it is likely to become the victim of a time lag between the desire for reform and its actual implementation. That is, much of the pressure to pursue "experiments" in higher education came from the students of the Sixties, the children of Woodstock and before. But if the current proliferation of Jesus freaks and other cults is any guide, a return to some kind of orthodoxy will be the theme of the Seventies. Like any other experiment, the University Without Walls is subject to fickle public taste: "In" today, on academia's relic heap tomorrow.

If University Without Walls is to become a lasting and valid educational alternative, it will have to reassess what experimentation can do and to whom it should appeal. Not all students adapt well to free learning environments. At Summerhill A. S: Neill allowed children to choose their own learning conditions; he found that disciplined students responded well to freedom. He also clearly demonstrated (and this is often forgotten) that undisciplined children learn most effectively under conditions of constraint and undeviating standards. There is no simple answer. But the dialectic remains critical in education regardless of the level or degree of experimentation. From my observation, those students with basic research skills, maturity, a sense of direction, and the capacity to do work independently can derive the greatest rewards from experimental education. In most cases this does not include the average seventeen-year- old who has just graduated from high school. It probably also excludes the ritualist who is at the university because of peer-group or parental pressure. And it certainly does not include those who seek a college degree only as the "calling card" for a better job.

After touring this nation from coast to coast in my effort to discover the meaning of "experimental programs," I feel entitled to say that there is rarely anything genuinely new in education. Yet, that should hardly make a difference. There are palpably things worth doing that have been done before. But whether they invite the new or resurrect the old, reforms depend for their success on modest objectives. Experimental education is not likely to change the basic character of higher education; it is merely an alternative track for a small group of students. If that were occasionally recalled, few would take the revolutionary rhetoric seriously and even fewer would make exaggerated claims in the name of experimentation. □

Getting It Together (101-102) For Credit
Human Behavior, September 1974
from *Fitting In: Crosswire at Generation Gap*

Since 1971, I have been involved in—I'm chary of saying committed to—something called experimental education. It's not that I think conventional education cannot involve experimentation, but my belief is—that in, recent years it hasn't—at least not sufficiently to accommodate the children of Woodstock, who saw rigidity everywhere. As someone who is cautious about change, yet willing to entertain new ideas when I believe them to be reasonable, it was natural—or so I thought at the time—that I be involved in these experiments. However, I am also a product of Intergenerational Confusion, a curious psychological state afflicting those who identify with neither Consciousness III nor the Organization Man. It usually means, in effect, that one is too old to "Do It!" yet too young not to try. IC is not something I discovered. The symptoms are *quite* apparent to any atavistic Nixon hater who, at the same time, found the McGovern candidacy abhorrent. Would you believe that products of IC preferred Hubie? Not the Humphrey of L.B.J., but the one who supported the civil rights plank in the Democratic party platform of 1948, the one who initiated the nuclear test ban.

As an IC type, I thought that higher education could use an infusion of energy, even if it did little more than discourage professors from reading their yellowing notes to somnambulant students. On the other hand, I found it difficult to accept the reform zeal of pseudo-intellectuals with rocks in hand who were intent on publicity for their own ends. I argued that only those changes likely to survive and that represented genuine needs would I endorse. It was, therefore, no wonder that from a student point of view I was a fence sitter, simultaneously an ally and a critic.

During a harangue with one of my students, in which I absolutely rejected the idea of offering eighteen academic credits for telepathic communication, my recently appointed assistant good-naturedly interjected, "Herb, you're the Barry Goldwater of experimental programs." I never could identify with Goldwater—the right wing always evoked fears of Westbrook Pegler in me—but that description perfectly characterized my attitude toward the programs I was asked to direct. After serving as director of experimental programs for less than a year, I could appreciate why William Shannon referred to experimental educators as the "new barbarians" From my observation, it became apparent that anything goes—as long as it is labeled "experimental."

The attitude of experimenters was best captured during the following recent conversation with a director at a nearby college:

Yours Truly: What activities do your students engage in when they are not taking courses?

Other Director: Crazy, man. They do everything. Of course, most of the time we have great rap sessions.

YT: But how do you know whether they get anything out of these sessions?

OD: How do I know anything, man?

YT: Well, if you don't have students in conventional courses and you don't require tangible evidence of performance, how do you know when they have completed the degree?

OD: Man, I just know. I just know!

As a giant lump formed in my throat, I looked at this popular, aging guru and said as politely as I could, "I think we have a different philosophical orientation. You *see,* I'm not quite hip; I still believe in papers, research, and assignments." Our acquaintanceship was fading rapidly. As this guy slammed the door he muttered; "That's experimental? Crazy!" If this director is at all representative, and I think he is, you can see why I readily subscribed to my designation as the Barry Goldwater of experimental education.

For someone as unattuned to the demands of this position as I was, it is curious that I got the job in the first place. My insatiable need to live several Walter Mitty lives and my IC sense of uneasiness in most institutional—settings determined my motives. But my selection was another story.

After having been an ombudsman for a year, I paraded my battle scars like a Congressional Medal winner. I was neither universally admired nor was I vilified; limbo is a place to which I am accustomed. When a university commission was organized to investigate and reform undergraduate education, I was one of the first appointees. Since the position required one additional committee meeting a week, I greeted the news of my appointment with the same enthusiasm I reserve for filling out my annual tax statement. But there were compensations. A reformist fervor permeated our meetings. One could really get the impression that we were changing the university. It was also true that we often met at an Italian restaurant that served sensational baked clams.

After several months of meetings, we produced a document, redolent of garlic that expressed our zeal for reform. The commission chairman, who was already an official "change agent" became the director of the first genuine experiment at the university. I was content in the knowledge that a good man had been placed in an influential position; the cessation of committee meetings also marked the start of my much-needed diet. These results were obviously quite related to each other. However, after one month on the job, the stress of being pulled in different directions took its toll; the director rather sheepishly asked if I would assume the responsibility for educational experiments. Without any hesitation I accepted the offer. It was hardly a dramatic moment; some colleagues argued that it wasn't even an opportunity; but it certainly was different. Considering my general state of ennui at the time, that was a considerable plus.

One of the things I learned very quickly is that you shouldn't accept a new job if you have to inherit your predecessor's staff. My assistant had all the warmth of Belau Lugosi after a hard night's work. I also discovered that, she had as much enthusiasm for organizing a filing system as my three-year-old daughter had for putting her toys away. As a consequence, I avoided, coming to my new office for fear that I would continually ask, "Where is it?" Fortunately, she got tired of my penetrating stares and left. Unfortunately, that meant that I had to single handedly write a proposal for the program, design a budget, prepare a statement for the University Senate, obtain New York State accreditation, generate a publicity program, interview students, hire a faculty, gather an executive committee, and answer more questions than were asked during two decades of "20 Questions." Without any assistance I became an institution: I was clerk, secretary, news bureau, registrar, admissions office, bursar, program developer, and dean. For the first time I truly understood what Chairman Mao was talking about when he said, "Every leader must be a laborer." I moved furniture in the morning, typed letters in the afternoon and made grand decisions in the evening. And it all paid off. If something went wrong, I had no one to blame but myself. To avoid creeping schizophrenia, I stopped trying to define my role. When someone asked, "What are you doing, Herb?" I replied, "Everything."

It was easier to justify what I was doing than what everyone thought I should be doing. The faculty was generally disposed to resist experimentation with varying degrees of intensity; this response was based on dedication to some transcendent liberal arts ideal.

On the other side of the fence were the professional experimenters, those individuals who made criticism of academia a career. At a conference on experimental education held in California (where else?), participants were asked to "stop armoring" (Reichian jargon for lowering one's defenses) by means of a sensitivity session. This approach, I was told, was the answer to the "educational doldrums." Eager to find a panacea, I willingly complied with the rules of the exercise. First, I held a portion of a puzzle in my hand while scores of people milled about in an effort to find me and a proper fit for their parts of the puzzle. This is presumably an important symbol for post Freudians. Once my "cell" (since we were in Orange County, a hotbed of Birch ideas, I became a bit paranoid about the term) was organized, we were asked to select one person seated around the table and draw his (her) portrait. I proceeded to draw one fellow as diligently as I could—which was not too well. However, when the convener came by to "analyze" the results, he asked me to describe my feelings by observing my own imprecise lines

I said, "my drawing doesn't reveal very much; I draw very poorly."

He replied, "That's a copout. That drawing reveals hate. You hate the man but won't admit it. C'mon, admit it. You'll feel better if you do."

All I could honestly admit was little aptitude for drawing. But that was obviously the wrong response. "Honesty," in this case, would have been a dishonest "gut" response. I've come to realize that you can often identify sensitivity training by its general insensitivity. I have also come to believe that if this is California's answer to problems of higher education, then the voters probably deserved Max Rafferty.

Confused by the Neanderthals on the left and annoyed by the rigidity of academic patricians on the right, I retreated into my characteristic IC position of invoking a plague on both their houses. As usual, I also found myself with very few allies. When I went to national meetings with experimenters, they always discussed our community of interests. But whenever I insisted that without a consistent tuition schedule student exchange, an avowed ideal was impossible, I was immediately ostracized from the community. Pragmatists are not welcome among experimental educators. Unless the former are prepared to speak the praises of reform with the evangelical spirit of redemption, their colleagues will regard them as quislings.

The direction in which experimental education was headed also caused me considerable dismay. Since university faculties are often rigid and high priced, it should come as no surprise that most experimentation avoids the use of the regular campus offices and faculty. More often than not, educational experiments utilize adjunct faculty whose negligible academic qualifications are matched by correspondingly lower salary demands. The student's "education" continues in a community institution or wherever else he can find it. With relatively few resources, the student has to depend on his own ingenuity—a method which may encourage budding Eric Hoffers or create a generation of Uncle Hymies. It was Uncle Hymie who always told me that experience was more important than anything I could learn in books. Judging from my own teaching experiences in a university, the Hoffers are offering little competition to the Hyrnies. In fact, many universities have so extended the definition of "appropriate" educational activity that participation in student government may now earn the student four academic credits. Many universities now award credit retroactively for work experience. While the granting of credit was a needed reform for those who had educated themselves without the anguish of soporific lectures, it opened a Pandora's Box of administrative headaches. How, for example, does the administrator decide which type of work is worthy of credit? Does he (she) offer credit to anyone who has held that type of job or only to those who specifically apply to the program? Is it possible, or desirable, for someone to qualify for a degree without having attended any courses? These questions are not raised facetiously; surely some students should receive recognition for their informal study. But the abuses inherent in the credit-granting process remind me of a *New Yorker* cartoon in which a king announces to his subjects: "It is my wish that this be the most educated country in the world; toward that end, I hereby ordain that each and every one of my subjects be awarded a diploma."

My own professional experiences tended to reinforce my suspicions of credit being granted for life experience. One applicant requested fifty academic credits for raising four healthy sons. Another student argued that she was a superb cook, an accomplishment which she thought warranted twenty points of advanced standing. Still another contended that her philanthropic activity was "at least worth BA." There were no limits to the claims, unlike the narrowing limits to my patience. I do believe that the granting of credit is valid if it does nothing more than certify the years of research performed by those scholars who have labored anonymously in the dusty stacks of the New York Public Library. I have met people without high school diplomas who knew more about the Civil War than all the American history students twirling Phi Beta Kappa keys taken together. And I am also certain that one can learn more in museums, libraries, and zoos than in all the hours spent in a Philosophy I class playing "battleship." Nonetheless, not every-one wants to learn. More important, everyone's experience is not automatically translatable into academic terms.

In a society where everyone "must" have a degree, where academics are unsure of their roles, and where the student enrollment in private colleges is rapidly decreasing, reform is on the rise. Subject requirements are abandoned at the first whimper of student dissatisfaction. Grades are a legacy of the uptight 1950s, a system of competitive neurosis. And professors vie for popularity by being progressive, committed, groovy, cool with it, and even stoned, but rarely scholarly. Experimentation has become a way of keeping up with the times. The word has a magical attraction; it has been transmogrified from its ordinary usage to become a nostrum for the educational blues. I have no way of proving it, but I am firmly convinced that if Greek and Latin were offered in a so-called experimental program, students would be clamoring to enter. I've already suggested that all traditional programs be called experimental. Unfortunately, some people still take labels seriously.

On the other side of the educational barriers are the four-eyed, intellectual specialists who seemingly cannot stand up without a vest. They view anything that resembles experimentation with scorn. "There is no substitute for a classical education," they insist. "People who use their hands are usually disagreeable and all but a handful of graduate students are philistines." These specialists can spend hours arguing about the exact dates of the Navigation Acts and yet experience difficulty in negotiating the passage from Manhattan to Queens. They can write book length critiques of Norman Mailer, but wouldn't be found dead drinking a draft of beer with him at the Lion's Head. It is also this group that invariably views any modification in standards as the thin edge of the wedge of philistinism. For them, the 1960s was a nightmare, a bad dream they hope to avoid in the 1970s through additional committee meetings. Of course, their suspicions are well founded, but their actions are hopelessly naive. Even the most productive hours of nit-picking research will not transport them out of the twentieth century.

Having labored in the field of educational reform for a short but significant period of time, I thought I would share my findings with others. I was not egotistical enough to believe that what I wrote would make a difference, yet an irrepressible optimism forced me to try. After having visited several college programs that were advertised as being experimental, I wrote an article for *The Saturday Review*, the most popular educational journal in the country. To my surprise, it was published. And that's when things began to happen. Although the article was, in my view, well balanced, several experimenters argued that I had broken the faith. I was branded as a turncoat who had violated "the trust and openness" of experimental programs in a way that "demonstrated [my] irresponsibility." One friend who had read some of the critical letters I received sympathetically noted, "Now I know what Melvin Laird wrote to Daniel Ellsberg after the publication of the Pentagon Papers." I was criticized for using egregious examples (all of them were true, and by no means exaggerated); I was vilified for extracting information under false pretenses (of course, I had no intention of writing an article when I visited the institutions in question); and I was condemned for being an educational reformer who condemned educational reformers. In one month's time, I had become a *persona non grata* at national meetings of experimental educators; and when I heard two reformers chatting about "the bastard," I knew precisely who they had in mind.

This wasn't the only problem, though. The patricians had read my article as selectively as had the reformers. All they could see was "a ludicrous matter" being taken seriously by a "semiliterate educationist." As far as they were concerned, the article wasn't a matter worth considering, except for those who have little else to do with their time but hatch schemes to destroy the university. They did embrace several of my negative criticisms as confirmation of their prejudices, but they rejected my conclusions as a product of misguided zealousness.

Still, I have found that the role of experimental educator suits me. As usual, most people don't understand my motives, nor I theirs. We work side by side, but at cross-purposes. Like so much that had preceded the furor over the article, I suspect that this, too, is a function of IC.

I always liked going to school and I always liked to learn. Sure, I took basketball more seriously than physics, but I still recall that mass equals weight times velocity and that if one is driving a car there's a good reason to recall that equation. I also knew that some guys were dumb—the word has fallen into disuse—and some were smart. If I wanted to learn something or to borrow someone's homework, it wasn't from the local Denny Dimwit. I also knew that some experiences belonged in a school and some indubitably didn't. I remember pitching pennies in the schoolyard and taking bets on whether or not three baseball players would get a total of six hits, but I would have been eligible for Happy Home if I considered these experiences worthy of academic credit. While in college I wrote poetry, painted, and traveled, but I wouldn't have had the nerve to suggest that these activities represented learning experiences. As is the case with most college students, my poetry resembled badly written Gibran with a dash of existential angst, my painting echoed late Kandinsky without the early stages, and my travels confirmed George Bernard Shaw's axiom, "You can take an ass around the world, but it won't become a horse." In short, I was a fairly typical student.

What makes me unusual, if I may be self-indulgent, is my continued admiration for standards that are generally rejected by my peers. Very few students are willing to do hard academic work. The best evidence of this is that, in all the research papers I've read, not one student has been able to demonstrate an appreciation of research techniques. Grand theories, paradigms, models, and proposals are proffered as if generalizations are synonymous with conclusions. But where is the student who still engages in the unglamorous job of serious research? He is probably writing

books like this one, without even a modest gesture to the anonymous academics who make popular works possible.

Experimental education may be right for the person who can
study without much guidance. But it is unfair to the average student
to propagate the myth that any moderately resourceful person can
educate himself. In my experimental programs there are people
who perform well; but they are invariably individuals who have a
sense of discipline, a capacity to work independently, and a maturity that enables them to continue after the first disappointment.

Experimental education emerged in the 1960s as a response to
the so-called desensitizing trap of college—job, success, family,
wealth, frustration. That was the inexorable ontology of middle-
class America and the cancer of its children. As the identity crisis
became more fashionable, the multiversity grew less acceptable.
Education became more than an exposure to the great books; it
was a way of "finding oneself." If one expression characterized
the period, that was it. In the 1970s, it has become chic to say,
"I'm putting it together," but in the 1960s mothers in Miami Beach
hotels would say, "My son Herbie is finding himself." It makes
you wonder where his "self" was all these years.

Most of the time, the finding of oneself occurred at an educational institution and, with increasing frequency, in an experimental
program. It wasn't that experimentation made the search any easier
it was just that experimental programs allowed you to do things
besides study. It used to be that you took a trip and considered it
a vacation, an interlude from study; now it is interpreted as the
study itself. If there is anything that makes the older generation
angry, it is being told that play is study and vice versa.

Few things change attitudes more quickly than a recession. With
belt-tightening more prevalent today than a decade ago, the trends
described by most social commentators may be little more than
aberrational shifts. One now has to take three courses on how to
pass a law school entrance exam; the debris from medical school
applications could be used for a ticker tape parade up Broadway
more impressive than the one held to celebrate MacArthur's return
from Korea. Maybe that is the actual trend. Yet experimentalism
gains in popularity even as medical school applications soar. Per-

haps five years from now there will be nothing but experimental programs and medical schools, and, after ten years have passed, we may have experimental programs in medical schools. At that point we may be saying, "Heaven help the patient with a doctor who is trying to find himself."

Experimental education, like almost anything else, is as good or as bad as the experimenters. There is nothing inherently wrong with experimentation—with the exception of unsubstantiated claims made in its behalf. Perhaps it is worth recalling the obvious: every accepted practice was once an experiment. Yet, for an IC type like myself, there is something objectionable about all the furor. I was and still am a confirmed skeptic on this matter. Before I take a hard line one way or the other, I'll need many more answers. □

Accountability and the Role of the College Professor in Experimental Programs*
College Student Journal, **Spring 1976**

In the past ten years, with the widespread introduction of experimental programs in higher education, the professor has perforce had to confront the problems and possibilities that are attendant with programmatic change. This article attempts to describe the position that the professor has been placed in, as well as the kind of questions he should ask regarding the introduction of alternative study patterns. Originally prepared as a speech at Skidmore College, this paper is neither a defense for experimentation, nor a plea for the status quo. It is a modest effort to illustrate the issues and point out the potential hazards in educational experiments from the point of view of someone who administers a series of alternative programs.

From some fairly undisciplined reading in the field and from my own observation, much educational experimentation is not what its supporters endorse and certainly not what its detractors decry. The range of alternative forms of education, as any student of Plato and Dewey knows, is limited. Yet the climate in the sixties compelled every administrator and his surrogates to find alternative ways of educating the growing number of disenchanted students. What emerged has been a rash of innovative, some not so innovative and some very traditional programs, all called experimental. Experimentation became the magic word in the sixties; it was transmogrified from its ordinary usage and became the counterculture. And to some extent it was true: Experimental programs became the plural in pluralistic university models. They were, in many cases, an alternative route to the Bachelor of Arts degree.

While there were enough students to go around, this alternative was tolerated by academic patricians and even heartily endorsed by administrators who viewed it as a safety valve for campus turbulence. But when the student constituency declined, experimental programs became target. What had been going on for almost a decade now suddenly caught everyone's attention.

Experiments in education affect an infinitesimal portion of American college students. The University Without Walls, for example, has approximately 3,500 students in the participating institutions. But the effect of these programs, at a time when dramatic changes were demanded, was more significant than their numbers would indicate. The fact is experimental programs do challenge some of the fundamental assumptions on which academic programs are created. For example, if learning is not separated from living (to use a popular cliché often attributed to Dewey) why retain a campus at all? And if students can select their own advisors, why retain a permanent faculty? Similarly, if democratic principles are to prevail, how can students be evaluated and given degrees by the faculty?

While the effects of experimentation do have ramifications that affect every aspect of education, the most direct effect is on the faculty. Lest I create the impression that this is a one-way street, let me state the obvious and say faculties invariably affect the character of these programs. Since most experimentation goes on within a larger university setting, programs are usually not introduced without review, discussion, deliberation, and revision; spontaneity, as you well know, does not characterize faculty action. Nevertheless, in the last analysis, it is the faculty that must live with the decision.

And the decision has several critical consequences: First, notwithstanding the limited number of students involved, experiments often generate the fear of job displacement. If a professor reads that he can be replaced by an adjunct, he suspects the worst is in store. Second, experiments often require skills, e.g., counseling, that many academic specialists do not possess. The idea of having to retool to accommodate undergraduates is not what most academic researchers consider fair play. Third, alternative programs are willy-nilly, competitive programs. By example and their ability to attract students, experiments are competing against traditional programs for an even larger portion of the university's finances. And last, the experiments often generate a psychological dilemma for detractors. To oppose them means meeting the Zeitgeist head-on; yet to accept them without criticism is sometimes a violation of the academic standards one was taught to respect. Let me consider each of these consequences in some detail.

Although there have been several instances of wholesale faculty firings (New York University being one such instance), they cannot be attributed to experimental programs. Nonetheless, there is the implication that the expansion of external degree programs and the more extensive use of adjunct professors may indeed create an even more precarious position for the non-tenured facility member than the one that already exists. Please keep in mind that for a middle-class parent it is logical to ask whether the benefits that accrues to attendance at private colleges outweighs the savings often times derived from an external degree program. If the answer lies with the latter case, an unsettling period is in store for many young professors. Obviously, this is all speculation, but recent events clearly invite my tentative conclusions.

It is also the case that when exams and prepared materials become the focus of the Bachelor of Arts program, as in the Open University, the legitimacy of the traditional academic role is tarnished. The variation of views, heated exchanges, and personal idiosyncrasies (factors that account for student interest at the moment) are replaced by standardized exams and general reading matter.

After spending ten years and thousands of dollars for a Ph.D., the average professor is dedicated to his own field of interest. Without too heavy a reliance on William Arrowsmith, it is apparent that the price he pays for this objective is the substitution of a universalistic for a particularistic viewpoint. He doesn't deny the liberal arts and is indeed increasingly using sources outside his area of expertise, but he identifies primarily with his discipline. The idea of counseling a student on matters relating to mundane library questions (one of my students recently asked me, "what is a card catalogue") or on redefining the liberal arts is both foreign and sometimes objectionable to that academic. Some critics maintain that this is the clearest evidence of the failure of higher education and, to be sure, there is a point there even if turgidly made. Of course, it is equally true that the generalist without a knowledge of and a passion for a discipline, is also at a disadvantage. He may grasp a general view but the definition of specific events will be lost to him. But both views are irrelevant if the professor is trained and prefers to work as a specialist. He is then either an inappropriate candidate for an experimental program or someone who after years of training requires retraining in an area in which has no special interest or aptitude.

In the University Without Walls, for example, each student and faculty advisor plan a contract that includes courses and independent study and work related experience. The advisor is usually selected because he has the same area of interest as the student. But what is neglected or left up to the advisor's hesitant decision is the basic liberal arts training—the exposure to the proverbial great books. There are times when they are ignored. I've heard dozens of unconvincing arguments for this decision and times when the advisor starts thumbing through *The Iliad* again to identify an appropriate reading assignment. In my opinion, these options are both unsatisfactory, albeit they are not the only options.

Another argument I hear very frequently, is that new programs—even those that attract new students—are competing for the already depleted resources of private colleges. During a period of financial retrenchment, the argument is particularly persuasive. Afterall, a new program may attract students for a time, but public tastes are fickle and there is the likelihood that an experimental program, like many others, will require financial assistance to survive. Despite the attractiveness of laissez-faire any academic knows the market system could literally destroy many academically valid departments. So what usually occurs is a special nurturing of programs that allows them to become entrenched. As long as experimental programs pay their way there will be no problem, but when that is not possible (e.g., Old Westbury) competition is brought to the surface and so are survival instincts. Moreover, there is just no way of predicting the outcome. In the last analysis, programs with lower overhead have a better chance of surviving in private institutions. That isn't my jeremiad, just my observation of recent events at New York University—admittedly a situation that may be quite unique.

The last problem is by far the most difficult to confront. It is the schism engendered by a willingness to try something different in order to accommodate dissatisfied students and the compromises of values and discipline that occur in doing so. This is by no means an either/or situation; there are indeed many experiments that inspire the confidence of a faculty. But that tends to be the exception. More often than not reforms are accepted with skepticism. Even when they are justified, many faculty members view them as one more concession to the Zeitgeist. This, by, the way, despite the temptation, is not a view to be dismissed lightly. Experimental programs are dependent on the consensual or at least tacit support of the faculty. With considerable resistance any program, regardless of its value, faces the imminent possibility of extinction.

Now that I've defined what I consider the problem, let me explain why I'm involved in the enterprise. In spite of the problems, particularly faculty problems that can result from the introduction of so-called experimental programs, it seems to me that there is a place for alternative structures. It is cliché ridden but true that not everyone responds well to a lecture-reaction-exam approach. It is also true, albeit Machiavellian, that universities may be able to retain dissident students in a parallel structure. These are the students who are first to demonstrate, first to dropout, and first to demand an experimental program. It is equally true that experimental programs attract dissident faculty as well as students. In fact, I can be described as one of those people. I have reached a point of exasperation when something isn't valid because it doesn't conform to the computer program. On the other hand, I am not so much a dissident that I can cavalierly discard academic proprieties. In fact, I've maintained, to the dismay of some of my colleagues at the New York University Without Walls, that our students be asked to meet the most rigorous requirements that apply to an undergraduate program. Simply put, I would say experiments are justifiable when they comply with the highest standards. And I enjoy working in experimental programs that are defensible economically and educationally.

That, of course, still does not answer the problems associated with the faculty. It is my suspicion that two educational systems with several permutations will emerge that are classified as traditional and experimental. Coexistence will be difficult for the foreseeable future, but the existence of each remains a goad to the other. Faculty members will choose, as many already do, their program of primary loyalty, even though they may hold an appointment in both traditional and experimental centers.

It also seems likely that experimentalism will have a relatively minor affect on the number of university students for at least a decade, even though the total number of students in these programs will increase. That, I might add, will do more to mitigate the problems of faculty members than any solution I can cite. It is also the factor that may reduce resistance to the experimental idea. Of course, there are unanticipated factors such as the large-scale introduction of the British Open University or widespread cable television programs that could alter my estimates. But this, it seems to me, is not probable—at least within the next five years.

It should also be noted that tastes change, often more quickly than we might like. The idea that is popular today may be ignored tomorrow. What ever happened to programs for the gifted? And even interdisciplinary studies? Does the same fate lie in store for experimental programs? I think not, but the jury is still out on the subject.

Another consideration which is already apparent is the training of some Ph.D.'s in a way that gives recognition to teaching as opposed to research. Although I never did see teaching and research as mutually exclusive, it seems reasonable that the teaching-tutoring-counseling function will be the focus of experimental programs. And those who have that orientation may well have more employment options than their research oriented counterparts.

What I've circuitously contended is that experimental programs do present hard questions, but the problems may not be subject to reform. Yet with basic characteristics of the faculty role being called into question, there are still few answers to such fundamental questions: What is an appropriate faculty role? On what basis does a faculty confer a degree? What criteria establish permanent entry into the guild? How does the faculty make judgments about what constitutes an "appropriate" learning experience?

As is the case with many academics of both the traditional and experimental variety, it is easier to ask the questions than provide the answers.□

Liberal Arts: Learning from Past Mistakes

Is a liberal arts education passé? In the United States, students have been fleeing traditional liberal arts fields in droves for courses in business, management, and computers. Between 1974 and 1984 the number of bachelor's degrees granted in English fell by 39 percent, in the social sciences by 38 percent, and in the life sciences by 20 percent. Many think the tight job market facing much college graduates completely explains this decline. I think it also has something to do with how liberal arts education was trivialized in the late 1960s and early 1970s.

Many experimental liberal arts programs set up at the time ended up convincing both parents and students that they were nothing more than a one-way ticket to a post-graduation unemployment line. In fact, a degree from some of those programs had unintended effect. As a dean, I recall a young man who introduced himself to me as a "budding playwright." In discussing his program, I suggested that he read several of the highly regarded modern playwrights—Chekhov, Ibsen, Miller. He responded by looking at me quizzically and saying, "I don't learn by reading; I learn from living." I sometimes wonder how this young man is now living.

Despite such egregious examples, a student who is disciplined and goal-oriented enough can profit from flexible educational programs such as apprenticeships and independent study, especially if they are adapted to today's career-oriented times. And one way that students could again be convinced that a liberal arts education is useful and practical would be to take what was valuable in the experimental programs and adapt it to today's career oriented times.

Higher education has long tolerated nontraditional structures. Antioch and Oberlin for decades have been considered experiment institutions with their own unique programs, but their status was accepted because they maintained rigorous standards of admission and their influence on higher education in general was marginal. Everything changed in the late 1960s. It was difficult in those turbulent days to resist the call for change. I remember a graffito on a wall near my office that captured the student sentiment of those years: "Make them [professors] teach you only what you want to learn." With this abandonment of general education requirements at many schools, it appeared as if many professors agreed with that advice.

"Relevance" was in vogue and everyone scrambled to "innovate." Not everyone knew what innovation meant, nor were they always sure of its implications, but it was assumed the risks in doing nothing were far greater than in acting. And act they did. By 1973 almost every major UC university had an experimental college or a division devoted to reform.

Programs included the creations of evening and weekend classes, as well as the University Without Walls and work-study arrangements; degree-by-exam programs; individual study based on learning contracts, adult and continuing education; and even communal education projects in which students and faculty members lived and studied together in the same residence. Many of these programs emphasized flexibility to the virtual exclusion of rigor. "No-grading" and "pass-fail" policies were all too common.

The unanticipated consequence of these reforms was to delegitimize all liberal arts courses in many minds. In many colleges, the liberal arts program was expanded to include dance, film, and the studio arts. In still others, it was a hodgepodge of offerings based on student predilections. Many students came to regard the undergraduate curriculum—traditional or nontraditional—as essentially meaningless to their future. While business leaders invariably tell students that a liberal arts education is the best preparation for the world of work, few students actually believe them.

This is a pity, because while experiments in high education in the late 1960s and early 1970s often vitiated the quality of many college programs, my own experience suggests that there was much to be learned from this period. Most of the reforms introduced at that time were completely abandoned, and those programs that offered courses in "finding oneself" or encounter sessions are now gone. But a few programs, such as the Gallatin Division at New York University and Evergreen College in Washington state, that combine flexibility with rigor and student options with traditional standards, have prospered. It is worth recalling that every accepted practice was once an experiment, but that experiments that do not adapt to changing conditions and the test of common sense are doomed to failure.

The attempt to expand educational opportunity while maintaining academic standards is difficult but not impossible. As long as educators do not abdicate their responsibility to provide a quality of education, and as long as they stay away from a freedom so rigid that it inhibits the very qualities it was designed to promote, colleges may be able to combine selective nontraditional approaches such as contract learning, apprenticeships, and independent study options with high academic standards. Programs that take individual differences into account could yield extraordinary benefits for both colleges and their students. They might even have the added benefit of helping to prepare this generation of students for employment. □

Questions of Viability in Nontraditional Education

Before I attempt to discuss some of the conditions for the viability of nontraditional programs let me start my remarks with a brief parable.

A starving grasshopper ran into a very healthy tiger and asked, "How can I be as healthy as you?" "It's easy," the tiger replied, "find an unwary antelope, kill it, and eat the meat around the carcass." Incredulously the grasshopper inquired, "How can I possibly kill an antelope?" The tiger looked at him for a moment and said, "I gave you the idea. Now you take care of the details."

The moral of the story is that spokesmen with general solutions should be distrusted.

Despite the fact that I am committed to experimental programs, I do not believe they can be viable until some aspects of traditional education are incorporated into nontraditional study. Philosophically I am committed to a set of transcendent values associated with Western and Eastern traditions. Although we might disagree on some of the sources that constitute this tradition, I think there is a body of thought that an educated man should be exposed to. In the last decade we have pushed pragmatism so far, particularly in so-called nontraditional studies, that if a student can do something or change something he is deemed worthy of a degree whether or not he is an educated man. The liberal arts tradition has been so maligned that for me to use the phrase "great books" *or* "an educated man" at a conference on nontraditional study seems incongruous at best and finally bizarre, if you've been raised on a pabulum called "progressive education." But from what I have observed, the experiments that work are precisely those that do not lose sight of historical antecedents and a vision of the "educated man."

Education is not existential. Whether we like it or not we are tied organically to the past. To neglect that, means that in every class or alternative-learning session we merely reinvent the wheel. Either we recognize and use the past or we are caught in the seamless web of enigmas and relativism. Dewey notwithstanding, I believe that Aristotle was right: education of either traditional or nontraditional character must pass on the previous contributions of human thought.

Invariably experimental programs ignore this tradition. In name of all that is new or relevant, Plato and Confucius become the flotsam and jetsam of history and Malcolm X and Hermann Hesse, the only heroes. In the name of egalitarianism, academics ignore their roles and let students decide what is worth reading. And in the name of self-actualization an encounter session leads to personal growth while an evening reading *The City of God* is considered an exercise in futility.

Curiously, some of the most exciting experiments are occurring at relatively "straight" institutions. At Columbia University and at the Claremont Colleges an effort is being made to combine in some coherent way career objectives with those social and philosophical values implicit in every discipline. That seems to me an experiment too long in coming and too often ignored by the very experimenters who can apply its lessons.

But just as nontraditional studies disavow tradition, they often simultaneously dismiss traditional standards. I am, of course, not referring to a grading system that lost its legitimacy some time ago, but to requirements such as research and papers, and skills such as the tools of analysis and communication. It seems to me that while it is desirable to do things other than sit in a lecture hall, it is undesirable to ignore academic proprieties. There is, for example, no reason to believe that because a student engages in field study he has necessarily had a learning experience. The fact is that without sufficient preparation many field experiences are useless. You can take a student on every conceivable field trip, but without some perspective he will remain clueless. Similarly, credit for life experience is an idea whose time has come but whose legitimacy is questionable. No one, I think, questions the validity of offering advanced standing to self-taught scholars, to an Eric Hoffer, for example. But most students I've encountered do not have Hoffer's study regimen. Do we categorically give credit to someone who has travelled, or is married, or has children, or is a good cook? The only rule of thumb that gives this practice justification is when the experience translates into the desired outcomes of a course.

Perhaps the most flawed assumption that experimenters often have an unmitigated faith in freedom. "If he wants to do it, he'll learn," is a refrain I hear so often I do not even bother to challenge its illogic. What I have encountered is so much freedom in experimental programs that students spend all their time deciding what to do and as a consequence are even more inert than their counterparts in traditional institutions. Let me cite a recent case in point.

A twenty-two-year-old student from California stopped by my office quite unexpectedly and said he wanted to rap. Since I spend half of my waking hours talking to students I found his request not at all unusual. However, despite an inclination to rap he had nothing to say. "Why are you in the East?" I inquired. "Oh, just bumming. You see I'm a playwright and I've got to get my thing together." "Well, I'd be happy to discuss drama with you or read your plays. I am interested in Brecht, Pinter, and Grotowski." Oh man, I don't even know those cats," he volunteered, "and I haven't written anything yet. I've got to see the world before I write." "But don't you think you should at least study your craft and read other playwrights?" I naively asked. "Oh no, that would just screw up my head," he replied. "I've got to keep myself open." Of one thing I was quite assured: his head was very open. He was probably not representative of students in experimental programs, but neither was he atypical. Freedom for him and for many with his worldview means no constraints, no regimen, no serious study. Andre Gide wrote, "Art is born of discipline and dies of freedom."

When Sidney Hook wrote his book *The Paradoxes of Freedom* (1962), he noted that a freedom cult can develop an orthodoxy so rigid that it inhibits the very action it was designed to promote. How, it might be asked, can students write novels when they have never read novels? Do we produce filmmakers by merely giving our students cameras?

And do we determine who our social scientists will be by how well meaning they are? The test of experimentation should be the same as in traditional programs: How knowledgeable are students and how well can they use scholarly tools? It would naturally be desirable if they also matured, developed, actualized (you can insert your own cliché), but these are the unanticipated consequences of an education. The fact is, despite everything written by adherents of the human-potential movement, psychologists do not know how to plan for self-actualization.

It also seems equally obvious to me that a professor who presumably knows his discipline can offer a student some counsel. Student initiative should be a goal of nontraditional programs, but this does not happen by willing it or by leaving students to their own devices. Students must be nurtured, advised, and criticized until they are prepared for independent study. Independence suggests a divorce from the professor, a state of confidence engendered by the mastery of skills. That does not happen so easily. Students should earn independence in the same way a tadpole works to leave the pond and separate himself from the limitations of his youth. He works to be free.

What is the BA for experimenters? Is it nothing more than a student declaration of self-awareness? Is it a one-project certificate conferred on the student because he writes a satisfactory twenty-five page paper? It seems to me that without a reliance on some traditional standards—for example, competencies, knowledge, and skills—there is no way to measure performance except by intuition. And that is an article of faith, not scholarship. If judgments are to be that arbitrary, I would just as soon rely on the *I Ching* or random selection for a graduating class. I am not being facetious. At several recent conferences I have been told that my "uptight standards" do not distinguish those who are good. Since I am often unable to distinguish between good and not-so-good except at the extremes and since I am not sure how goodness relates to degree recipients, I asked my critics to tell me how their judgments are made. One fellow looked at me incredulously and "Man, you know, you just know." You can see why I need the *I Ching*.

Since I am an inveterate cynic, it is not at all coincidental that I associate the rise of alternative educational systems with the financial crunch in higher education. Although this is by no means the only reason for its rather sudden rise or the reason that its disciples honor, I am convinced that in many institutions, including my own, it was the overriding reason for the acceptance of nontraditional programs should also add that if I am right, most of these experimental programs will last only so long as their costs are minimal and their ability to produce income formidable. But is this sufficient reason to experiment, and if it is, can an experiment last when it is established on this basis? Educational experimentation should have a logic of its own, a logic unrelated to financial vicissitudes or even student demand. And despite some notable efforts in this direction—for example, the Carnegie Commission Report and the Newman Report—I remain unconvinced by the arguments. So, might I add, are most of my colleagues in this field and many of the students I meet.

Now that I .have told you why I think many nontraditional programs are not viable, please indulge me while I speculate on how I think they can be. Any system that has legitimacy depends on a shared-value orientation. Before 1960, most colleges shared a view of the baccalaureate degree that included the accumulation of credit, the satisfaction of a major requirement, a final project or dissertation, and an oral exam or its equivalent. There were of course exceptions to this rule, but this was the pattern. A degree meant something. Whether you accepted it or admired the standard is irrelevant; it did have common coinage.

This is obviously no longer the case. And to complicate the issue, each degree from an experimental college has a special meaning all its own. Even within programs supposedly sharing a philosophy, it is obvious that no two institutions share similar degree requirements. I should point out that as a pluralist, I am not advocating national and homogenous standards; I am merely suggesting that experimental programs that presumably share some common goals have some common degree standards. But the fact is, if there is an alternative-education movement in this country, it suffers from incurable entropy. What it translated into, of course, is an additional burden on students. A law school admissions officer recently told me that he ignores college transcripts and undergraduate records. When there are so many idiosyncratic record systems and when each college has a different value orientation, the only thing that counts is the LSAT scores. At least that has the advantage of some general meaning. I find this conclusion understandable, but still depressing. I also realize that with the proliferation of many new programs, each with its own philosophy, the trend toward standardized testing will increase. Here is the ultimate paradox: in order to accommodate a variety of needs, we have been forced to rely on a national standard.

The answer—and it is certainly chimerical at this point—is to develop a shared-value system about the goals and characteristics of a degree program as distinguished from a nontraditional program. The particulars of the model, which might include such issues as credits or another system of evaluating achievement, how to allocate life-experience credit, the utility of field experience, a minimal liberal-arts background, the qualifications and expectations of a faculty, still do not result in a philosophical harmony on the meaning of nontraditional study. But the resolution of these particulars is the route to greater understanding.

I am convinced that in the effort to merge work and formal study lies the philosophical framework for experimental programs. But the leaders of this movement should know why work is critical in the educational amalgam. They must be precise about what it can do and they must find a way to measure its effect. I think we share some disenchantment when the liberal arts student describes his degree as an aggregate of 128 points. Yet, however specious its meaning, that is a description. What, I ask, are the assumptions in a nontraditional program and how are its degrees conferred? Until such time as nontraditional study has common assumptions—not attitudes, I might add—it is absurd to discuss its viability. Napoleon once said, "A form of government that is not the result of a long sequence of shared experiences, efforts, and endeavors can never take root." So it is with experimental programs. □

5

Off Track at Specific Institutions

It is one thing to discuss general conditions in the academy, quite another to discuss specific instances of institutions that, in my opinion, have lost a sense of their mission. Cited herein are the illustrations.

Experience with American Law Schools and Attitudes to the War on Terror

On October 15, 2004, I gave an address at Temple University Law School on the theme "Balancing Security and Civil Liberties in the New Century." On my panel were three "distinguished" scholars, one from the ACLU and two with university appointments.

To my astonishment, these panelists represented a unanimous opinion that the United States was violating the civil liberties of collaborators in the war against radical Islam. They spoke passionately about civil liberties violations from the Red Scare in the twenties to the internment of Japanese Americans during World War II.

In fact, they seemed confident that the government had overreached in its security concerns. One fellow discussed the many flaws in the Patriot Act and another, the degree to which the US violated the Geneva Accord with the Abu Garaib atrocities. The names Padilla, Hamdi, and Lindh were employed as a broken record. If one hadn't any knowledge of recent history and walked into the auditorium, they might have assumed these men are national heroes.

Overlooked in the discussion were other names: Bin Laden, Zaquari, Sheik Omar. With the exception of the points I made, one might well conclude the US is not fighting a war abroad but rather fighting against its citizens at home.

That future lawyers might be engaged in the web spun by these civil libertarian purists is enough to offer chilling prospects for the nation.

Are American law schools only concerned with pettifogging legal issues? Is there concern about the threat we now face? Is there a realistic appreciation of what the terrorists have in mind for us? As I see it, the answer to the first question is yes and the answers to the last two, no. Something has gone awry in American legal education.

It appears that courses on Constitutionalism start with the assumption that government is always wrong and is intent on compromising or eliminating basic liberties. Clearly, people should be vigilant about the loss of rights, but they should also appreciate the nature of the present menace and face it with a realism rights obsessions do not permit.

Moreover, the threat at the moment is difficult from any in our past. Deterrence is predicated on basic rationality, a belief that bloodshed can be avoided if both sides in a conflict would prefer to survive rather than die.

If, however, many people want to die in order to serve Allah, deterrence isn't possible. All one can do is eliminate the enemy before he eliminates us. That is the situation we now confront, notwithstanding the unwillingness of many law students to deal with the new reality.

This horrible scenario is complicated by the existence of weapons of mass destruction (biological, chemical, and nuclear), which the terrorists are eagerly seeking. Does anyone doubt that Al Qaeda would be willing to use this deadly force against the United States?

As I see it these law students and faculty members reside in a bubble, a kind of academic womb that protects them from the ugly dimensions of reality. They fight the legal battles of the past: Indian rights, McCarthyism, Chicago Six. They don't realize our world has changed. The threat doesn't come from Washington; it festers in dysfunctional regimes around the globe and in a culture of nihilism.

At the end of the conference an elegant speaker rose to say the US is a "rogue state" because it refuses to adhere to the dictates of the International Criminal Court. I was inclined to laugh at the comment, but resisted doing so because the speaker was quite earnest. It hadn't occurred to him that the US might be hesitant to accept the legal opinion of judges from the Sudan, Libya, and Zimbabwe, among others. For this naive student, America is "the tyranny" we must oppose.

This position was reinforced at a debate organized by Indiana University Law School and Butler University several weeks later. The debate entitled "Civil Liberties and National Security" pitted Nadine Strossen, president of the ACLU, against yours truly.

Ms. Strossen delivered a passionate defense of civil liberties and an equally passionate condemnation of the Patriot Act. The focus of her fevered critique was John Ashcroft, erstwhile attorney general, who she mentioned at least half a dozen times during her remarks. Omitted from her critique was Osama bin Laden, Zarqari, Sheik Omar, or any of the other terrorists whose actions inspired the Patriot Act in the first place.

As I listened to Ms. Strossen and the dozens of students who made comments and asked questions—as you might guess most of the students were inclined to support her contentions—I had a strange sense of *deja vu.*

During the Cold War the United States had communists, anti-communists, and anti-anti-communists. The latter group, while generally unsympathetic to the communists, concentrated their criticism on the anti-communists who they accused of overreaching or of undermining civil liberties. Lost in their calculus was the threat of communism, a threat the anti anti-communists considered greatly exaggerated.

For those like the editors at the *Nation,* communists were merely union supporters, benign critics of income disparity and idealists caught in the web of great power competition. As a consequence, they concerned themselves solely with the actions of the anti-communists condemning at every turn judicial or legislative action designed to thwart communist espionage.

Curiously, as I see it, history has repeated itself. Now we have terrorists, anti-terrorists and anti-anti-terrorists. Those in the latter group either resemble the leftists of yesteryear or, in fact, are many of the same people.

Their enmity is not directed at those who would kill and maim Christians and Jews, Americans and westerners; their anger is directed at anti-terrorists who believe modification in judicial procedure and covert action may be necessary to track down a shadowy and deadly band of global fanatics. Hence, Ashcroft is regarded as a more sinister figure than bin Laden. It is not coincidental that anti anti-communists regarded Joseph McCarthy as a more sinister historical figure than Joseph Stalin.

The only conclusion that I can reasonably reach from these discussions and debates is that there is an ideological plague at American law schools that overlooks or underestimates the threat to national security and overestimates the damage to our liberty through legislative action like the Patriot Act, however imperfect it may be.

Clearly, law is the foundation stone of the American political system and neither I nor John Ashcroft has advocated wholesale violation of Constitutional provisions. Yet it is useful to recall what Justice Jackson wrote in the majority opinion of the Kuramatsu Case: "The Constitution and the Bill of Rights do not constitute a suicide pact." If only the anti-anti-terrorists would remember that statement. Then again, if law professors would consider the balance necessary for national security and civil liberties, they might not have any way to arouse their students. □

Princeton Then and Now

As a basketball player at Columbia College in the late 1950s, I'll never forget the coach's admonition to a Princeton player who cursed and was generally rowdy on the court, "Son," he said,

"You're not acting like a Princeton man." I wasn't sure how a Princeton man was supposed to behave, but from the embarrassed look on the face of this basketball player, he obviously wasn't living up to the Princeton requisites of a gentleman.

This tale enters the realm of nostalgia mythology when one considers the contemporary scene at Princeton. Lest I confuse a couple of examples with hard evidence, let me acknowledge that on a campus with thousands of students, facile generalizations are often not accurate. It is also the case that fashions change, not only from one generation to the next, but from year to year. With these cautionary reflections in mind, I will relate two stories appearing in Princeton publications that seemingly reflect some unknown portion of student opinion.

The *Daily Princetonian* had a story of a lecture given by Suzi Landolphi before a capacity crowd in McCosh 50 entitled, "Hot, Sexy and Safer." Landolphi, a comedienne, discusses sex frankly with audience participation. According to the report, she went down the aisle holding an oblong microphone and said to one young woman, "Why don't you just grab this and hold it tight, honey?" Pulling a Princeton student from the audience, described as a "super stud," she said, "the clitoris, it's about time it got the respect it deserves. Most of you guys haven't found it yet." She then turned to another student and said, "Say vaginal fluid." When he did not respond immediately, Ms. Landolphi squealed, "You sound like it got caught in your throat."

She also encouraged students to be "comfortable with condoms" by tasting, touching, and smelling them. A male member of the audience was asked to have a condom stretched over his head. One member of the class of '90 said, "It was the most amazing thing. I've never seen anybody be so honest about things that you're usually not (honest about)." This student concluded by noting, "I'm sorry that everybody wasn't there."

As a member of the same class of '90, Maia Batlin writing in *On The Campus*, describes several shoplifting incidents at the Wawa, a convenience store near the campus. The most recent incident involved a Princeton junior who was handcuffed and taken to the local precinct for stealing a sixty-nine cent pack of gum. Prior to this case, there were several examples of petty theft by Princeton students. The store manager, Joseph Bendas, estimates "shoplifting occurs approximately 25 times a day." Bendas believes only a small percentage of the shoplifters are Princeton students, although "every person arrested this fall has been an undergraduate."

Given the penalties for shoplifting, Ms. Batlin asks why students would take such risks. She answers her own question with several hypotheses. The first is that students think of the Wawa as "an extension of the university's dining facilities." Said one student, "We go there so often, and spend so much money there, that it doesn't seem like a regular store."

It is also pointed out that the shoplifters are protesting Wawa's high prices. "It's so damned expensive," says a senior. "Who pays sixty-five cents for a can of Coca Cola? It's highway robbery there, and when a store rips you off, you feel like ripping it off back." For other students, Wawa is a convenient target to ventilate dismay with the cost of a Princeton education. As one student explained, "It seems that everywhere we turn at Princeton we're paying another fee. It's awful that we feel this way, but students sometimes lose their perspective and steal from Wawa to get back at the system."

Still another student contends that minor theft is not inherently wrong. He justifies shoplifting as a statement against capitalism. "The Wawa Corporation writes off millions of dollars a year to shoplifting, so prices go up," he says. While he concedes shoppers pay for thievery in the form of higher prices," the people who steal get a break....I think that capitalism and shoplifting are both ritualized theft."

While these views are unquestionably in the minority at Princeton and, assuredly, shoplifting is not in any way countenanced by the Princeton administration, it is worth asking who says this is not the way for a Princeton student to behave. Who tells students that sex is a private matter? Who tells Princeton students that "letting it all hang out" is not the appropriate way for a student to conduct himself even if this act masquerades as honesty? And who says theft is wrong, period, notwithstanding budding Marxists who have rationalizations for their miscreant behavior? Clearly,

Princeton circa 1990 is not the same as Princeton circa 1959. But I'm confident it would be advisable if the old Princeton basketball coach walked around campus saying, "You're not acting like a Princeton man."□

Sex, Politics, and the State University of New York

A virtual firestorm has erupted at the State University of New York at New Paltz over a conference on women's sexuality. This normally placid liberal arts college has been transformed into a bastion of heated free speech debate.

On November 1, 1999 the New Paltz campus played host to a women's studies conference that featured sessions on sadomasochism and sex toys. The explicit dramatization of sadomasochistic techniques and recruitment efforts, as well as a demonstration of sex toys, including dildos, vibrators, harnesses, eroscillators, was enough to inflame the ire of even disinterested observers.

Lee Bell, the presiding officer of the faculty said, "It' s clear they [the critics] were looking for something to use in the service of something bigger." After all, she noted only a little more than $1000 was spent on the conference. "The attacks are a dereliction of duty by the people who are supposed to be protecting the university."

A number of students sounded a similar refrain, suggesting that education requires openness and the expression of many points of view. But the high-sounding rhetoric in defense of the conference overlooks the fact that lesbianism was promoted, sadomasochism was discussed as an alternative to "plain vanilla sex!" and sex toys were on display.

George Morton, a member of New Paltz's college council, an advisory group named by the Governor, attended the conference and said the sadomasochism workshop "was like a recruitment event." Mr. Morton also noted he was revolted by a stripper and s/m aficionado who mounted a male colleague and began whipping him. At least one faculty member shared Mr. Morton's disapproval arguing that "the Women's Studies Program…should not be a platform for lesbian issues."

In the eye of this hurricane is Roger Bowen, a political scientist who serves as president. Mr. Bowen gave the welcoming address for the conference in which he invoked Milton, John Stuart Mill, and former Supreme Court Justice William Brennan as defenders of free speech, "no matter how odious." He called the conference "an important one" because "we are the last chance to help students develop a sense of civic responsibility."

Alas, if a conference on "Revolting Behavior: The Challenges of Women's Sexual Freedom" that emphasizes lesbianism, sadomasochism, and sex toys is how a university president thinks civic responsibility is developed, there is little hope for the redemption of higher education.

It should, of course, be kept in mind that New Paltz is a state institution subsidized by the taxpayers of New York. I wonder how taxpayers feel about spending $1000 to have students learn about sadomasochistic techniques.

Moreover, despite invocations of Milton, Mill, and Brennan, I doubt that any of these figures would defend sadomasochism as an appropriate expression of free speech. So far down the rabbit hole of depreciated expression have we gone that perversity and tastelessness are defended as First Amendment rights. Surely, Jefferson would be turning over in his grave if he heard Bowen's defense of the conference. Not only is the allusion to the First Amendment absurd, but the evolution of women's studies from objective scholarship to an emotional screed for lesbian politics is a betrayal of scholarly standards.

On a more mundane level, the expenditure of public funds for a conference on lesbianism, sex toys, and sadomasochism suggests that the state university has lost a sense of priorities. Wouldn't it be more appropriate to provide a $1000 scholarship to a poor student than underwriting this women's studies conference? Couldn't the library use a new computer?

While university officials contend this was an insignificant expenditure for an event that in the end fostered free speech, I wonder if the administration would have been willing to spend $1000 for a conference on the inheritability of IQ? Would the free speech position have been adopted for Shockley or Jensen, geneticists who believe in race IQ correlations?

Although it is impossible to generalize from one experience in SUNY, it does appear as if universities have adopted a double standard in which politically correct ideas, including the promotion of lesbianism, are accepted and politically incorrect ideas are taboo.

It is indeed peculiar that at the New Paltz campus the once taboo subjects are taken out of the closet and students with little experience are asked to reflect on the perverse and obscene. This is now called *higher* education. □

Divinity Condomized
"From The Editor's Desk," *Academic Questions*, Fall 1992

Little that occurs in higher education any longer surprises me. Segregation by race, banned in the rest of society, flourishes in the academy; meritocratic standards have retreated before quotas, or what are euphemistically called goals; and radical orthodoxy has insinuated itself into the curriculum at the expense of rational discourse. Numbed by these now familiar offenses to decency and good sense, I thought I had become shockproof. But I hadn't taken the Harvard Divinity School into account.

Once a bastion of conservative religious thought and a center for the training of establishment Protestant ministers, Harvard Divinity now rides the wave of radical chic. Its latest outrage is to have sponsored an art exhibit of colorful objects and tiny sculptures—one a bust of C. Everett Koop, the former surgeon general—constructed with condoms. There are condoms covered with beads, condoms covered with fur, with yarn, leather, charms, and feathers—the most colorful sculpture is called "Carmen Miranda" featuring dolls dressed in condoms, images of condoms as if fossilized, and condoms filled with honey, alphabet soup, a baby's sneaker, tiny globes, and sunflower seeds.

According to Karen Norberg of the child psychiatry unit at Boston City Hospital, "The idea is to move away from the embarrassed, secretive, forbidden kind of association to making [condoms] acceptable." "Putting condoms on display," she notes, "pushes things as far as possible in the opposite direction." It certainly does. Carmen Miranda? I guess sex is just a lot of fun, and our only responsibility is not to give, or get, a disease.

Despite Dr. Norberg's zeal to influence social mores, the divinity school has kept this artistic display, entitled "Sacred Condoms," largely out of public view. The exhibit had been open for only ninety minutes a day, and only when the student body was on spring break. Andrew Rasanen, a school spokesman, said the exhibit was "used in teaching students at the nondenominational school how to counsel people about sexuality." "We're really hoping that this doesn't turn into a huge public event," he added, "It is largely/intended to be an in-house educational tool for ministerial students."

If "Sacred Condoms" is to be an educational tool, let us see what we can learn from it. We can learn, first of all, that Harvard Divinity School has elevated secular over spiritual concerns. If guilt interferes with good hygiene, then let us do away with guilt. So what if promiscuity erodes all that is of spiritual value in sexual intimacy? Just be sure to use a condom.

Next we learn that a new aesthetic has replaced that which prizes the exquisite use of line, volume, and color as in, say, the sculpture and stained glass of the cathedral at Chartres. According to the revised standard, something is art, even religious art, if it manages to discover a new depth of vulgarity and plunges in. The point is to thumb one's nose at conventional morality, and not even a sophomoric level of cleverness is required.

Our third lesson pertains to lessons themselves. What now counts as educational? If Harvard's divinity students agree that gazing upon honey-filled condoms is educational, what must the rest of their education be like? Can we continue to assume that a graduate of the divinity school has been steeped in Aramaic, Hebrew, and Greek texts and in the arcana of theological disputes, or that his mind has been honed on fide distinctions to razor sharpness?

Finally, what may we conclude from Harvard's schizophrenic desire both to make condoms "acceptable" and to keep this good work from public view? If those in charge lack the courage of their convictions, perhaps that is because, deep down, they know their convictions are indefensible. They play at being bold reformers, but only when responsible adults are out of the room. They are willing to sap the foundations of society, but not to risk alienating the sources of their financial support.

This furtiveness is not unique to Harvard Divinity School. It has become a pattern throughout higher education, where deans and presidents (with some notable exceptions) regularly deny the existence of the phenomenon known as "political correctness" even while they foster it on their own campuses. Students who report what is really going on in classrooms, on campus, and in admissions offices have frequently been punished or threatened with punishment for telling the truth. An ivy curtain is being drawn, officially to protect the "privileged" communication of teacher and student, but in reality to shield the indefensible substitution of social reform goals for educational goals from public scrutiny.

"Sacred Condoms" may not be much good as an "educational tool," but it is a perfect emblem of what's wrong with higher education today.□

When Language Loses Its Meaning
"From the Editor's Desk," *Academic Questions*

In an open letter to the Duke University faculty, Professor Stanley Fish not long ago claimed that the National Association of Scholars was "widely known to be racist, sexist, and homophobic." Although Fish could not provide any evidence to substantiate this charge, a colleague later defended him in a letter to the *National Review* (25 February 1991), asserting that he "was merely advancing an opinion couched in the inflammatory rhetoric of our time." This colleague went on to note that while one might agree or disagree, with Professor Fish on the merits, "Surely no one today would be *foolish enough to try to find 1950s-style literal meaning* in phrases of this sort" (emphasis added).

Here in unadorned form is where deconstruction has brought us. Words mean whatever we want them to mean; hence, who would take literally terms like "racist," "sexist," and "homophobic?" This remarkable argument leads us down a linguistic path that even

George Orwell didn't imagine. Words don't mean the opposite of what is intended; they mean whatever we wish them to.

Yet simultaneously, "political correctness," deconstruction's ideological sister, has managed to establish an elaborate standard of usage to chastise those whose criticism takes the wrong direction. Several years ago, for example, a Yale University student was placed on probation for a sign he made poking fun at "gay pride week," despite his denial of malevolent intent and citation of First Amendment rights. While his punishment was eventually overturned, he could have probably saved himself a lot of trouble by using the better defense of deconstruction in what, after all, was then deconstruction's stronghold. "How dare you take my words at face value," he might have cried, "I am merely using a language of symbols. Do you suffer from a 1950s literal-mindedness or, worse yet, logocentrism?"

Or perhaps the Brown University student who was recently thrown out of school for shouting anti-semitic and racial slurs should have said, "Don't be so unsophisticated. Attending a prestigious university like Brown, and exposure to Derrida, Foucault, de Man, and Bloom (Harold, not Allan) has taught me the absurdity of precise meaning. How can I be held accountable for using words that haven't any literal significance?"

Of course, on the modern-day campus these "defenses" would be of no real avail, since the self-appointed interpreters of meaning have arrogated to themselves the right to cut through the Gordian knot of indeterminacy whenever it is convenient. Words are illusions only so long as these arbiters do not choose to transform them into something more concrete and sententious.

Can you imagine the outcry, if based on no evidence at all, NAS officials had called Stanley Fish racist, sexist, and homophobic? In the unrelenting onslaught that would have followed, any defense that relied on "mere rhetoric" would undoubtedly have been laughed out of court. Apparently, only literary radicals can tell what is genuine, and their standard is invariably solipsistic. This condition certainly helps explain why rationality is in retreat at many American colleges, and why the victors in intellectual debate are usually those who bully their adversaries with pretensions to a level of knowledge they would deny to everyone else.☐

Inverted Puritanism at Brown University
"From the Editor's Desk," *Academic Questions*, Spring 1991

In yet another concession to the prevailing sentiment on campus, Brown University's fraternities and sororities voted to end "ethnic-minority theme parties." The particular party that sparked the uproar was advertised with invitations depicting a Mexican cartoon figure wearing a sombrero and napping, as if on a siesta. Tequila was served, but there weren't any other examples of the theme's accoutrements, such as costume or decoration.

Commenting on the subsequent ban, John Mohr, president of Psi Upsilon and a member of the Greek Council, remarked that it had been adopted "to show our sensitivity to the issue....Some theme parties can be taken to the point of ridicule and discrimination." John Robinson, Brown's dean of student life, observed that, "The desire to ban ethnic parties may [be] an effort to stay so far away from even unwittingly insulting another culture."

Campus thought controllers, known at Brown as the "p.c."—the politically correct—have insinuated themselves into every dimension of academic life, including extracurricular activities. Karen Hirschfeld, a Brown sophomore, called the theme party decision "the most recent symptom of the festering disease of paranoid pluralism which seems to infect Brown, seething and boiling underneath the surface of our p.c. campus." As Hirschfeld noted, most students and faculty members are actually "inverted Puritans" who will happily engage in drinking and revelry as long as no ethnic or racial group is offended by their antics.

Sensitivity training reigns in an age of mind controllers. Even unwitting insults must be purged lest a group of "designated victims" show offense. It is no longer possible simply to speak one's mind. The Salem witch hunts have resurfaced nineties-style.

But while there is now considerable concern about some subjects, there is almost a complete callousness with regard to others. It is especially ironic, for instance, that many of the college students who seek to restrict other forms of campus expression will go to the mat to defend artistic displays that outrage religious or moral sensibilities. And, apparently, it hasn't occurred to these inverted Puritans that the sale of condoms on each dormitory floor might also slight the feelings of certain students. Finally, they might well consider the possibility that there are conservatives, moderates, and liberals who find the notion of a "politically correct ideology" to be offensive.

But such double standards are hardly new. Inverted Puritans never want their ox gored, but are happy to plunge the knife of defiance into perceived enemies. At today's colleges, a joke about blacks, Hispanics, Native Americans, or homosexuals is unacceptable, even if hostility or disparagement isn't evident. But a tasteless comment about Catholics and, in most cases, Jews, is quite acceptable. That we have come to such a pass has far less to do with sensitivity than with an increasingly strident campaign to impose conformity.

Great strides have been made in national tolerance in the last thirty years, but the tolerance called for today at our colleges is highly selective in its coverage. Not all groups receive the protection of the cultural police. Thus, in the present climate, it is imperative to be exceedingly careful about what you say and how your remarks can be interpreted. If you are not, a metaphorical *auto-da-fe* is being prepared.□

In a Time Machine at Grove City College

Now that the political-correctness police have bared their teeth at the University of Pennsylvania and Hillary Rodham Clinton has told the nation that colleges and universities must commit themselves to diversity (she didn't say diversity of views) higher education is unquestionably in a political hot house. What was once an atmosphere of serenity with occasional winds of controversy has been converted into an environment of political bickering with rarely a moment of serenity.

It was with this in mind that I entered a time machine and went to the commencement at Grove City College in Grove City, Pennsylvania in May 1993. At Grove City, the clocks don't move it feels as if it is 1955. No, this wasn't Bill Murray in "Groundhog Day," it is a real world of manners and morals, of discipline and respect, of sweetness and innocence, characteristics seemingly lost in the rush to modernity and the politicization of universities.

Grove City College is perhaps best known for its unwillingness to accept government money or government mandates. It is indeed the last bastion of independence in higher education. It is also an anachronism. Students follow parietals: young men *call on* women for a date, curfews exist, and students respect the well-manicured quad—no Frisbees allowed.

Students routinely say "sir" and "madam" and, with the exception of one obvious rebel, every student wears a suit or dress to the graduation ceremony. Men are asked to take off their hats in public places and, to my knowledge, a formal protest against this regulation hasn't been registered. Students are required to read classic texts—in fact, the supermarket approach to the selection of courses is frowned upon. Learning of basic subjects is admired and emphasized.

The college is located in an idyllic corner of Pennsylvania far from the maddening crowd. Doors are left unlocked in town. Grove City is a "dry" town. There is one movie theater that charges $2 to see "Aladdin." The kids in this city are refreshingly bright-eyed and bushy-tailed, as if they walked off a set at Disney World.

I compare this scene with what I usually observe: the jean and tee-shirt set I refer to as "unmade beds"; the profane talking and hip swinging poseurs who believe that sophistication comes from converting a four letter noun expletive into a seven letter adjective the defenders of a new orthodoxy based on race, class, and gender and believers in a "democracy" dependent on breeding and privilege.

Grove City College is most certainly a new world for me. When a faculty member said he wished to comment on my remarks, I responded reflexively expecting unvarnished scorn. Instead he said, "I agree with what you said—the speech was wonderful." I almost passed out. Could it really be that a faculty member somewhere in the western hemisphere agrees with me?

As I was about to leave a student came rushing up to me saying "Dr. London, I would really appreciate the opportunity to introduce my parents to you." The parents looked and sounded like Ozzie and Harriet Nelson. I wanted to put them in a cryonic state so I could take them back to New York and occasionally remind myself of the way the world used to be.

On the trip back to Pittsburgh I found it difficult to believe that what I experienced is real. Is there a place where sweetness exists? Are there other places like Grove City College or is this an oasis separated from the higher education desert? A college administrator driving me to the airport said, "this place is unique." He must have been reading my mind.

When I returned to the foul odors of Washington Square, the ubiquitous drug dealers on the street, and the shrill sound of student radicals, I wanted to go "back to the future," to recapture another time as Grove City College manages to do so well. Grove City is not merely a center for learning; it is a place for the development of character and the deepening of the soul. Undoubtedly, the college is appropriately named for a grove. □

A Double Standard at the University of Pennsylvania

In response to several allegedly controversial articles in *The Daily Pennsylvanian*, a group of black students attempted to remove all 14,000 copies of the April 15 edition from the university's distribution points. The students claimed they were merely expressing their disapproval of what they described as "racist editorials"; their actions, they noted, "were protected by the First Amendment."

A disciplinary committee at the University of Pennsylvania concluded that confiscating newspapers is not an approved form of protest, although erstwhile President Sheldon Hackney responded to the incident by referring to the need to balance free speech with diversity. As has been noted by others, this equivalence defied common sense and the provisions of the First Amendment.

Now, however, a recent report suggests the "culprits" in this incident are security guards who "should have recognized that the removal of the DP's...was a form of student protest and not an indicator of criminal behavior." Several officers were singled out for censure. According to the report one officer attempting to arrest a "protestor" "behaved in an unprofessional manner." Presumably, campus police are not supposed to intervene in even "misguided demonstrations." John Kuprevich, commissioner of the university police department, said the role of security officers in the situation described is to record names, interview witnesses, and contact administrators. Arrests and giving chase are verboten.

To say this response is peculiar is an understatement. The *Wall Street Journal*, among several newspapers, noted that logic was sacrificed on the altar of appeasement in this incident. Editors at the *Daily Pennsylvanian* have also suggested that ever since the April incident, university administrators have been more worried about offending minority students than protecting free speech. And one of the campus security guards, reprimanded in the report, echoed this sentiment. After all, in the most recent explanation of the event, he was deemed to be one of the culpable parties.

As one might guess in this era of political correctness, the report recommended that university security personnel receive "training on working and interacting with people from diverse backgrounds." It is no wonder that Alan Kors, a professor of history at the University of Pennsylvania, suggested that the university's name be changed to the University of Peking. Presumably, if one isn't sensitive to a designated minority group, reeducation is in the offing. It is instructive that the security guard who tried to apprehend the students said he didn't think about the race of the self-described protestors when he gave chase. "I really think I would act the same way no matter who took the papers," he said.

That the report makes every effort to accommodate the students is hardly surprising in the present campus climate. Suppose, however, a group of conservative students offended by editorials in a black student newspaper decided to destroy the edition. Would university officials side with the conservative students? Would they seek a sacrificial lamb among security guards?

It is apparent that when it comes to black students in higher education there is a double standard. The cowardice of university administrators is evident whenever incidents of this kind arise. Actually, the security guard demonstrated more sense than his scholarly colleagues. Of course, the students should have been discouraged from taking the newspapers. One would hope that when disciplinary proceedings take place in the fall, they result in an appropriate penalty for the self-appointed protestors, albeit I'm not sanguine that will occur. At this time it is more likely blame will be leveled against security guards trying to maintain order and civility rather than the trespassers who violate one of the fundamental principles of the Constitution. After the report was published a security guard said, "I still don't understand what I did wrong." Neither do I!□

Yale Then and Now

Early April is a nail biting period for high school seniors eager to learn where they have been accepted to pursue a college education. Parents scour mailboxes and e-mails for the anxiety-laden teens.

In the end, of course, everyone will gain admission somewhere since, as America advertises, we have a college for everyone. What we don't have is a space for all the applicants to elite institutions, those ivy colleges dripping with tradition and influence.

Arguably the most influential is Yale, former home to Clintons and the Bushes, among other notables. According to *Newsweek*, Yale may receive more applications for available spots than any other college in the nation.

With that in mind, I recently had the occasion to compare the 1894 Yale College prospectus of elective courses with the 2006-7 Yale College program of study. In doing so, you can't help but be struck by the dramatic change that has occurred in 113 years. Moreover, if evolution infers progress, there is something fundamentally wrong with this comparison.

The 1894 catalogue was fifty pages long. Each course was described succinctly, e.g., "The History of Europe since 1789" or "The Phaedo of Plato," Literature courses are simply named after a playwright, author, or poet, such as "Shakespeare" and "Browning."

The introduction merely indicates how many courses must be selected. A statement of aims doesn't appear. Course descriptions when they exist are brief and very much to the point. For example, in "Latin Philology" "such features of the language are studied as its historical development and decay, relations to other languages, forms and syntax, pronunciation, adaptation to literature, etc."

Courses associated with biblical literature are prominently mentioned, but all, of what we now call, the liberal arts and science are included.

By contrast the present catalogue is 620 pages. Some of that additional content can be attributed to relatively recent developments in the sciences such as neuroliguistics and computer science. While many traditional courses are retained, the college has clearly embraced the concerns of the *zeitgeist*. For example, in the women's gender and sexuality program, one can find courses such as "US Lesbian and Gay History," "White Masculinity and Sexuality in US Popular Culture," "Queer Ethnographics," and "Introduction to Queer Cinema."

At the beginning of the catalogue, Yale officials state their purpose: "Yale College offers a liberal arts education, one that aims to train a broadly based, highly disciplined intellect without specifying in advance how that intellect will be used." The goal is "exploration," stimulating curiosity, and discovering new interests. These platitudinous claims stand in stark contrast to the simple educational goals implied in the 1894 catalogue. Presumably the 620 pages in the modern catalogue, 12 times the size of the 1894 document, are needed to enhance the exploration. The good, the bad, and the ugly must be explored along with the trivial, the fashionable, and the puerile.

In a real sense, the college education of fewer course offerings had a more solid foundation than its modern counterpart. After all, 620 pages of courses can only confuse the teenage mind. How does one separate the wheat from the chaff? The modern catalogue also suggests that the faculty has either lost a sense of what a liberal education ought to be or it has been coerced into the "Chinese menu" of educational selection, i.e., so many from column A and column B.

For me, less is more. A course simply devoted to Plato has more to offer than one called "Plato's Philosophical Psychology." In an effort to satisfy the yearning of professors who seek courses in areas narrowly defined, e.g., "Music, Law, and Sexual Desire in Medieval Europe," the administration has lost control of the curriculum.

Rather than promote a vision of the academy, professors have abdicated responsibility through choices of every variety, a veritable bouquet of experiences. If you cannot find what you are looking for in the extraordinary course list, you can always engage in that old stand-by independent study. Now you can determine what you want to learn without paying much attention to the guidance of an instructor.

Six hundred and twenty pages of courses reduce to fatuity the notion of a central "core" or what it is a student ought to know. At the moment, a student decides what he should know from a vast reservoir of courses.

Is there any one way to manage a university? My guess is Cardinal Newman wouldn't countenance the present curriculum nor, for that matter, would those who attended Yale University more than one hundred years ago. □

Leveraging Feminism at Barnard
"From the Editor's Desk," *Academic Questions*, Spring 1991

The New Age has arrived in higher education. No matter how extreme the prognosis about the future of the educational enterprise, it is unlikely the guess can keep pace with actual events.

Recently the *Barnard College Bulletin* reported on the deliberations of the First Year Seminar Committee, which is composed of two social science and three humanities professors. This group has decided to use a grant from the Ford Foundation to incorporate the works of "minority women" into the college curriculum.

According to the report, the director of the committee, Helena Foley, indicated that the grant will be used to provide a stipend to professors who put works by minority women onto their syllabi. Moreover, Ms. Foley noted, "The money will be used by the professors to buy time to discover and read works, so that he or she can seriously incorporate these works into his or her syllabus."

Aside from the mangling of language in an effort to accommodate modern gender etiquette, the phrases "buy time" and "seriously incorporate" speak volumes about the feminization of the curriculum. "Buying time" translates *into* plain and simple bribes for instructors willing to meet the demands of the seminar committee. "Seriously incorporating" means, in effect, that the works selected must actually be assigned, as opposed to being merely placed among the recommended readings. The committee is obviously serious about achieving its goal.

So far six professors have chosen to take advantage of the grant opportunity. But others will probably be lured by the prospect of money, prestige, and time off. How can a professor easily say no to such bait?

"The spirit of the First Year Seminar," Ms. Foley contends, "is to develop the first year students' ability to write and read about important texts chosen without regard to whatever culture these works come from, [and this] will not change." She added that the selections need not be part of the Western canon, "but the books cannot be junk either." What "junk" may be in this context is impossible to determine. However, it is rather easy to determine that the Barnard curriculum will not rely on the work of dead, white males.

Last year this same committee sent a questionnaire to graduating seniors asking if they thought "diverse" works should be included in the First Year Seminar. About 61 percent of the respondents said they would like to see additional texts by minorities and members of non-Western cultures and about 59 percent said there was a need for additional works by women. As a result of the survey a group of minority and white students were invited to speak to the faculty involved in the seminar. According to Ms. Foley, some time after this meeting the committee accepted an offer made by the director of Barnard's Center for Research on Women to participate in the Ford Foundation grant.

Now that faculty indecision dominates academic deliberations, many actions, especially decisions about curriculum, are determined by a student plebiscite. After all, such recourse always allows the faculty to fall back on the defense that they just offer what the students want. But in assessing this decision, I'm reminded of graffito on a New York University wall written by a radical group circa 1970: "Make them (instructors) teach you only what you want to learn." It is now demonstrably evident that this aim is common practice.

The Ford Foundation gives grants to various institutes at colleges and universities designed to foster research on women. And in order to be eligible for the foundation's largess the applicant must already be a member of the National Council for Research on Women. But as incestuous as this arrangement most obviously is, its most disturbing feature is the leverage it has given to a special interest group. Consider the likely faculty response to a request by a corporate sponsor to alter the syllabus in introductory economics by adding the works of the Austrian school. Although the substance of such a request might be unobjectionable to a few professors, particularly serious economists, most instructors would justifiably balk at the idea of a corporation dictating curriculum change.

Here, of course, is the rub. Foundation money can now provide influence and standing for fringe groups who under ordinary circumstances would be at best peripheral to the academic experience. Instead, they gain real clout, buying time and handing out rewards. Endowed by angels at the Ford Foundation, they themselves become the angels and benefactors of their peers. Is it any wonder the curriculum is in disarray and the defenders of Western civilization are often hiding in their office bunkers? □

Farewell Old-Fashioned Dean
"From the Editor's Desk," *Academic Questions*

Eight male Purdue University students were recently arrested by campus police for running naked across a dormitory quadrangle. They claimed they were participating in something called the "Nude Olympics," an event banned by the university. Shortly thereafter, a Purdue spokesman announced that the students would face a variety of criminal charges ranging from public indecency to resisting arrest.

At a southern university, two male students were apprehended after taking female undergarments from dormitory rooms. A university official declared that this event constituted a serious violation of the rights of women and would be dealt with accordingly.

These incidents and the subsequent reactions by university officials represent a significant shift in attitude. Throughout most of this century, a consensus prevailed that undergraduates would occasionally behave in bizarrely immature ways that included swallowing goldfish, imitating sardines in a telephone booth, engaging in panty raids, or "streaking" simply because they were adolescents. The appropriate remedy was to bring them before an avuncular but stern dean who would upbraid them for their transgressions, while offering both advice and encouragement. This recollection is not simply borne of nostalgia and watching old Hollywood films. On one occasion, my own student high jinks elicited a stern lecture of precisely this kind. I didn't particularly enjoy the experience, but I subsequently realized that it was good for the soul.

Today, university administrators wax eloquent about being sensitive to the needs of a "diverse" campus community, but they have apparently lost sight of a broader responsibility in abdicating their duty as role models and counselors who can combine discipline with understanding. Who would have assumed that "streaking" (or in my generation, "mooning") would call down the full force of the law? Perhaps college executives have simply become too busy raising money, meeting affirmative action quotas, and cultivating alumni to remember what it was like when they themselves were young.

Today's adolescents are not very different from their predecessors. They will be rowdy, naive, irrepressible, and cocksure of their immortality, but still crave limits while seeming to deplore them. Most of them continue to need a warm, supportive shoulder to rely on and a mature person with whom to talk. There wasn't any magic to being a university administrator in the past; a higher degree in educational administration certainly wasn't necessary. Rather it was balanced judgment, tempered authority, and an appreciation of adolescent behavior that tended to serve administrators well.

In an age when parietal rules are shunned and administrators are decidedly not surrogate parents, a contractual, impersonal relationship has emerged, rendering these traditional qualities "obsolete." Students merely "pass through" the educational system and administrators no longer consider counseling them to be their charge. Indeed, such counseling is often among peers, or dealt out by "professionals" hired to provide guidance and apply fashionable theories of psychology and intergroup relations learned in graduate school. Mr. Chips is gone. He has been replaced by a bureaucrat who talks passionately about "needs," but responds to high jinks by calling the police. Common sense and the Dutch uncle have become casualties of an era in which adolescents are treated like toddlers, except when they act as adolescents. Then they're treated as adults. It is hardly surprising that colleges advertising a hospitable environment for learning rarely provide it. Currently, "hospitable" means an army of professional counselors, state-of-the-art computers, and a student lounge filled with video games. It certainly doesn't mean someone who combines gentle solace with firmness. Farewell old-fashioned dean.□

The Rites of Spring at Hunter College
"From the Editor's Desk," *Academic Questions*, Winter 1990-91

There are the old rites of spring and the new. There was a time when a young man's fancy turned to baseball, and couples immersed in romance could be seen strolling in the park. But during the sixties these old rites began to change. As the weather turned congenial, activists seized the opportunity to demonstrate about the war, the academy, the environment, or whatever else elicited youthful indignation. So accustomed have academics become to these new rites of spring that there is now a general expectation that student demands will seasonally emerge like animals from hibernation. Rarely are they disappointed.

Take, for example, the unusually long shopping list of demands submitted to the administration of Hunter College in the spring of 1989, whose contents suggest a great deal about what is on the minds of students, that is to say, the most politicized ones. Paramount on the list was condemnation of the state legislature by the activists for proposed budget cuts, and a demand for "a tuition freeze and rollback." But this was only the beginning. They also wanted to see the Hunter College budget for the last ten years and the asbestos report of the New York Department of Investigation. They wanted an Asian American studies program funded by September 1990. They wanted new elevators. They wanted additional security guards. They wanted 68th Street closed during the period set aside for student activities. They wanted the use of recycled paper in all departments, "recycling drop points for newspapers," and the replacement of "all Styrofoam with recyclable paper products." They wanted all tutoring services to be free of charge. They didn't want college classes held at Julia Richmond High School. They wanted selected administrators and faculty members removed from their positions. They wanted locks on female bathrooms and condom dispensers readily available. They wanted a new gymnasium floor and permission to take children on the campus shuttle. They wanted a student housing placement center. They wanted three students to work with the college's affirmative action officer. They wanted the college to procure buses so that City University of New York students could travel to Albany for "political mobilization." They wanted a citywide convention on "the crisis in public education" to be funded by Hunter College. They wanted to establish and maintain "a multicultural core curriculum reflective of the ethnic composition of the Hunter College student body." And, finally, they called for a "legitimate evacuation plan for disabled students." (Presumably whatever plan was in place at the time didn't qualify as legitimate.)

The demands were predictable; they are part of the *zeitgeist* on college campuses. Yet the audacity and silliness of most of them should be considered without the usual dismissal: "Oh, what can you expect, they're only students." I, for one, do expect more than sophomoric thoughts. Is it too much, for example, for them to realize that a rollback in tuition will block the additional expenditures they also call for?

What judgments would these students make from an examination of the budget? The only thing that could be confidently predicted is a rejection of the present pattern of allocation. Should administrators and faculty members be dismissed because students don't like their views? If they go, wouldn't everyone become a potential candidate for dismissal? Should condom dispensers be available at the college even if this display offends some students? Aren't they already available in the drugstore down the street? Should the college procure buses for overtly political purposes? But if students really wish to demonstrate or organize a convention, why couldn't they do it without the subvention and support of the administration? Should the curriculum reflect the college's ethnic composition? But wouldn't that undercut the City University's historic mission, deepening divisions and failing to address the universal questions that cut across ethnicity and race?

What these demands reveal is an insulation from the world as it is. These student activists are poseurs. They say what they believe the administration wants to hear from them. Their views are formulaic—a dash of ethnic loyalty, some environmental concerns, the *de rigeur* fiscal investigation, an acknowledgment to sexual openness, a nod to political activism, and voila! The soup is ready to be served. If administrators had backbone, they would take such proposals and use them as an exercise in logical exegesis, pointing out with some irony the internal contradictions. This wouldn't alter the new rite of spring, but it might introduce a degree of levity appropriate to the nature of the exercise.☐

Whither PC?
"From the Editor's Desk," *Academic Questions*

Media attention to political correctness has probably run its course, another victim of the insatiable appetite for what's new and fashionable. PC remains. The academic establishment, though chastened and defensive, has not reformed. It continues to subordinate education to social engineering and to shield its more radical efforts from public scrutiny. If proof of the latter claim is required, one need only look at the ways in which many of those in the academy have responded to criticism.

The most curious example is the creation of two groups dedicated expressly to combating the National Association of Scholars: Teachers for a Democratic Culture (TDC), formed by Professors Gerald Graff and Gregory Jay, and the Union of Democratic Intellectuals, formed by Professor Stanley Aronowitz. Among the charter members of TDC are such prominent denizens of the academic establishment as Graff, Stanley Fish, and Houston Baker. Baker, for example, is also the President of the Modern Language Association. These are the people who inhabit the mighty castles of PC. Why do they find it necessary to sally out on the open plain, erecting siege engines of their own? Is it to draw attention away from the fact that they are the establishment?

Next, consider the sad case of the American Association of University Professors, an organization with a long and honorable history. The AAUP has never failed to defend academic freedom from its enemies outside the academy, and it has never even tried to defend that same freedom from its enemies within the professoriate. Adding sins of commission to those of omission, the AAUP has now joined the PC league: a special committee of four, appointed by AAUP president Barbara Bergmann, wrote a "Statement on the 'Political Correctness' Controversy" that denies the PC phenomenon and then proceeds to exemplify it. It fulminates against charges that PC is "the new McCarthyism," and in the very next sentence adopts the late senator's style of baseless slur: "For all its self-righteous verve, this attack [on PC] has frequently been less than candid about its actual origin, which appears to lie in an only partly concealed animosity toward equal opportunity and its first effects of modestly increasing the participation of women and racial and cultural minorities on campus."

Contrary to the AAUP's normal practice, its general secretary, Ernst Benjamin, released this committee's work to the national press as a formal AAUP statement, without a draft first having been circulated for review by other bodies within the AAUP. Apparently, the AAUP's leadership does not trust its own membership to do the politically correct thing. This is another indication that

PC proceeds from the top down: the tenured left is not a majority within the ranks, but it has captured leadership positions in the academy and treats the professoriate with the same arrogant disdain that it treats the public.

After protest, the AAUP republished this same statement, now designated merely as a committee report, in the September-October 1991 issue of its bulletin, *Academe*. The same issue features a long article by Cathy Davidson, a professor of English in Duke University's by now legendary department, in which she attacks PC's critics with the usual virulence: "The media," she says, "has *[sic]* done little to examine the connections" between "the demand that courses in Western civilization be restored to the curriculum" and "the ultraright hate rags springing up on campuses." "This is hardly surprising," she adds, "considering the interconnections between the hate rags, mega corporations, the government, conservative policy institutions, and the national media."

Davidson, who is another of TDC's charter members, also assures us—with, I might add, the same total lack of evidence—that in newspaper stories on PC, "the same half-dozen or so horror stories are endlessly recycled." This itself repeats, almost to the word, the considered and widely publicized judgment of the American Council on Education, a Washington, D.C. organization that represents the top administrative echelons of American colleges and universities. ACE surveyed its own members about whether there was any PC on their campuses, and, most reassuringly, they reported that everything is going along swimmingly. "Fewer than one in twenty reported dissensions," we read in a news item in this same AAUP bulletin. "We were not surprised by the finding," an ACE staff member is quoted as saying—not for the obvious reason of the study's methodology—but because "we had a feeling that the whole PC controversy had been overblown." And she is said to have noted that "many anecdotes have been recycled in the press."

In our lead essay, Heather MacDonald shows how PC's defenders react when they confront more than a few anecdotes: they then reverse course and disparage facts as being no more than a "rhetorical strategy." Their own rhetorical strategies, however, are pure, since they avoid fact altogether. Instead, as MacDonald amply documents, they rely heavily on branding their critics as racists or, "only slightly less damning," as Republicans. Who could deny that on American campuses PC remains alive and well?

Another rhetorical strategy is to exaggerate the charges being made so that one can then truthfully deny that those (exaggerated) charges are true. "Thought control is simply not a problem," Davidson helpfully informs us about Duke. Others have alleged that no one has been fired for uttering politically incorrect sentiments. Although what we are hearing indicates otherwise, it is in their nature that these cases are difficult to prove. Be that as it may, many untenured professors have *Academic Questions* sent to their home addresses rather than risk being identified by their colleagues as NAS members. And, in this issue of *AQ,* we learn of two cases where professors were forced out of their department or program by reason of their heterodox insistence on speaking their minds and upholding standards.

Julius Lester tells us that six months of ostracism by his department did not prevent him from writing what he wanted to, but that there were periods when that "took every bit of steel I had within me." Clearly, it is not necessary to fire dissidents in order to inhibit inquiry and expression. An important decision by a federal judge, excerpts of which are printed in this issue, recognizes that academic freedom means more than job security and that it is violated by the "corrosive atmosphere of suspicion and distrust" that has come to be called PC.

The educational establishment's defensiveness testifies to the NAS's relative success. We have gotten the public's attention and have marshaled the evidence needed to convince it that something is rotten in the halls of ivy. The manner in which the establishment's counter-attack has been mounted serves only to provide us with further evidence. We should use it. For despite their facile calls for debate, it is clear that debate is not what PC's defenders are interested in. We must continue to appeal to a broader public, who, by bringing pressure on the establishment, will help to restore the conditions necessary for genuine debate, open inquiry, and unpoliticized teaching. □

In the Bunkers of Binghamton
"From The Editor's Desk," *Academic Questions*

On March 14, more than two hundred angry students jammed a lecture at the State University of New York at Binghamton given by Professor Richard Hofferbert, entitled "Letters from Berlin 1990: Fall of the Wall." The lecture was intended to be a discussion of the new wave of intellectual and political freedom sweeping through Eastern Europe. Few of the students, however, had come out of any interest in the subject. For most, attendance had been prompted by a vicious rumor that members of the Ku Klux Klan would be present, and that the National Association of Scholars promoted racist views.

Before the talk began, the students congregated outside the lecture hall to listen to Gonzales Santos, an adjunct lecturer, and Edward Pichardo, president of the black student union, excoriate the NAS. According to press accounts, Pichardo told the students: "We must let the [NAS] know that we are not going to stand for their discrimination against minorities....We must question what the NAS is about." Santos added, "We will not allow them to paint us as the barbarians."

Once inside the auditorium, several students verbally abused and menaced the meeting's participants. Some brandished sticks. One, holding a cane, paced behind Professor Hofferbert as he attempted to proceed with his lecture. When Professor Hofferbert passed around a framed photograph of his grand daughter perched on the shoulders of both an East German and a West German border guard, a second student hurled it across the room, narrowly missing several people. The student then lunged at another professor who tried to admonish him, and was only barely restrained by those around him. Shortly thereafter, the same student blew his nose into a tissue and then conspicuously stuck the tissue in Professor Hofferbert's drinking glass.

Among the members of the SUNY-Binghamton chapter of the NAS are some of the university's most distinguished scholars: Aldo Bernardo, Saul Levin, Michael Mittelstadt, Otto Ulc, Anthony Pelligrini, and Giovanni Gullace. All attended the Hofferbert lecture. It was Levin, an admired professor, who was threatened with violence.

After the meeting ended, another student, Adam Bromberg, was punched in the face and knocked to the ground outside the hall because he admitted to having gone to the meeting to hear Professor Hofferbert discuss Eastern Europe. While Bromberg was able to walk away without injury, his assailant, though questioned at the scene by a university official, was not detained.

Clearly these actions beg for an expression of outrage. Yet neither the president of the university nor the faculty has condemned the occurrence in unequivocal terms. In fact, President Lois De Fleur has repeatedly insisted that the reports of the incident were "overblown." Worse yet, the faculty senate specifically refused to censure this effort at intimidation, and in a report on the matter approved in July, actually suggested that, given the NAS's outlook, it was hardly surprising that disruptions might occur.

It is instructive that Dr. De Fleur seemed to be far more interested in containing the publicity than in dealing directly with the incident. Like too many college presidents, she appears unwilling to defend academic freedom if that means risking demonstrations by campus radicals. If not out of a desire to placate radicals, how else can one interpret her contention that campus disruption and intimidation could be explained by "festering social ills in the nation?"

In the aftermath of this affair I was asked to lecture at SUNY-Binghamton. Almost every member of the Broome County Police Force had to be in attendance. Sticks were confiscated at the door, and a security officer brought me to the auditorium through an underground passageway.

It may be an exaggeration to describe the audience as contemporary Brown Shirts; they were more on the order of "Tie-dye Shirts" suffering from sloppy thinking—mere pawns of self-serving ideologues. Their questions at my lecture bespoke untrained minds filled with fashionable clichés about race, gender, class, and the "evils" of Western civilization. It is difficult, of course, for these students to appreciate a canon they generally have not read, or to criticize a society of whose institutions and history they are largely ignorant.

Ignorance should never be underestimated as an explanation for strongly held ideology. It would appear that ignorant rumor incited the disruption at the Hofferbert lecture. And it is the manner in which that ignorant rumor was manipulated that led directly to the unconscionable behavior of several *bien pensant* students.

As ignorance explains the students' actions, cowardice explains faculty and administration inaction. The consequence of this cowardice is the emergence of a bone-chilling attitude that students need not be censured for brandishing sticks at a university lecture. Using the tortured logic of apologists, some faculty members at SUNY-Binghamton rationalize this by arguing that the lecture was given and no one was injured. Indeed that is true. But in permitting hooligans to threaten both the speaker and the audience, academic freedom was irreparably harmed.

The message to me and to students is that intimidation still works. SUNY Binghamton is not a place for the free exchange of ideas. Students and faculty who do not share the fashionable orthodoxy are in jeopardy of physical harm. The administration will not speak out forthrightly on this matter, and the members of the faculty—with rare exceptions—hide in their bunkers. □

The Non-Readers at Nassau County Community College
"From the Editor in Chief," *Academic Questions*

There is little doubt that colleges and universities are not what they once were and, if recent trends are a guide, will not retain even the marginal quality they presently have. As I see it, there are many reasons for this condition, including the politicization of the curriculum and the dumbing down of standards. Yet no matter how absurd the scenarios of university life I imagine, they fail to match present reality.

Take, for example, a report in the Nassau County Community College student newspaper on Literary Day. Three sessions were held on this occasion with the titles "Alienation in the Classroom," "The Imperfect Decoder: Penalties for Non-Standard Language Production," and "Negotiating the Text before You Read."

The first session dealt with the problems that occur in classrooms between professors and students. Speakers explained how statements like "Half of you won't be here at the end of the semester" prompt student alienation.

The second session, "The Imperfect Decoder," addressed the problems attached to reading "difficult" textbooks. And the last session encouraged students to "Get a Mind Set" before reading the text. Students were told to "read the title of a book before reading the contents."

If Literary Day were the focus of a "Saturday Night Live" skit, viewers might regard it as too extreme for plausible satire. However, reality defies logic. No longer is it possible for a professor to say some things that are empirically valid, e.g., "half the students will drop out." After all, John and Mary may not like this statement.

"The Imperfect Decoder" is little more than a euphemism for semi-literacy. A demonstrated need to discuss this topic suggests in unadorned fashion that students at Nassau Community College cannot read college-level texts. In effect, colleges have gone from remediation centers to kindergartens, all the while using a language of obfuscation to deny student deficiencies.

And then there is my favorite discussion: getting a mind-set. One gets a mind-set, it is argued, by reading the title of a book. I wonder what mind-set semi-literates get when they read a title like *The Iliad.* Since Homer is unknown to most students and since the author can easily be confused with Homer Simpson, *The Iliad* might well be conceived of as a television program instead of an epic poem.

This educational experience—I use the phrase generously—is not "trained incapacity," to borrow Thorstein Veblen's term. It is untrained incapacity. How can you train non-readers? This isn't a student group propagandized by Derrida's abstract logic, it is a student population trying hard to read Donald Duck.

That taxpayer money to the tune of $17,000 a student is spent on this nonsense is an outrage. The fact that such silliness is countenanced at Nassau County Community College and similar institutions is cause for profound concern. Not only are many students poorly prepared for formal higher education, but the public is being asked to subsidize basic reading programs for college students in the name of "imperfect decoding." The college experience, for many of these students, is a replay of elementary education. In the process a great deception is being fostered.

Students and parents often believe they have received a college education when, in fact, students have been engaged in child's play. Taxpayers are led to believe this investment in human capital is worthwhile, even though the return on investment is negligible. And university-trained professors are obliged to foster the ruse so that a justification for their efforts and salary can be found.

All of this raises a serious question about truth in advertising. Should an institution engaged in elementary education call itself a "college?" And if it is not a college, then what purpose does it serve, and is that purpose worth the price?□

6

Sports and Educational Standards

Having played big-time basketball at Columbia, I realize that sports can play an important part in one's life. It did in mine. Yet at no time did I compromise scholarship for athletics. As contemporary conditions now suggest, that claim has a distinctly anachronistic ring to it.

The NCAA, Discrimination, and the Corruption of College Sports

Recently trial lawyers for Public Justice (TLPJ)—the title is a dead giveaway filed a national race discrimination class action suit against the National College Athletic Association (N.C.A.A.)—charged that the freshman eligibility rules discriminate against black student athletes.

The NCAA, which governs intercollegiate athletics, requires potential student athletes to achieve a 2.0 grade point average in eleven academic courses and attain at least a combined score of 700 on the Scholastic Aptitude Test (SAT) or a 15 on the American college Test (ACT). Because of opposition to this standard (Proposition 48) by coaches and a group of black educators, it was modified (Proposal 42) so that students who graduate with a 2.0 grade point average but fail to meet the minimum SAT or ACT score may still receive an athletic scholarship if they lose a year of athletic eligibility.

The TLPJ lawsuit charges that these requirements—minimal and flexible as they are—violate Title VI of the civil Rights Act of 1964, which prohibits race discrimination by educational institutions receiving federal funds. According to Andre Dennis, the co-lead counsel, "minimum test score requirements discriminate against African Americans." The class action lawsuit, *Cureton vs. NCAA*, was filed on behalf of Tai Kwari Cureton and Leatrice Shaw who graduated from a Philadelphia high school and were recruited for track teams at several division I colleges. However, the recruiting abruptly ceased when these track stars could not meet the minimum SAT score requirement.

TLPJ lawyers contend that a "fixed cut-off score is completely unjustified." "Colleges," noted one lawyer, "do not even use fixed cut-off scores to determine admissions. The NCA A's reliance on this one-size-fits-all cut-off score arbitrarily denies athletic opportunities for African-American students."

Lest any of the TLPJ arguments be taken seriously, it should be noted for those unfamiliar with SAT scoring that students automatically receive 400 points for writing their names and addresses. Moreover, in an era of depreciated standards, a 2.0 grade point average, or C average, is achievable for all but the brain dead. And last, even if an athlete—I can't bring myself to say student athlete—cannot meet this minimum standard, the only penalty incurred is the loss of one year's athletic eligibility.

Notwithstanding this reality, the NCAA minimal requirements are still perceived by some lawyers as a form of race discrimination. Since any standard is tautologically a form of discrimination, the only thing the NCAA can do to meet the TLPJ objection is withdraw any academic standard for potential athletes. That would remove the stigma of discrimination; it would also deceive many athletes into believing that basic skills such as reading, writing, and computation are unimportant and all that counts is sinking a jump shot from twenty feet or catching a forty-yard pass.

It is instructive that only a small percentage of the black basketball and football players at Division I schools graduate from college. Since an even smaller percentage will go on to professional sports, the athletic scholarship deception is not without its victims. Young men from the inner city with glory dancing like sugarplums in their youthful imaginations assume they will ride the gravy train to fame and fortune. They learn about stars like Jordan and Sanders, O'Neal and Irvin; they don't hear the tales of misery and disappointment, of missed opportunity and youthful exuberance converted to despair.

With so many frivolous lawsuits in the courts, I am not surprised by the TLPJ discrimination charge. But if the TLPJ charge has any validity, then it follows that not having Chinese players on the University of California basketball team is a form of discrimination as well. After all, one-third of the student population is Asian and not one of them is on the team. Similarly, those under five feet five are routinely discriminated against in the selection of basketball teams with the exception of Mugsy Bogues, no one in the NBA is under this height standard; yet this diminutive group constitutes half of the population. Isn't it arbitrary having a basket hung at ten feet? Shouldn't shorter players have the same opportunity as taller players?

There isn't an end to this line of argument. If a standard is a violation of the civil Rights Act, then all tests in which results reflect a bell-shaped curve are unlawful. If all applicants cannot gain admission to an institution, whether it be the Military Academy or the Police Academy, because of some screen, then the law has been broken with radical egalitarianism, any standard is wrong. In fact, what TLPJ should note is that scores themselves are an arbitrary convention for selecting winners. Far better to give everyone a chance to play and don't keep score at all. Why, after all, should sports maintain a standard for victory when the presumption is made that college admission standards for athletes on scholarship are unlawful? I'd love to hear the TLPJ response to this question. □

Coddling of College Athletes
Only Damages Youths in Question
New York City Tribune, February 14, 1989

It is noteworthy that college basketball coaches have become concerned about educational opportunities for poor black youths. Lest these altruistic motives be seen for anything other than what they are, the opportunities are calibrated to the height and basketball skill of those in question.

It is one thing to offer educational opportunities and quite another matter to send a young man to a gym five hours a day and to basket weaving for one hour and call that an education. Who, after all, is kidding whom? The world of big-time college sports has been turned topsy-turvy. It was recently reported that an Oklahoma football player supposedly said, "We want a college that the football team can be proud of."

With millions of dollars at the end of the NCAA rainbow, college coaches are obliged to hide behind a facade of educational opportunity. What they mean is that the pipeline that sends inner-city athletes to colleges can't be shut down for something as trifling as academic admission standards.

The fact that most big-time athletes don't graduate from college doesn't seem to bother these coaches. Surely these kids were given an opportunity to learn. The tilt in college athletics is so severe that the players are coddled from the moment they enter a college. Athletes aren't expected in traditional courses; they eat together, room together and attend classes together. The classes have as much to do with serious subjects as the Red Cross life-saving program has to do with attendance at medical school.

When these coddled athletes are found guilty of some university infraction such as drug use or fighting; coaches, players, and the administration close ranks. It isn't the infraction that's wrong, it's what undermines the basketball program that counts.

Vernon Maxwell, the University of Florida's all-time leading basketball scorer, reportedly tested positive for drugs three times before his senior season, but school administrators failed to enforce their policy that calls for a one year suspension. Dr. Richard Shaara, the team physician, said that Maxwell was suspended for only three games because university officials wanted "to help" the star player. Maxwell now is the starting guard for the San Antonio Spurs of the National Basketball Association.

Syracuse basketball star Derrick Coleman and four other student athletes were reprimanded and given the lightest possible penalty for a fight that they started and two apartment break-ins. A university judicial board found that the students "engaged in wrongful behavior in violation of general university regulation" and agreed to sanctions varying from a warning to a reprimand. Syracuse Coach Jim Bocheim said, Coleman "admitted what he did was wrong and now he's been punished for it. It's over with."

What is not over, however, are criminal charges emanating from the same incident in which the student athletes tried to enter a fraternity dance without paying, subsequently punching one of the fraternity members without provocation. Had this altercation been prompted by anyone other than these basketball and football players, the penalty would most definitely have been more severe.

With the financial, stakes as high as they are in college sports these athletes can get away with almost anything. As a matter of fact, there is little they can't get away with. But the act of coddling these kids can hardly be described as humanitarian. In what sense is it humanitarian to create the illusion one is being educated in a film-appreciation course? These athletes are being trained for one job only: professional basketball. Those who make it will prosper; those who don't will be left behind to pick up the pieces of their lives.

It is unadorned hypocrisy to argue for educational opportunity so that a 6-foot 10-inch, 240-pound center can enter the university and then insist that all his time must be spent in the gym and the weight room. These coaches who now cry foul play over modestly tightened NCAA standards for admission should look at themselves in the mirror and ask why is it my humanitarian gestures don't result in higher rates of graduation and do I evince the same concern for those who drop-out as for those who are pushed in to the academy. I suspect that honest answers would lead to broken mirrors. □

Co-Education Causes Columbia Football Team to Suffer
New York City Tribune, December 17, 1987

Missed in all the heat that Columbia College has taken for modifying its admission standards for eleven football players—in the hope it can end its dubious record for consecutive game losses—is the fact that Columbia football fortunes began to sink at the same time the college went cooed. I am not arguing that co-education isn't desirable. In fact, by enlarging the pool of applicants, co-education had the effect of improving the academic profile of the college. Overlooked is the effect co-education has had on Columbia football.

Since roughly half the student body is female, there is simply a smaller pool of male students from which to draft a team. At the time co-education was considered, the Columbia administration and board should have anticipated the consequences. Columbia could have dropped out of Division I competition preferring Division III play instead, it could have asked for exceptions to the Ivy League admission standards at that time, or it could have said to its alumni, "Expect to see many losses." None of these approaches were adopted.

It has been widely assumed for some time that the Ivy League occasionally makes exceptions to its academic standards in order to keep teams competitive with the rest of the league. A current example of such an exception is the one being made for Columbia. Last week, the league publicly admitted the practice. However, Columbia officials were embarrassed by the modification of the rules since they had criticized such practices in the past. In fact the rules have been modified to so notable a degree for some football players, that it has been argued—no one outside the college knows for sure—that the Columbia admission standard is beginning to resemble the one imposed on Oklahoma University linebackers. This isn't good for Columbia and it isn't good for Ivy League football.

No one wants to lose, least of all the young men representing their school. Despite the unfortunate contention by a former Columbia coach who said his players were "addicted to losing," no one puts on football gear with the intention of losing. Fans should remember that losing athletes put in the same practice time and make the same physical sacrifices as winning athletes.

Football, however, has unique requirements. You need forty players for an offensive team, a defensive team, a punter and field goal kicker, and special teams. In basketball, by contrast, recruiting three fine players can make a fine team. Small schools can easily assemble great basketball teams, but small schools rarely assemble great football teams.

The last time Columbia won a share of the Ivy League football championship was 1962. During most of the period from 1963 to 1987 it has had losing teams. But until the skein of forty-one straight losses, it had teams that could win a few games each year. It even produced several pro-football players during this period including George Sharke and Marty Domres. The Columbia alumni might not be completely satisfied with the football program, but I've never met a Columbia alumnus who would trade in his degree for winning teams.

Apparently, the loss record has introduced a degree of desperation into Columbia decisions. Someone has convinced the president and the athletic director that Columbia shouldn't be the Ivy League whipping boy. The sentiment is understandable. What is not understandable is the reluctance of the administration to recognize the result of co-education on the football program. It is one thing to defend the role of the scholar athlete in college sports; it is quite another matter to cut the recruiting pool by half and expect Columbia to compete with its fellow Ivy League institutions.

My own belief is that Columbia shouldn't be in the business of modifying its admission standards for athletes. However, it is a minor indiscretion if the standards are revised slightly. This kind of modification happens all the time for selected ethnics and to preserve geographic distribution. But when Columbia starts behaving like Oklahoma, when officials are obliged to use sub rosa techniques that blatantly contradict stated admission rules, something is wrong.

Columbia College students are fond of singing, "Oh we own New York." They do because Columbia graduated some of the best students in New York's history and continues to attract superb scholars. The fact is few people really care whether Columbia's football team wins the Ivy League championship. What they care about is the quality of its educational program, not the quality of play at Baker Field on a Saturday afternoon.

That education was enhanced with a co-education admissions policy. Ifs time, I think, for Columbia officials to say that athletics paid a price for the maintenance of high educational standards. That would be the right thing to say and the sort of comment one would never hear at Oklahoma or Nebraska. It might even engender support from an alumni that doesn't expect winning teams at Columbia College. □

Here's a Fresh Idea for School Athletics That Wouldn't Sully Integrity
New York City Tribune, February 7, 1987

At Indiana University, the faculty council passed a "bill of rights" for university athletes that attempts to protect players from physical and verbal abuse by their coaches. In Indiana, this "bill of rights" is known as the, "Bobby Knight Amendment." At Auburn University the faculty senate will vote on a motion to rebuke the athletic director for allowing a football player to participate in a bowl game even though he hadn't attended classes in two months. At Southern Methodist University, faculty leaders have called for an end to "quasi professional athletics" and for a role in athletic decision-making. At the University of Maryland, faculty sentiments about athletics were aroused after the cocaine-induced death of Len Bias and the subsequent revelations about his absence from classes. Jan Kemp, an assistant professor at the University of Georgia, won a much-publicized legal battle after she was fired for protesting preferential treatment of athletes.

Some university officials have responded to this faculty concern by calling for oversight committees along the lines of accreditation procedures. The NCAA has responded by calling for minimum high school grades and a combined SAT score of 700 as the standard for athletic eligibility. Some faculties have requested an annual review of athletic programs, a suggestion that prompted Bill Mallory, Indiana University's football coach, to remark: "I don't buy that bit about someone telling us how to run our program. We don't tell them how to run theirs."

It seems to me that both sides in this controversy have been disingenuous. For years coaches in big time athletic programs have violated NCAA recruitment regulations. They often looked the other way when alumni boosters gave a new car to a seventeen-year-old basketball wonder-kid with a deadly jump shot from twenty feet. Preferential treatment for athletes in their academic courses has been an on-going practice for many years. It is a California cliché to ask: "How many USC ' football players does it take to change a light bulb? Answer: The entire team because they get credit for the experience." At some institutions athletes are obliged to major in "movie appreciation" and occasionally get credit for finding the library. (Mind you, they don't have to enter the library, much less read a book).

On the other hand, the ruckus faculty members now appear to be creating about athletic practices is hypocritical. There is scarcely a faculty member in the entire country who is unfamiliar with athletic malfeasance. For years, these practices were accepted because faculty members realized a major bowl appearance by the football team added significant funding to the faculty salary pool. It is one thing to decry the "dumb athletes"; it is quite another thing to cut off your nose to spite your face. By the way that is why I'm not sanguine athletic policies will change even with the recent faculty bravura over the issue.

It seems to me the most logical thing to do is also the most obvious. The NCAA can simply declare that Division I teams are clubs loosely attached to colleges. A portion of the proceeds from athletic contests would be given to the college for its sponsorship of these events, however, the athletes would be obliged to conform to the same standards as everyone else. There is simply no sense in engaging in the charade of establishing minimum standards for admission—often absurd standards—and then having many coaches cry that these standards are "racist." These clubs can fill the same role as teams. Games will remain an outlet for youthful exuberance and school spirit. The only difference, of course, is that the athletes students cheer for won't be their classmates.

With this arrangement in place the faculty could mind its own business; the administration would continue to receive money from athletic programs; students could still attend athletic contests at which school spirit is exhibited and athletes would have the opportunity to put their talents on display, Moreover, this plan gives athletes the opportunity for a real education. Those who can "hack it" will study and play; those who can't do both will simply play. The important point is that academic programs won't be vitiated to accommodate athletes.

Some might argue that these clubs are a form of professionalism. That is partially true, but only partially. The appropriate analogue would be amateur track and field clubs that are somewhere between professional and college teams. Since athletics are probably too important to leave for professorial review and too easily compromised to leave for the coaching fraternity, it seems to me it should have a niche of its own where coaches can run programs as they see fit, and college professors can tend their own gardens. □

Colleges Should Scour Their Consciences before They Admit Unqualified Athletes
New York City Tribune, January 7, 1986

Recently the NCAA presidents' commission proposed a modification in the rulings that govern freshman participation in intercollegiate sports. The proposal would combine cumulative high school grades and standardized test scores to determine eligibility.

In the original proposal adopted in 1983, freshman athletes in Division I schools had to have a 2.0 grade point average in 11 standard school courses (a C average) and a score of at least 700 on the Scholastic Aptitude Test (SAT) (350 math, 350 verbal scores or some combination resulting in a 700 score).

However, this proposal, which was due to go into effect in August 1986 was vigorously assailed by the presidents of black colleges who contend "that the standards were biased against black athletes." An NCAA sponsored study found that black athletes would be more directly affected than their white counterparts.

As a consequence the president's commission will propose a combination of a 1.8 grade point average and 660 SAT score. If a student has a 1.8 grade point average, he would have to score

748 on the SAT to be eligible to play intercollegiate sports; if a student scores 660 on the SAT he will have to have a 2.2 grade point average.

Although the commission's intention to assist black athletes in maintaining their eligibility is commendable, the statistical gymnastics and the attitude of the president at black colleges is lamentable. What most people don't realize is that writing your name and address on the SAT automatically gives a student a score of 400. Moreover, in high schools across the country where the effects of grade inflation are legion, an average of "C" is tantamount to a failing grade thirty years ago. If universities are in the business of education, an assumption that is not at all clear nor undeniable, then standards for academic competence must be achieved so that student athletes are not handicapped the rest of their lives. Success on the playing field does not usually translate into a professional contract. For every Magic Johnson, there are thousands of anonymous players who graduate from our universities without any discernible skills or even a reasonable chance for success. This is scandalous.

That university presidents are now inclined to modify admissions standards to accommodate athletes suggests more about financial motives than concern for athletes or for educational attainment. Admittedly, some institutions cannot survive without the revenues for Saturday's football game. But as much as I like these games and as devoted as I am to winning, something has to give. From my point of view, it can't be the admissions requirements for athletes.

It is also curious that the proposal should come from the presidents of black colleges. One would think that these schools would do everything possible to raise their standards, especially for black athletes. What happens to the black athlete who doesn't have the ability to make the pros and who reads at the seventh grade level and computes at the fifth grade level? What happens to the black athlete who is coddled at every college and is unprepared to face the harsh realities of life upon graduation? Is a differential standard of admission and academic performance in his best interest?

Of course, some minimal academic standard for eligibility is better than no standard at all. But what concerns me is that this minimal standard, very minimal standard, is already subject to political pressure and subsequent compromise. One can surely predict that when high school All Americans can't gain admission into Division I schools, there will be further efforts at watering down the admissions requirement. If sports are didactic then one must realize that the competition on the athletic field is in some sense related to the in the rest of life. To suggest to student athletes that they must compete in athletics, but need not compete in academics, is to insure possible success in sports and failure for the rest of their lives. I think the presidents of the NCAA commission ought to ruminate about the matter.☐

College Athletes Who Never Graduate
From the Editor in Chief

Clifford Adelman, of the Department of Education, argues that the graduation rates of athletes should be higher than those of other students since the former have a "safety net" of financial support and tutoring generally unavailable to others. Yet athletes have much lower rates of graduation. This is despite the fact that many are engaged in academic programs that could be generously described as fraudulent. (Athletes often study weight lifting, sports appreciation, and gym techniques hardly opening a book or exciting the concern of coaches largely indifferent to their academic progress.)

Unfortunately, all of this is most glaringly true in the case of black athletes. A recent survey conducted by the *Chronicle of Higher Education* indicates that at nearly half of 248 Division I colleges, fewer than one-third of black male athletes, graduate in a six-year period. At eighty of the colleges, fewer than one in every four black male athletes receives a degree in six years—a graduation rate two times lower than their white counterparts.

In three leagues playing big-time football—the Big Eight, the Big West Conference, and the Western Athletic Conference—the graduation rates for black male athletes are below 25 percent. For the Southeastern and Southwest conferences, the rate is below

30 percent. Senator Bill Bradley has called for research into the reasons for this gap between white and black. But this must be a disingenuous suggestion. Bradley and everyone else know precisely why black male athletes don't graduate.

Many of our superior quality black athletes are scouted, nurtured, coddled, and offered every conceivable privilege—except that of a good education from their sophomore year in high school until they enter college. As a result their attention is focused exclusively on sports. Were it not for their athletic prowess, probably 75 percent of these students would not get to college at all.

Doubtless, some of these athletes have the intellectual ability to become good, even outstanding, college students. But that's a side of them in which the universities have shown no interest. It is certainly not the side that is rewarded and developed. Worse yet, many disadvantaged black youths who are merely smart, but without any athletic gift, do not go to college at all. There has been a lot of empty rhetoric about "institutional racism." Here is the real thing, and it is conveniently ignored.

Many college administrators contend that more should be done to "close the gap." But as long as college sports is big business generating extraordinary sums of money, academic standards will be compromised for winning teams. The controversy surrounding the imposition of Proposition 48, which forced Division I athletes to meet minimum—very minimum—core curriculum, grade point average, and test performance standards suggests that most schools will subvert Proposition 48's intent in one way or another.

Similarly, the NCAA's plans to release graduation rates by race on a college-by-college basis will result in schools pushing athletes through regardless of their academic performance. Rudy Davalos, director of athletics at the University of Houston, which graduated just one of forty-nine black male athletes who entered as freshmen, has said, "The NCAA rules that have come into play have made a big difference, and the rates are going to be better." That may be true, but Mr. Davalos does not indicate at what price.

As the recent Olympics shows, the distinction between amateur and professional athlete is now hopelessly blurred. Perhaps a similar blurring among Division I athletic programs could have a salutary effect on degree requirements. Instead of vitiating degree standards to accommodate athletes, big-time sports programs should be disentangled from colleges.

Let those who wish to play big-time sports become semiprofessionals attached in a contractual way to colleges. Let colleges charge for the use of their football field and gymnasia. And let academic programs retain their integrity without any concession to athletes.

If this proposal were adopted, the disparity in graduation rates would become irrelevant. There would be no need for congressional oversight of big-time college sports. There would be no need for athletic scholarships. There would be no need for compromising admission or graduation requirements. The adoption of this recommendation would eliminate the cynicism that now surrounds student athletes and their "academic" programs. And, finally, we would be able to address more honestly our responsibility to provide quality higher education to black Americans. □

7

The Student Perspective

It is one thing to discuss my view of the academy or professorial attitudes. Ultimately, the way to judge an institution is the performance of students. What have they learned? What is the meaning of this four-year college experience? And what do they take away from it?

Commencement Speakers Merely Reinforce
Their Audience's Prejudice
New York City Tribune, June 17, 1986

The reputation of a university does not rise or fall on the basis of those to whom it gives honorary degrees. In fact, the reason for giving such degrees has more to do with finding a convivial speaker at commencement than with the academic enterprise itself.

This explains why Bill Cosby is this nation's most sought after commencement speaker. However, the selection of honorary degree recipients is not totally irrelevant; it does suggest who it is a university administration considers sufficiently noteworthy to be honored.

It is therefore somewhat astonishing that Winnie and Nelson Mandela—radical leaders of the African National Congress—have been accumulating such honors at various campuses in this country. Or is it? After all most students—dare I include faculty members?—are unaware of this communist domination of the ANC or its violent aspirations. For years now, certainly since the '60s, universities have been inclined to give honorary degrees to those people whose views are most compatible with the political orientation in the academy.

It is not coincidental that George Kennan, a man disheartened with American life since the turbulence in the '60s and obsessed with American disarmament, is arguable the most honored person at university commencements in the last two decades. It might also be said that Kennan is a person who might very well be described as out-of-touch with the sentiments of the American people.

Here is the rub. Those the university chooses to honor are very often the people who deplore the attitudes of typical Americans. Surely that can't be said of Bill Cosby. But in his case it is his celebrity status that is sought, not his views on arms control agreements or welfare programs. What one actually hears at graduation bespeaks splendid isolation.

At the New York University commencement, Speaker of the House Tip O'Neill gave the main address. It was an unvarnished assault on the Reagan Administration. Every dusty complaint, from the deficit cuts in aid to education, to the decision to abrogate the Salt II agreement, was trotted out for inspection by a generally respective audience. O'Neill made it sounds as if the venal Reagan was intent on destroying the Republic. Were it not for the vigilant O'Neill this might well have occurred in 1980. Modesty was never a characteristic in which O'Neill put great value.

What is most intriguing about his performance, aside from its obvious partisanship and egoism, is how thoroughly out of kilter it is with prevailing national attitudes. Speaker O'Neill looked and sounded like a dinosaur. In decrying the president's decision to ignore the Salt II agreement, he uttered not a word about Soviet Krasnoyarsk or the introduction of the SS-25 mobile missiles. He said nothing at all about the expiration of the agreement or even the fact it did not obtain Senate approval. Nor did he bother mentioning that President Reagan has said that the agreement is incompatible with our national security.

No, there was O'Neill vaingloriously defending his position as speaker of a House divided by pettiness, local interests, pet projects, and cowardice in the face of Soviet intimidation. On this, the day when students come together in ceremony and celebration, the anachronism from the Eighth Congressional District of Massachusetts said what most sensible Americans know to be either untrue or out of step with prevailing sentiments.

Such is the glory of our system that universities are free to honor people whose entire career is characterized by misjudgment. That, I suppose, is the way it must be. But what does the conferral of an honorary degree suggest about the state of the academy when it is given to a person like Tip O'Neill?

The answer is obvious. The cloistered benefactions of our campuses have convinced many academics of the superiority of their views. Tom and Jane from Peoria presumably don't know where it's at. This elitism is reinforced by the professional classes who send their sons and daughters to the "best" (read Ivy League) colleges.

What honorary degree recipients at these commencements tell the assembled throng is what they want to hear. Unfortunately that is often wrong, misguided, misleading, and generally bad advice. □

For Commencement Speeches an Igneous Athlete Sure Beats a Glib Politician
New York City Tribune, July 15, 1986

This is the season of graduation and speeches. Politicians collect honorary degrees the way gun shooters from Hollywood's Wild West collect notches on their gun belts. Having heard dozens of these speeches I am confident that this year's versions will be little different from the past. Advice will be given that is synthetic at best and wrong-headed at worst. Students will sit at this convocation anxiously waiting to let off steam. Parents will sit there beaming with pride, but generally out of touch with the speakers.

If I had to select a category of people to give graduation addresses, it would be athletes. Certainly not all athletes are prepared to deliver speeches. Nor are athletes always good role models. Quinton Daily and Michael Ray Richardson prove as much. Nonetheless, the view of this nation is much more realistic on the fields of play than in the halls of Congress.

Recently 400 student athletes met at Rutgers to attend on seminar on the transition from high school to college. Senator Bill Bradley, formerly of the New York Knickerbockers, started his remarks but saying "Be the best you can be." He argued that "half of them (in the audience) know they're not going to be a pro athlete. And for the other half who think they might make it, this is a toughening process." When was the last time a politician discussed a "toughening process?"

Other speakers followed Bradley with their own good advice. One athlete said, "Don't ever leave class early for your sport, the teacher will resent you forever." Paul Silas, former all-pro with the Boston Celtics, said, "The thing that turned me around at Creighton was that I flunked accounting. That was a blow to my ego. The next year I got an A in the same class. I went on to be an academic all American, play in the NBA for sixteen seasons, and be the president of the players association. So if you persevere, you can make it. No matter what your background." When was the last time a politician said you can make it in this nation regardless of your background?

Satch Sanders, also a former star of the Boston Celtics, argued that "You're an athlete for only a few more years. You have to live eighty or ninty years, so you better find more things to do." Julius Erving, "Dr. J.," reiterated this theme by talking about "opportunities and responsibilities." He noted, "Never look at your life in terms of one shot or one blown opportunity." When was the last time a politician said he wasn't concerned about losing an election.

When it came to drugs these established athletes waxed didactic. Sanders argues, "If you're singled out for something special, as a student athlete is, you've got to be careful. Sometimes you want not to be special. That's when you might tend to bend over backwards to be part of a group. That could lead to succumbing to pressure, which could create a situation that could lead to a loss of scholarship." Dick Anderson, the Rutgers football coach, concurred: "You've got to be your own man or your own woman when people are talking about getting drunk or smoking a joint." When was the last time you met a politician who was his own man or woman?

Because of the lessons of sports most athletes revere excellence. It is the cult of athletics. While mediocrity may be accepted in many fields of endeavor, I have never heard an athlete say he was satisfied with anything but "the best you can be." This translates into pushing oneself to a level of performance higher than the last. It means never being satisfied with what has been achieved because the next accomplishment may be the best one. Athletes don't rest on their laurels unless they're ready for retirement.

I don't think there are many athletes who will receive honorary degrees this June, albeit Julius Erving received a doctorate from the University of Massachusetts. But even if athletes don't receive these honors or give the commencement address, listen carefully to their message. It is bound to be more useful and rooted in reality then the speech delivered by the typical politician. □

Campus Language Police
With John M. Olin

The once idyllic setting at universities where the free exchange of opinion was promoted is over, a casualty of political correctness. At a recent SUNY Albany student picnic to honor Jackie Robinson's breaking of the major league baseball color barrier in 1947, campus fury erupted. A bizarre debate emerged when forty students at the university objected to the event being called a "picnic"—a term these students incorrectly alleged emanated from racial lynchings. (Actually, the word is derived from the French term *piquenique*, a social event where attendees bring the food.)

Despite the wrongfully placed angst, SUNY Albany student leaders forbade the occasion from being publicized as a picnic. But the problem did not end there. When the organizers considered calling the event an "outing," a gay student leader objected, noting the term's use to describe the public attribution of homosexuality. Eventually the event was publicized without a title.

SUNY Albany's Student Assembly Affirmative Action director Zaheer Mustafa told the *Albany Times Union*, "My job is to make sure people from underrepresented groups are heard. Whether the claims are true or not, the point is the word offended."

Now this is a curious standard. Presumably, if a word offends—whether or not the word is offensive—there is an obligation to prevent its use. I am reminded of a recent incident in which the word "niggardly" could not be employed because it offended black students who mistook it as an insult.

Self-appointed campus police are sensitized to any offense even when none is intended. What is emerging are affirmative action administrators whose job it is to ferret out insults, intended or not, to designated minorities.

America's campus Red Guard don't force perpetrators of language infractions to wear pointy hats, they just bring the "guilty" up on charges. Insensitivity being the one infraction for which there isn't any defense.

Try calling a female student a "girl" or a well-built male a "stud" and the campus police will descend. In order to stay on the straight and narrow students require orientation sessions that prescribe existentially acceptable speech.

Use of the correct terminology of course doesn't guarantee acceptance. Terms change. Who would have guessed that "picnic" would offend a group on campus?

There was a time when colleges issued a behavioral guide to students. Alcoholism was discouraged. At the moment, almost any behavior is tolerated, but colleges impose a form of thought control. Certain words cannot be used.

Moreover, anyone offended by a statement is ipso facto the judge and jury of the person who made the statement. Therefore, ordinary rules of fair play are meaningless. The explanation that "I didn't mean to offend anyone," no longer applies. If someone is offended, you are culpable, and evidence is irrelevant.

Social interaction is best engaged in with either an attorney or a member of the Red Guard who enforced prevailing campus norms. "Would you like to go out?" is not a question a young man may ask a female student. Like President Bill Clinton, the semiotician, the female will ask what do you mean by "like"? "What is the intent of 'go out'?" The young man who cannot answer these questions satisfactorily could be in hot water. □

What Happened to Professionalism?

The 1940 statement on academic freedom establishes an ideal context for discussion in this symposium. World War Two forced consideration of the survival mechanism for democratic republics. As the 1940 statement notes, scholars argues for the freedom to search for the truth (*lehrfreiheit*) and the freedom for students to learn (*lernfreiheit*) because these conditions in the academy insured against totalitarian impulses from without.

Furthermore, the authors recognized that freedom imposes responsibility. Without restraint, faculty freedom could become a license that jeopardizes the very legitimacy of the academy. As a consequence, the authors argued for prudent professional standards, i.e., cautions in discussing topics unrelated to one's field of expertise. Notice as well the use of the words "accurate," "restraint," and "respect for the opinion of others" in the original text. Professionalism could be defined negatively as the rejection of an inappropriate display of advocacy, unsustainable political argumentation, or propagandizing.

During the 1950s, the so-called McCarthy era, academic freedom was usefully employed as a shield from sometimes-irrational political attributions about the professoriate made from without. Standing its ground, the American Association of University Professors and others raised the torch of freedom to teach, to engage in research, and to learn. Although one might contend there were institutions that faltered in this struggle, on balance the academy prevailed over the accusers. Whether the accusers represented a totalitarian impulse, as was sometimes suggested during that period, was less relevant to the argument than a belief that threats to academic freedom cannot be countenanced in any form.

In the late sixties a different challenge to the academy emerged. Some students, having been suckled on the milk of participatory democracy and believing themselves to be the handmaidens of a new social order, demanded (usually in nonnegotiable terms) an altered college environment. Rather than the freedom to learn, these students demanded the freedom to reform and restructure the academy. While it is hard to make the argument that universities simply conceded to radical student sentiment, it is the case that parietals were abandoned; undifferentiated grades were introduced; faculty evaluations were routinely embraced; electives increased geometrically; students sat on university councils; and issues of ethnicity, race, and gender dominated the curriculum. In the brouhaha, what went unnoticed is that faculties abdicated responsibility to maintain professional standards. The words participatory democracy seared the imagination of professors who often did not have the courage to say the obvious: education is not a democratic condition. When the dust settled, professionalism was tarnished as a concept and a practice.

Many of those students and their sympathizers who carried the flag for participatory democracy in the student demonstrations of the sixties are now tenured professors. Having assumed—correctly it turns out—that internal pressure can reform the academic enterprise, these recently tenured professors have converted the academy into a center for reform. Verities of the past are candidates for excision. Parietals and other vestiges of orderly campus life are "anachronistic." Where once universities were cultural transmission belts, now they are launching pads for experimentation. Multiculturalism, semiotics, relativism, and radical politics are words pegged into the *zeitgeist*. What each suggests is an effort to overturn an established truth. For the experimenters there isn't any truth, except in the display of power to push one idea aside to make room for another.

Since academic freedom can only be discussed in the context of the university's mission, and since that mission has been altered dramatically in the last several decades, academic freedom as a concept has been transformed as well. As a shield from outside intrusion, academic freedom has served the academy well: as a standard for professionalism and the antidote to erosive ideas and irresponsible behavior, it has been a failure. In fact, the problem with the very idea of contemporary academic freedom is that it concentrates on threats from without that rarely exist and overlooks threats from within, which have violently disordered the academic mission.

The academy legitimately makes a claim to be an *imperium in imperio*. Throughout this century, there has existed a belief in self-regulation, which set the professorate apart from the larger society and constituted a form of collective academic freedom. More recently, academic freedom has offered protection for irresponsible behavior. Some faculty members have so redefined the profession that any resemblance between professionalism in the 1940s and their present behavior is merely coincidental.

A professor of English at the University of Wisconsin, who admits to seducing students, claims that she intentionally sexualizes the classroom in order to reduce barriers between students and instructors. When she was brought up on charges of harassment—a case where harassment charges are warranted—the protective shield of academic freedom was raised and university officials relented suggesting, in effect, that seduction could be tolerated if the students were no longer in the instructor's class.

Similarly, when charges of irresponsibility were leveled against Professor Leonard Jeffries at the City University of New York over lectures on "ice people" and "sun people," which did not provide a shred of evidence to support his contentions, he, in a state of high dudgeon, raised the banner of academic freedom. Jeffries was removed from an administrative post, but he continues to offer his highly questionable theories to unwary students as a tenured professor of black studies.

What might be concluded from this analysis is that academic freedom must be redefined for the present state of the academy. I would argue that academic freedom must retain its traditional and appropriate meaning as a force to maintain the aims of scholarship and learning untrammeled by outside political influence. Furthermore, academic freedom should uphold professionalism in terms far more direct and precise than those of the 1940 statement.

In my judgment, it should embody the premise that rational exegesis is the *sine qua non* of scholarship. Appeals to intuition and other vague mystical formulations should not be as persuasive in an academy of scholars as evidence. Moreover, propagandizing on behalf of one's favorite cause should be discouraged unless it can be demonstrated that such appeal is consistent with the canons of scholarship. Scholarship and teaching should be distinguished from advocacy and preaching. Behavior one would not countenance outside college walls should not be embraced inside those walls. While I have always been skeptical about a university's ability to instill moral and social virtue, the university should enforce a code of conduct for faculty members and students consistent with the requirements of the larger society. If drug use has specific legal restrictions, to cite one example, the university's stance should conform to society's position. And last, professional standards should imply rigorous academic pursuits. When latitudinarians define scholarship as "any learning experience," they undermine the meaning of scholarship. Academic freedom should be a bulwark against faddism, unsubstantiated claims, and mere social activism.

Responsible professors should not stand by and let the carrying of banners in behalf of a cause warrant academic credit; they should say as well that flabby exercises unrelated to disciplined reading and research will not receive the protective embrace of academic freedom.

Surely my detractors will find examples that challenge my model of professionalism. But, in the end, unless consensus of professionalism is established and well understood by the public, the spectre of irresponsibility will trigger interventions that may well curtail the freedoms that academics so cherish. Most people do not think of universities as change agents. They expect a university to be a place where high culture is transmitted, skills and knowledge are conveyed, and pure research is encouraged. These purposes allow much room for interpretation. When Socrates conceived of a center of learning, he recognized that thought experimentation and the free exchange of ideas can be risky. But certainly Socrates did not assume that the academic enterprise would be frivolous. Academic freedom must be brought to bear against frivolity in higher education today. □

The Culmination of Student Freedom
Academic Questions, Fall 1996

Most parents who spend $30,000 a year to send their children to prestigious private colleges across the country and state legislators who subsidize students to the tune of $12,000 a year in public colleges assume that graduates of our institutions of higher learning have some acquaintance with this mathematical principles; historical, philosophical, and literary interpretation; a grasp of science; and perhaps some exposure to great artistic pursuits. While there was an empirical basis for these assumptions during much of this century, it is increasingly difficult to justify such claims today.

A recent study by the National Association of Scholars (NAS), *The Dissolution of General Education: 1914-1993*, postulates that a "radical transformation" has taken place in higher education in which basic survey courses have been purged from the curriculum. To test this hypothesis, NAS researchers examined the requirement for a bachelor of arts degree at fifty of the top-ranked institutions in the nation. What the study demonstrates is what many academics have long suspected: the nation's leading institutions have abandoned the core academic requirements once considered the essence of a sound curriculum and the basis for a democratic society.

Overall, the study found that structured course requirements were the norm in 1914, 1939, and 1964, but, by 1993, these requirements had declined precipitously. Moreover, graduation requirements incorporating general education courses dropped significantly as well. There are now fewer mandatory courses, fewer clusters, fewer courses with prerequisites, and longer completion time than was the case heretofore. In addition, the study indicates that today's students at leading colleges are not held to the exacting standards that once prevailed in the academy. For example, more than 50 percent of the schools in the study demanded a thesis or comprehensive examination as a requirement for a baccalaureate degree between 1939 and 1964. By 1993, only 12 percent of the institutions in the study maintained this requirement.

With their roots firmly planted in the soil of the 1960s, academics willingly, and in some cases reluctantly, accepted the proposition advocated by radical students that judgments could not be made about what should and should not be studied. Very often a *cri de coeur* from the barricades later became official policy.

Commitment to structured general education requirements and rigorous standards for the completion of a degree have, as the NAS study demonstrates, been vitiated. For some, participatory democracy has had a natural and understandable effect on the curriculum. As Sidney Hook reported (*The Philosophy of the Curriculum: The Need for General Education*, ed. Sidney Hook, Paul Kurtz, and Miro Todorovich [Buffalo, N.Y.: Prometheus Books, 1975], 28), a student at a Washington Square College meeting (in the 1960s) said, "the intrinsic value or interest of a subject isn't enough to justify prescribing it. Every subject has intrinsic value but not to everybody, and judging by some of our teachers, not even to those who make their living teaching it. If education is to be effective and relevant, it must be related to the personal needs of the students. Without us, you have no justification for your being teachers."

Here, in unadorned form, was the challenge of that decade and beyond, a challenge from which most academics have retreated. Some scholars contend that students should have the choice of a college curriculum, not merely the college one wishes to attend but open-ended opportunities to select any course within the university's catalogue of offerings.

It seems to me there are two conditions this point of view underscores. The first is that an education having any value should be related to individual needs. Second is that students know what they want to study and the consequences of their decisions. After thirty years in the academy, it seems to me almost axiomatic that propositions one and two are mutually incompatible. What students want is often not what they need, need being defined as that common frame of reference that sustains a liberal society such as ours. To balkanize the curriculum by suggesting students, as unfettered actors on the university stage, can select any course they wish is to admit that professors, with more experience and presumably more knowledge about what to study, should abdicate their responsibility and transfer it to untutored freshmen and sophomores. Yet, *mirabile dictu*, this is precisely what has been occurring for several decades.

As the NAS study notes, broad exposure to areas of knowledge and the attainment of skills have been declining dramatically since

1964. To cite one example: the percentage of institutions with composition requirements administered by English departments slipped from 86 percent in 1964 to 36 percent in 1993. The present university curriculum has gone very far down the road of student participatory democracy, leaving in its wake a hodge-podge of general education programs and ambiguity about priorities in undergraduate education. Granted, students will ultimately make career decisions and select majors on their own and, granted as well, we have experienced a knowledge explosion. Nevertheless, it is incumbent on professors to identify what is to be studied within our social context. It is not arbitrary and inappropriate for the faculty to say that in its considered judgment there are indispensable courses all students should experience. Surely, curriculum decisions are not entirely one-sided. They unfold from the debate about curriculum that is never-ending. But a faculty, as I see it, should not abandon its authority to be at the very center of these decisions.

A former dean and present vice-president for information technology at Middlebury College, Eric Davis, argues that it is desirable to have fewer required courses. "To expect all students to take the same course, read the same books, hear the same lecture, is a format of study that's too rigid and too restrictive for the modern world," he says. What Professor Davis does not say is that the humanities are predicated on an understanding of our common humanities. The humanities are, in fact, based not on the superficial differences that separate us, such as race and ethnicity, but the common bonds of empathy, sorrow, loyalty, love, bravery, and cowardice, which unite us.

A culture divorced from its common bonds does not have the amalgam to cohere. When students are unaware of common cultural cues, when the voices of deep human understanding (e.g., Shakespeare) are ignored, when the achievements of Western civilization are derided and subsequently subordinated to the study of other civilization, then the die for cultural dissolution is cast. I have given lectures with passing reference to phrases rooted in the culture, such as "Panglossian," "Achilles' heel," "Alice's rabbit hole," "The Ides of March," "Hobson's choice." Yet, to my astonishment, the college students I encountered did not know the meanings. Admittedly, this does not exhaust the range and depth of liberal education, but it is symptomatic, in my judgment, of a shift in cultural understanding. ☐

Parietals Then and Now
Chronicles, September 1997

As a Columbia University undergraduate in 1956, I resided in Hartley Hall, a stately building on the Morningside Campus. During my orientation week, I was introduced to my floor counselor who said in an unambiguous way that hijinks would not be permitted on his watch. He highlighted one rule that could never be disobeyed: women were not permitted in what was then an all-male dorm unless it was during designated hours on the weekend. When visitation was allowed, women had to sign in and a book had to keep one's dorm room door open. Closed doors were considered a violation of the dormitory deportment code and subject to penalty. Of course a few clever students used matchbooks as a door wedge, but they were the exception.

While there were those who balked at the rules and occasionally adolescent men were rowdy (I readily admit to infractions) there was not any doubt about the university's expectation. In fact, the freshmen student guide said Columbia is a place where the "whole man" is developed—including mind and character. In those days character development was taken seriously.

When I played on the basketball team, my coach, Lou Rossini, insisted that we wear ties and jackets when traveling to other schools. On one occasion when we played against the University of Maine and temperatures plummeted to minus 10 degrees on the streets of Bangor, I wore a turtleneck and a blazer. Rossini, noticing my attire, said, "If you want to play at Columbia you'll follow a gentleman's code of conduct. I expect all players to wear shirts and ties even if the temperature is 50 below zero." I got the message.

Columbia was not alone in assuming the role of *in loco parentis*. It was believed by administrators at the time that student deportment was an essential part of the university experience. Many students resented these regulations, choosing to exercise their freedom by renting apartments off-campus or joining fraternities and living in frat houses in the hope that the vigilance of student regulations could not easily be maintained.

At the University of Pennsylvania, the student handbook of 1961 noted that it is a "privilege being a University of Pennsylvania student," which "carries with it certain responsibilities." When a student lives up to these responsibilities, "he brings credit not only to himself, his family, and his friends but also to his university. The converse is true when a student fails to meet these responsibilities."

In every handbook I read during this period in the early 60s, before the maelstrom of student discontent, the concept of enforcement was predicated on self-discipline. Universities set down the regulations for responsible behavior and students were expected to meet them. An emphasis was placed on order, propriety, and decorum with specific censure of intoxication and bad manners.

Dorm regulations were universally applied. Specified visiting hours for "escorted women" were posted, and in most instances fraternity houses were obliged to adhere to similar rules. If women were visiting men off-campus, it was expected they would receive permission from their parents.

It is instructive that social regulations for men and women were written separately. Women were asked to reflect on the question of whether an individual act might adversely affect "the reputation of the university" and whether this act reflects poorly on all women students. It was customary for women's residences to have their own governing body. The large majority of cases in the early 60s dealt with the violation of drinking regulations and an occasional problem with curfews, which were routinely 11:00 P.M. for first-semester freshmen (a word now in disuse) and midnight for other students. If there was no evidence of infractions, a curfew of 1:00 A.M. would be considered for the weekend.

Casual attire was prohibited in all academic buildings, laboratories, libraries, and administrative buildings. In one student document after another, women were expected to be "ladylike" and men "gentlemanly." Although rarely elaborated on, the intention was clear. Women were chaperoned at parties and men were expected to be well mannered, especially in the presence of women.

In addition to academic violations such as cheating and plagiarism, which automatically resulted in expulsion, students culpable of flagrant violation of parietals would face suspension. On one matter the university in the 1960s was confident: it had an unequivocal standard of correct student behavior.

Sic fugit. From 1972 to 1992, I was a dean at New York University. During that period I not only observed an incremental but continual alteration in parietals at my home institution and at other institutions across the country. While there are several exceptions to my generalization, Grove City College comes to mind, in most instances the student code of conduct based on a standard of correct behavior surrendered to a standard of "correct" thinking.

For example, in the Harvard Handbook for Students for 1996-97, all students are expected to ''behave in a mature and responsible manner." But mature and responsible have less to do with behavior today and more to do with a way of thinking. Most of the section on "conduct" deals with complaints of discrimination, harassment of several kinds (sexual, racial, gay, lesbian), and resolving differences.

Clearly, unwanted sexual behavior in colleges and universities should be thwarted, but verbal suggestions in an environment in which hormones are coruscating through adolescents are not easily deterred. Similarly, a mere charge of discrimination is often sufficient to initiate a hearing or complaint procedure whether or not the evidence justifies such investigation. Discrimination now exists in the eye of the beholder.

While I could not locate one student handbook of the early 60s that made specific reference to homosexuals, almost every contemporary student guide makes specific reference to this subgroup. The language invariably notes that principles of respect and toleration must be honored. Conspicuously absent from these declarations is respect or tolerance for orthodox religious groups that do not countenance homosexual behavior.

Several handbooks also assume that gay (the word "homosexual" rarely appears in these guidebooks) students have been subject to harassment by members of the student community though evidence is not in print to substantiate this claim. Several student codes indicate that students must be especially cognizant of abuse leveled at lesbians and gays.

Implicit in these statements is a belief that students enter the university with crude sexual stereotypes, racial antipathy, and an aversion to homosexuals, and that it is incumbent on university officials to change these assumptions. It is not coincidental that at several elite colleges students are obliged to engage in an orientation session that deals primarily with student prejudice and ways to overcome it. After observing these sessions in which unwary students are obliged to admit harboring prejudicial feelings, several commentators have described this psychological intimidation as "reeducation." One colleague describes colleges engaged in this training as "the University of Peking in the United States."

Current orientation sessions involve another curious ideological entrapment. At such meetings seventeen-year-olds are often asked whether they are sexually confused. If they answer affirmatively members of the Mattachine Society or the Gay and Lesbian Alliance are asked to counsel these students. The fact many seventeen-year-olds are confused about their sexuality is no reason to believe they are potential homosexuals. Yet legitimacy exists for gays and lesbians to engage in active recruitment, notwithstanding the general lack of any heterosexual counseling service on campus. It is also the case that since males can select their roommates, homosexuals may live together even though heterosexuals cannot. At some colleges recognition of this condition has led to separate dormitory floors being designated for homosexuals only.

For a typical first-year student inexperienced in the ways of the world, this orientation to university life is jarring. If the university maintains the status of *in loco parentis*, then it is substituting its own code of ideological adaptation for a traditional parental code most students imbibed from childhood. The university says implicitly, and increasingly explicitly, that everything you have learned about right and wrong must be relearned using the university's ideological litmus test.

As one might suppose, confusion is often the result of this culture clash. Several years ago, a young man residing in a university dorm told me the following story. A young woman with a "crush" on him visited his dorm room late at night. She proceeded to beseech him for sexual favors in a most direct way. The young man, from a traditional home, was perplexed. If he allowed himself to be seduced, he would violate his religious convictions; if he rejected this woman's overtures, he feared being mocked by his peers. Torn between tradition and peer group pressure, he sought counsel.

A psychology professor told him to do what feels best, let your instinct be your guide. I said let your conscience be your guide, which in the present scheme of things is a retrograde point of view. In the end, I do not know how this student resolved his dilemma, but I do know he was distraught over the incident.

For those students who assume religion is communal obser-vance, there are many problems on campus. Theme dorms (a euphemism for ethnic or racial segregation) are countenanced on many campuses, but religious segregation is usually frowned on. The assumption is that religion is a matter of personal inclination, while racial and ethnic affiliation are perforce communal.

It is obvious that the early 60s and the present are worlds apart. Rules based on civility and morality have retreated before an ideo-logical steamroller. Students are now in the position of having their thoughts manipulated and any traditionalist stance ridiculed. A so-called code of conduct is actually a code of conformist thinking.

Admittedly, the era in the early 60s demanded conformity as well. But this was the conformity of deportment, a way for gentlemen and ladies to behave in polite and refined company. Of course, even the mention of deportment has a quaint ring to it. Now students and faculty members address one another by their first names, use the "f" word routinely as an adjective for everything from tests to institutional food, and generally dress as if they are unmade beds.

Much has been lost in the last twenty-five years. Charles Eliot, the erstwhile president of Harvard, once said, "The reason there is so much intelligence at the university is freshmen bring so much in and as seniors take so little out." Unfortunately, what students bring in today is not what they take out. It is not merely the abandonment of deportment rules, albeit they are more important than contemporary students assume, but the brainwashing in relativism, multiculturalism, and the critique of religion and tradition.

The university is still a surrogate parent, but not one who worries about the emotional well-being of progeny. Rather the university is a self-designated revolutionary changing the rules that promote social order, while fostering confusion and undermining a moral sensibility. It was not easy adjusting to life in the academy several decades ago. Nevertheless, a student knew what was expected, was told how to behave, and recognized a standard of gentlemanly behavior. That world is now lost and, at least for me, lamented. In the interest of truth-in-advertising, most universities should say to incoming students, "Welcome to the brave new world where truth is relative, everything you've learned before must be forgotten, and sensitivity training awaits you."□

Freedom To/ Freedom From: Reconsidered
The New Federalist Papers

Entering my consciousness like a half-forgotten dream is a song that was part of my pre-adolescent memory bank: "The Best Things in Life Are Free." There was nothing particularly haunting about the melody and the lyrics were nonsensical but it did establish my faith in a mystical kind of freedom, for if the best things are free, then freedom must be free. The logic is somewhat convoluted but what can you expect from a ten-year-old who imbibed pop music lyrics the way most kids devoured ice cream sandwiches? When I would say things that would prompt my contemporaries to shout, "hey you can't say that," I would steadfastly reply, "I can say whatever I please; this is a free country." So well had I learned my lyrical lesson that I was an unwitting defender of absolute freedoms long before I ever heard of Justice Black. It was also a time before I considered the ramifications of my posturing. I simply looked at an American flag and thought of my freedom.

It was not until I reached high school that the matter of freedom became somewhat enigmatic. One day as I walked through the corridors of Jamaica High School two thugs stopped me and requested my change, in language that I used exclusively in schoolyard basketball games. Since I had walked two miles to school in order to save the fifteen cent carfare, I was not about to give up my change to an army of King Kong's, much less these two thugs. So when I said, "no way," they started to pummel my stomach and face until the one teacher who had the courage to intervene said, "Enough!" When this teacher asked for an explanation, these thugs said, "None of your business; this is a free country." It was exactly at that moment that freedom began to mean something different from the notion of my nave past. It is also this scene at Jamaica High School that I recall every time I hear Oliver Wendell Holmes Jr.'s quotation, "Your freedom ends where my nose begins." My nose could testify to the judgment. My conscience could testify to Edmund Burke's claim that "society cannot exist unless a controlling power upon will and appetite be placed somewhere, and the less of it there is within, the more there must be without."

From this episode, it is rather easy to understand why I was so sensitive to the intrinsic excesses of freedom. It was not that I loved freedom any less, only that I recognized with a certain poignancy what it can become without limitation. It was this lesson that I returned to many times thereafter.

Like most college youths educated at a liberal university the fifties, I was entranced by the apparent verities of existentialism. "Life is meaningless," I told unwary girls on park benches only half understanding the full import of my claims. And I am not even sure which half I understood the existence or the essence. I read and repeated lines from Albert Camus with all the gravity I could muster. It was during one of my several readings of *The Rebel*, that I rediscovered what I intuitively considered true. "There is no justice," noted Camus, "there is only limitation." Could it be, I asked myself, that Camus meant to say freedom instead of justice? It would have been consistent with this text; moreover, it seemed to me the real controversy undergirding rebellion. Freedom exists only with its inherent contradiction. A rebel without a cause is like Jimmy Dean and the thugs at Jamaica High School: a threat to others and ultimately a threat to the freedom that gave them license.

This analysis of the precarious character of freedom is by no means new. It is simply a case of balancing those shibboleths learned in school with the truths of the street. "Of course freedom has limits," shout dissenters who won't let me respond. It was always freedom for them and limits for me. Events in the sixties and seventies confirmed this observation. The children of Woodstock learned—perhaps over-learned—the value of freedom, but they did not learn about restraint. When, as a professor, I engaged students in discussion, I was at a distinct disadvantage. They were free to say what they wished; I, on the other hand, was encumbered by proprieties and a well-developed sense of fair play. When they would shout "bullshit," I would say, "What is the evidence for your claims?" It is obvious who got the better of those exchanges.

As Freud has noted, freedom must be restrained through the development of a conscience. Yet those weaned on the "Con III" value of "let it all hang out" considered conscience a trick of the establishment to ensure social order. And they are right. Conscience does mean order, but it is as much a trick of the establishment—whatever that is—as the belief that concentration in order to learn something is a trick of the FBI to keep you out of trouble. If desire is not harnessed, the pleasure principle is subject solely to utilitarian standards. Consider this extrapolation. If in the act of rape the rapist derives twenty units of pleasure, compared to ten units of displeasure he gives the person being raped, his freedom to act seems socially desirable. This syllogism is logical, but the initial assumption is wrong. There are simply some acts that should not be done regardless of the pleasure obtained. Rapists, of course, do not know that; neither did these *enfants terribles* of the sixties who performed their deeds with extraordinary vanity and little regard for restraints.

"Do your thing" often meant reject the uptight standards of the public (read: bourgeois) conscience. In the afterglow of university riots, expression was everything. Freedom became an absolute right in the puerile minds that were sure laws only secure the advantage of the privileged class. Since most of these rebels were members of that class, there was something paradoxical about the claim. Yet this view was more than an adolescent beating on his chest for an emergent manhood. Freedom without restraint was fast becoming a goal of the larger society in the same way my adolescent belief in doing what I wanted made what I wanted worth doing. This analogy is not so far fetched. With adolescence extended into the thirties, it is not unusual to find aging students who maintain that their desires must be recognized. One student, confusing himself with Patrick Henry, told my class that "even if what I want is wrong, my importance as a human being warrants consideration of my desires." Indeed! Then all human beings, who by virtue of their birth are important, have desires that warrant consideration. This was not what the Founding Fathers had in mind when they spoke of unalienable rights

If freedom is equated with desire—as is often the case—then in the tradition of musical comedy, anything goes. Laws are subordinated to feelings of satisfaction. The hero of *A Clockwork Orange* is a prototype for the "new freedom." His cruel acts make him feel good, so why should he not do them? Is it any wonder that our criminals, when they are apprehended, consider themselves "political prisoners." After all, the society guarantees their freedom—or so it is naively believed—why then should their actions be punished?

With freedom's meaning unraveled, with many people in society unwilling to accept conventional restraints, freedom as we've known it has lost her loveliness. We are in jeopardy of losing this value completely at the same time that we vocally defend its importance.☐

SARS —The Campus Disease

The SARS epidemic metastasizes across the globe as scientists frantically pursue a cure for this rapidly mutating virus. In my own life, I have encountered a psychological virus that is virulent, communicable, and goes by the same acronym SARS. It stands for Self Absorbed Repugnant Snobbery. While anyone can catch it, the disease has a political pedigree of reflexive urban liberalism.

Let me point out the characteristics of this "disease" from personal encounters. Recently I went to the thirtieth-year anniversary of a college I created at NYU, the Gallatin School. It was a chance to see old friends and former students and, incidentally, to receive an award for my efforts about which I was somewhat self-conscious.

As background it should be noted that while I am an unapologetic conservative and ran for public office with this label attached to my candidacy, I scrupulously avoided partisanship in any management decision during my more that two decades as dean. In fact, I hired a communist and assorted radicals on my faculty including a minority of conservatives. Politics simply wasn't in my management equation. I am interested in outstanding teaching and maintaining the canons of scholarship, ideas that once served as the basis for higher education.

What I did not expect is the forwardness, indeed the arrogance, in the way students and colleagues addressed me. SARS was very much on display at the anniversary celebration.

Although I don't wear a scarlet "c" on my chest, the husband of a faculty member greeted me by saying, "I never expected to celebrate May Day with you." Well, in fact, I never did join the parade in Red Square or Washington Square Park for that matter, but I also never asked my protagonist to raise the flag on July 4th.

Several former students came up to me to say you did "a wonderful job; I just hate your politics." This is curious since I never once in thirty-five years in the academy said to a student "I enjoyed your paper, but I hate your politics." Alas, there was probably much to hate, but I would never be so audacious to say so.

Then there were examples of indirect SARS. "You're a fine fellow; I assume you aren't serious about your political views." Most of these well wishers have never met a Republican in the university and treat me as some exotic but dangerous animal. Could anyone really believe that tax reduction can result in an expanded tax base? How quaint!

A whole group suffering from SARS noted that I had not discussed my political views in class. While I regarded that as a compliment, they meant to suggest that had I admitted to my "misguided political allegiance" they would have been pleased to contest my claims.

At no point did any of these people feel the least bit self-conscious. They were direct and assertive. They were confident and absolutely certain President Bush is a fool and anyone who supports his policies must be foolish as well.

In fact, I'm convinced Bush has been a successful president and it is an eminently defensible position. However, I don't believe I should have to engage in that defense at a celebration; nor do I believe it is appropriate for former students and colleagues to try to put me on the defensive.

I realize good form and civility have gone the way of bell-bottom trousers, yet I had hoped that SARS could be held in check, a period of remission during the anniversary celebration. Needless to say, I was mistaken.

SARS is a plague, in both viral and political forms. The political form may be more frequently found at places like NYU, but it has spread to other campuses and cities. As I write this screed, many social critics are hard at work trying to find an antidote for this contagious problem. But like its viral relative, no known cures are as yet available and I'm confident none will soon be found. □

Universities Search for Answers to the National Threat

For much of the twentieth century universities served a public function. Despite a liberal orientation, they cultivated patriotism, a respect for the free market, and a belief in exceptional American traditions.

It was not coincidental that college students volunteered in large number during World War II. Nor was it coincidental that the OSS (the forerunner of the CIA) was composed almost entirely of Yalies.

Needless to say, this condition changed with the Vietnam generation. In the sixties and seventies college students lost confidence in their nation. They burned flags, spelled American with a "k" and were fed a pabulum of American venality.

Students grew soft and decadent. Although the word appeasement wasn't used, peace at any price became the standard. There weren't any conditions they noted in which reason wouldn't prevail.

So sacrosanct was this belief that harpoons couldn't penetrate the wall of liberal illusion. Yet it was precisely this appeasement that made terror more likely. It was precisely the scent of weakness that the terrorists found irresistible.

In the minds of the cultural relativists who came to dominate the university curriculum, American students were obliged to understand our enemies, to empathize with their condition. After all, there was no higher principle than tolerance, the emerging god of campus debate.

The *Wall Street Journal* editorial page contends that this condition changed on September 11. Even the Harvard *Crimson*, the editorialists note, printed a poll showing 69 percent of the student body is in favor of military action against those who attacked America. More telling was the *Crimson's* response to 38 percent of undergraduates who said they were unwilling to take part in military action themselves. As the editors observed, one worries about students that favor military response "only as long as they can continue to sit comfortably in Cambridge."

The *Yale Daily News* asks plaintively, "Will we serve?" It answered the question by noting, "We must answer the calling of our time—for if we don't who will?"

Is it possible that several generations trained in moral obtuseness have awakened from slumber? Is it possible that student hearts and minds were not captured by aging baby boomers still immersed in Woodstock nostalgia?

I am not persuaded. There is considerable counter evidence that cannot be easily dismissed. A University of North Carolina lecturer said if he were president he would apologize to "the widows and orphans, the tortured and the impoverished and all the millions of other victims of American imperialism."

Professor Paul Kennedy at Yale asked his audience to understand the reasons people have for their hatred of America—notably our military power and culture.

University of Texas Professor Robert Jensen wrote that the attack "was no more despicable than the massive acts of terrorism...the U.S. government has committed during my lifetime."

A rabbi in downtown Manhattan in the shadow of Ground Zero told her congregation of many students that we must "build bridges" to our enemies rather than "feed the dog of evil."

A recent NYU graduate said he was unwilling to defend his country because it "has been something of a bully."

Another NYU student that saw the towers fall said, "this is all America's fault anyway."

At Hunter College a student on a soap box said the best response to terrorist attacks is "fighting American racism."

Professor Bill Crain at CCNY said, "he wants peace not war. Our diplomacy is horrible."

I suspect that the post-Vietnam generations have stripped the gears of public moral judgment. A flaccid form of tolerance and moral slovenliness intrudes on the unequivocal denunciation of evil. It is hard for someone raised on university banalities to accept the view espoused by Hamas leader, Sheik Hasan Josef: "We like to grow them from kindergarten through college." He was referring to Islamic martyrs.

John Maynard Keynes once wrote: "Madmen in authority who hear voices in the air are distilling their frenzy from some academic scribblers of a few decades back." The madmen of the present take their lead from scribblers of many years back. It is the contemporary college crowd that in my judgment hasn't yet unloaded its scribblers.

Is America's youth ready to learn something about its obligation to a free if imperfect society? Can they withstand the orthodoxy of relativism so many of their faculty members embrace? Can they overcome a history of appeasement and fight for what is right?

History awaits the answer and history is an impatient master.☐

Herbert London—Advice to Students

The best advice I can provide any student is to be armed with a healthy dose of skepticism. Accept no comment, however artfully framed, on face value. Search for the telltale signs: Is that comment supported by evidence? Is that claim subject to proof? If everyone nods affirmatively, does that mean truth is revealed?

Academics filled with the ardor of contemporary orthodoxies balkanize the study of any discipline by reducing it to class, sex, race, and ethnicity. As an antidote to these rather predictable preoccupations, it is healthy to ask whether there are any questions that cut across time and place, and recognize our common humanity. Is there, in fact anything at all that can be said about human beings who face the inevitable derision of death, yet seek to find some meaningful way of leaving their mark on civilization?

Should you find yourself in a classroom with the growing legion of professorial deconstructionists, hoist these charlatans by their own petards. If any position is true, ask "How do you know?" In fact, how does Derrida know? In the world or relativists, only authoritarians know the truth. The ultimate logic of deconstruction is that intimidation justifies one's opinion.

If inquisitiveness does not have its desired effect because your grades suffer, do what previous generations have done: follow the dictates of your instructor for examination purposes and ignore his advice for the rest of your life. □

"Theme Programs" in College Dorms

In the era of special interest politics it is hardly surprising that students wish to separate themselves by race, ethnicity, or sexual preference (to use the vernacular of the moment.) Homosexual students at Cornell University lobbied vigorously for their own dorm spaces, albeit the proposal was rejected by the president, Frank Rhodes. Rhodes explained his decision by saying he had "the deepest reservation about the increasing tendency within the campus to define ourselves in terms of groups and factions." Alas, he is right in my judgment, but one wonders whether this opinion is widely held among Mr. Rhodes' colleagues.

Even at Cornell there are "program houses" for American Indian culture, black culture, international life, and environmentalists. If Rhodes is right, what is to be done about housing arrangements that systematically balkanize the campus? And if homosexuals are denied separate residences, why should the university countenance such an arrangement for blacks? Presumably what is good for the goose is good for the gander.

According to the *Chronicle of Higher Education* the University of California introduced Asian-Pacific and Hispanic "theme" floors in a new dormitory and Wesleyan University approved a "queer positive" house much like the space requested by homosexuals at Cornell. Those who live in these separate quarters invariably justify the separation by noting that "they feel at home with their own kind" or "this is a space free of racial tension."

The question that remains, of course, is whether segregation either voluntary or involuntary is a racist echo from the past. It may well be that the voluntary segregation of the present inspires the very discomfort among white students that justifies further acts of separation and a gulf in interracial relations. As I recall when I enrolled in a university for the first time many years ago, I was told that I had stepped over the threshold of a narrowly defined community and entered one without boundaries called the academy. The very definition of the academy was ecumenical, universal, and open. How different most campuses have become.

Many white students I've discussed this matter with lament a campus torn by racial enclaves, yet only a disturbingly few have the courage to speak out against the practice. It is the enclaves themselves that promote racial tension and, ironically, are the rationale for an environment "free of racial tension." So powerful is the peer pressure for racial separation that if a black student breaks ranks and resides with a fellow white student, he could be chastised as an "Oreo" or "Uncle Tom."

If college administrators had the courage—surely in short supply in higher education—random selection would be employed as a housing policy for freshmen and "theme" housing programs would be abandoned as inconsistent with the essential mission of the university. Needless to say, I don't expect this result in the near future. But what the Frank Rhodes decision does indicate is that there is a growing realization that balkanization has gone much too far, transforming colleges from centers of openness for all kinds of people to parochial ghettos.

If one also realizes that the overriding purpose of a college education is to liberate youngsters from their narrowly perceived background and open them to the received wisdom of civilization, it becomes clear that housing separation, and its current curriculum variant multiculturalism, often undermine the college mission. This act of liberation doesn't suggest a negation of the past, but rather an embrace of the new. It isn't an attempt to trivialize racial or ethnic history, but to contextualize it against the backdrop of the global experience. President Rhodes admitted as much when he finally vetoed the housing plan for homosexuals at Cornell. The next step is for a college president to assert the danger separation represents to the purpose and goals of the academy. I eagerly wait for this hero to emerge.□

Non-Chemically Free Dorms

My goddaughter, who attends a small, prestigious liberal arts college in New England, was asked on her application whether she prefers to live in a "chemically-free dorm." When we chatted about this decision I didn't know what was meant by the phrase.

I soon learned. Chemically-free dorms are dormitories where students sign a pledge they will not drink alcohol or use drugs. What this means, of course, is that non-chemically free dorms are those where drug use and alcohol consumption are countenanced.

Never mind what the laws of the land suggest, colleges are a sanctuary for seventeen- and eighteen-year-olds who want to get high and plastered. Presumably those who sign up for chemically-free dorm spaces are the nerds.

While this generation of college students may not be so different from their predecessors who also engaged in hard drinking as an act of adolescent rebellion, what distinguishes the past from the present is that authority figures of yesteryear frowned on this practice. All dorms were once theoretically chemically free.

It is instructive that this New England college does not stand alone. Most colleges have chemically-free and substance-free dorms or dorm floors. At one large urban university marijuana smoking is tolerated in non-substance-free dorms as long as it is conducted in the privacy of one's room. At another, a floor counselor has to catch a student in the act of smoking marijuana three times before expulsion proceedings can be considered.

In fact, even though every college has stated parietals against drug use, non-substance free dorms are places notorious for pill popping and marijuana use. As my goddaughter has affirmed, youngsters in the tolerant dorm spaces are often strung-out, a condition administrators choose to ignore.

At one large university, drinking and drug use start on Thursday night and go on untill Monday morning. Invariably someone gets sick and an ambulance is called. A dorm counselor told me this is a regular weekly occurrence.

While university officials will invariably decry drug use, university hypocrisy is palpable, especially to students. Those adolescents who opt for non-chemically free dorms know that drug use will be tolerated. And university officials who give lip service to a zero tolerance policy defy their own regulations by averting their gaze to what happens in some dorms.

As the *Chronicle of Higher Education* recently pointed out, several students lost their lives to alcohol consumption and drug overdose. What this report did not note was university complicity in these matters.

When students under twenty-one consume alcohol in states where twenty-one is the legal limit and when students buy and then smoke marijuana joints, they are in violation of the law; and universities, by extension, are in violation of the law as well.

Last year there was a controversy at Yale over Orthodox Jewish students who refused to live in the dorm. The dean defended dormitory living as part and parcel of the college learning experience.

However, if Yale is at all like other colleges, the level of permissiveness challenges traditional standards of behavior. The very fact that there are dorms that disapprove of drug use and others where it is tolerated clearly demonstrates this point. For students who adhere to religious precepts most colleges are an invitation to Sodom and Gomorrah.

When I asked my goddaughter how students make a decision about dorm life, she said, "those who don't care whether they're thought of as nerds, will stay in the chemically-free dorms. The others think it's cool that drinking and marijuana smoking are permitted."

This issue is not a secret on campus. Parietals were abandoned decades ago. Fraternities may have a reputation for permitting hard drinking, but dorms often allow the same kind of behavior.

Every university catalogue I examined said drug use is a reason for dismissal. Some even said the university will apply the full weight of the law when drug rules are violated. Yet curiously, these same universities have non-chemically free dorms. What college administrators do is wink as they refer to strict drug use regulations.

That wink is a manifestation of gross hypocrisy. It is a demonstration that universities have become agents for undermining any aspect of traditional culture. Should a college administrator challenge this view, ask him what is meant by a non-chemically free dorm.□

Students as Customers

I have recently attended several meetings where students were routinely referred to as "our customers." In an effort to be accommodating, university administrators often call students customers whose concerns must be addressed. If any statement reveals the current absurdity of higher education, this is it. Students *qua* customers means that every attempt must be made to keep them satisfied.

In the university context, that usually translates into high grades, lax standards, permissive rules in dorms, sufficient parking spaces, and competitive football and basketball teams. It also means that students shouldn't be held to the "tyranny of grammar" or the "dictatorship of scientific precision," terms I actually heard employed by several administrators.

What they should be held to remains elusive. Undifferentiated grading and inflated grades are a response to open admissions

policy; students as judicial arbiters and on university committees are a reaction to the demand for "participatory democracy"
and student evaluations are a reflection of the need to keep them
satisfied.

Clearly contemporary university officials do accept the idea of
students as customers. That explains why extracurricular activities
have taken on so much importance and why students are considered
a vital constituency in all university-wide deliberations.

It is useful to recall in these somewhat absurd times that students
were once in the system of higher education to learn. Hence democracy, however the word is defined, did not apply to students.
Their fate was determined by their instructors and the process of
grading was decidedly undemocratic, albeit on rare occasions a
student argument for a higher grade might be persuasive.

Students were expected to behave as ladies and gentlemen,
terms that have an anachronistic tone. If they became boisterous,
intoxicated, unkempt, a dean would offer a warning and then a
punishment. It was considered a privilege to be on campus.

If anything the student is a client, someone you work for but
someone with whom you must be honest. If marginal work doesn't
deserve an A grade; students should not expect it and faculty
members shouldn't grant it.

Clients don't have to be satisfied, but they do have to be in-
formed. If in the process the student as client isn't happy with
the education he receives, he is free to go elsewhere. Universities
once acknowledged, even if they didn't welcome, high student
transfer rates.

But university life has undergone substantial—and in my judgment largely negative—change since the late 1960s. Competition
for students resulted in a "sale" of university seats. The university
became a corporation selling its primary product: degrees. Even
course credits were put in the cauldron of commodification. Accu-
mulate 120 credits and you get a degree, a little like green stamps
in the supermarket.

Students even talk as if they are customers. "I'm having a great
time"; "the social life is terrific"; "I'm pledging at a fraternity";
"football games are super"; this represents the language of satis-

faction. Rarely, if ever, have I heard someone say, "the studies are demanding" or "I appreciate the rigor."

If one relies on faculty evaluations, most especially letters of recommendation, every student is a combination of Einstein, Thoreau, and Jefferson. Too bad Johnny can't compose a coherent memo or Mary cannot solve a quadratic equation. But after all, they are expressive and imaginative and, most significantly, they are sensitive.

The upshot of consumerism is that no one tells the truth about students. In fact, students often believe the lies until at some point in their lives they are put to a real test and found wanting. Then the rationalizations begin.

Parents have a stake in the student-as-consumer model and so do most of the institutions of higher learning organized as corporations. For them money in the form of tuition or, better yet, alumni gifts is sacred.

Where this will end is already clear: the student as consumer will buy what he thinks is necessary to launch a career whether or not it has any value. This isn't merely a case of the blind leading the blind, it is more the vendor offering the consumer temporary satisfaction. It is unfortunate that the expression *caveat emptor* isn't employed. Then again, no one studies Latin on campus anymore. □

8

The Heroes in the Halls of Ivy

As I see it there are many villains—mostly inadvertent ones—in the university system. But I've been privileged to know several heroes, people who have risen above the others and stood by standards of excellence.

Political Pilgrims and the NAS
Academic Questions, Summer 1998

It is a cliché of the visual age in which we live that seeing is believing. Yet, as Paul Hollander suggests in one of the most profound books of the last four decades, *Political Pilgrims: Western Intellectuals in Search of the Good Society,*, believing is seeing. A class of intellectuals has developed the morally debilitating idea that belief is a filtering system in which the evidence that challenges suppositions is discarded and rendered irrelevant.

Daniel Bell asks of these intellectuals "why did not the young zealots read and learn about the history of revolutions, and why... did one and does one, see the continual 'process of enchantment,' the aching need to embrace revolutionary romanticism which recurs time and again?"

Paul Hollander has an answer. Many intellectuals, nurtured on relativism, do not have the capacity to differentiate among political systems. Filled with a romantic ideal, they embark on peregrinations around the globe searching for a system that confirms their vision. At its core this belief system is anti-intellectual, anti-rational. Those who share the faith engage in pilgrimages that invariably affirm their belief. They see, or choose to see, only that which legitimates a deeply held orthodoxy.

As a consequence, many intellectuals can rationalize political violence, alas even the gulag, rather than challenge the atrocities in front of their eyes. They have built a Potemkin village of the mind, one that sees violence as a necessary means to a desirable end. Not only do they see what they believe in so-called progressive states, they usually hold their own Western political systems in great contempt.

Their credulousness, as Professor Hollander points out so effectively, knows no bounds. When Western pilgrims are given special treatment in revolutionary states, they come to feel insufficiently recognized in their own countries. They do not question; they do not probe. They are the dupes Lenin described, who are so intoxicated by their faith in revolution that even childish propaganda is swallowed whole hog. If mention is made of torture and arbitrary imprisonment in the Promised Land of the moment, these *soi disant* intellectuals refer to class stratification in the United States or cruelty to animals in England. This is moral equivalence with a vengeance, one in which distinctions exist only in the mind of the true believer.

While intellectuals rail against the slightest violation in the United States, they steadfastly refuse to issue any criticism of human rights violations in Cuba or Nicaragua. Even when the evidence is overwhelming and devastating, the true believers find excuses or seek solace in another activity that seemingly justifies their loyalty. A cultural elite cannot let go of its illusions. To do so would be demoralizing; it would shatter its worldview.

Moreover, those who engage in systematic acts of denial are rarely, if ever, discredited by their academic peers. How can they be when the conviction is so widespread that no evil committed anywhere in the world can possibly measure up to the evils ascribed to the United States? The academic pilgrims discover that Soviet people, or Vietnamese, or Cubans are like ordinary Americans, except (as true believers note) their housing is less expensive, their medical care is free, and their loyalty is unshakable.

It is instructive that when revolutionaries visit the United States they are convinced that what they see has been organized solely for their edification. They often assume that their American hosts employ tactics comparable to those at home. I can vividly recall visiting Marine training operations with a Soviet general who had made up his mind that the young Marines he met were carefully screened and put on display to impress him. When I argued this is not how the Marine Corps operates, I was dismissed with a wave of his hand.

What he saw had to confirm what he already knew. He was the mirror image of the West's intellectual pilgrims. It is not co-incidental that Lincoin Steffens's famous phrase about the Soviet Union, "I have seen the future and it works," was written on a train to Stockholm, long before he entered the land of his revolution-ary dreams. In fact, it would not have made any difference if he made the claim after visiting the Soviet Union; he was prepared to affirm his faith.

As Hollander notes, there would not be any political pilgrims unless an elite group did not feel "a strong aversion to their own society and its culture, that is Western culture." Emotional dis-position, a faith in revolution, can prove to be decisive for many intellectuals who often have the capacity to create an intricate web of rationalizations and denials. It is hardly surprising that many intellectual pilgrims have embraced deconstruction that traduces objectivity and common standards of scholarship, as well as mul-ticulturalism that relies on wrongheaded interpretations of history in order to produce current resentment.

When *Political Pilgrims* was first published in 1981 it had a profound effect on those who recognized intuitively that something was wrong behind the walls of ivy. The organizers of the National Association of Scholars resisted the *zeitgeist* by suggesting that academic life should be based on a rational exchange of ideas and civil discourse that relies on evidence and knowledge. Those who had totalistic visions resistant to the canons of scholarship represented a threat to the academic enterprise precisely because of their intolerance, their overweening belief in a system of ideas that could not be challenged.

More than any other scholar, Paul Hollander offered documentation of a condition we observed on campus. The political pilgrims had come home as tenured professors and their beliefs metastasized across the body of higher education. Inspired by his example, the organizers of NAS sought to decry the subjectivists and the romance that accomplished a reflexive faith in revolutionary regimes.

We recognized that criticism of the West was necessary and welcome, but it had to be based on evidence, not hearsay. We recognized as well that true believers are often polemicists who seek only what confirms their assumptions. Just as political pilgrims are blind to the flaws in revolutionary states, their counterparts in the academy are emotional purveyors of knowledge who filter all information through an ideological prism.

Paul Hollander forced us to ask the appropriate questions about intellectuals and about ourselves. The fact that the phrase "political pilgrim" has entered the vernacular of scholars attests to the power of his discourse. In ways Professor Hollander cannot possibly fathom, he and his powerful book served as a catalyst for the National Association of Scholars. Recently reprinted with a new introduction, the fourth edition of *Political Pilgrims* not only reminds us of what we must be vigilant against, it is above all a model of impeccably careful scholarship and sound judgment. When the history of our organization is written, Paul Hollander's book deserves to be remembered as a compass that has guided us. It has helped establish the bearings for the NAS's humble efforts to elevate canons of objective scholarship from the debasement they have suffered at the hands of naive true believers caught up in pursuit of any number of impossible dreams. □

An Obituary for a Friend: Eugen Loebl
"From the Editor," *Academic Questions*, Spring 1988

Eugen Loebl was truly a man of this century. As a youth, he imbibed communist dogma as a catechism. The Nazis were his enemy. As a Jew and a communist intellectual in Czechoslovakia during the 1930s, he was the target of persecution and torture.

Spared by the grace of God, Eugen's torment would begin anew.

In the newly created Czech government after World War II, this talented economist was rewarded with a position as First Deputy Minister of Commerce. He hobnobbed with the leading lights of the Soviet Union. He was invited to high-level meetings of party officials and was privy to state secrets. He entered the inner sanctum of Stalin's East European empire. He also was a victim of state-inspired paranoia.

In 1948 Eugen was accused, along with Arthur London, Rudolf Slansky, and several leading Czech Jewish intellectuals, of selling state secrets to the recently created state of Israel. This was one of many staged trials by the Stalin regime. Eugen was found guilty. In this purge—bloodletting is a more accurate word—lies were made legitimate. The Slansky trial eviscerated the old Czech communist officials and set the stage for a full-scale installation of Soviet puppets and finally Soviet domination when tanks crushed the Czech rebellion in 1968.

Eugen Loebl was an unlikely hero. He was gentle, warm, and reflective—by no means physically threatening. But his mind was an enemy to bureaucrats who feared resourcefulness and possible disloyalty. Eugen described his torment during the Slansky trial with words etched into the terror—stricken history of the century. His book *My Mind on Trial* told the tale of torture; the admission of lies to support a fabricated Soviet case; and the Orwellian world that engulfed him, in which lies were truth and the party was the instrument of mind games.

Eugen was sentenced to eleven years in the Gulag, that vast wasteland forgotten by Western intellectuals unwilling to recognize an enemy on the Left. His first five years were spent in an isolation box. Yet in Eugen's case, his spirit could not be broken. He always noted that his "real education began in that box." The hours became days, the days months, the months years. All he had was time. His mind wandered over the map of his life. Every detail of his economics training was recalled. His political experience was treated as a virus to be isolated and identified.

He challenged the assumptions of his training, particularly the Marxist dogma that imperiled sound economic policies. He recalled conversations with Soviet party officials as if the words required Talmudic interpretation. Eugen reeducated himself using his collected experience as a textbook. He was the quintessential autodidact. If Arthur Koestler in *Darkness at Noon* excoriated the inherent totalitarian temptation in Stalin's purge trials, Eugen Loebl's *My Mind On Trial* is testimony of mankind's indomitable spirit even in the face of total domination. The more he was persecuted, the more his spirit soared. "I wasn't courageous," he said, "I simply had nothing to lose."

Several years ago at lunch, I expressed my dismay at Eugen's chain smoking, noting how bad this practice was for his health. He looked at me with a gentle smile and, said, "Bert [his name for me], if the Nazis couldn't kill me and the Gulag couldn't kill me, what makes you think these things can kill me?" I never again said a word about his smoking.

When Gene came to this country, he secured a teaching position at Vassar College. His good will and extraordinary intelligence made him a favorite instructor among students. But, as he often contended, "My faculty colleagues dismissed me as a cold warrior, in other words, an untrustworthy Eastern European afflicted with contempt for the Soviet Union."

Of course, there was some truth to this claim. Eugen understood Marxist Leninist ideas as few people have. For him, the party was not simply a dictatorship of the proletariat, it was a form of spiritual dismemberment allowing any atrocity for the survival of the system. When critics would say, "You are most certainly exaggerating," Gene would offer his kind smile and the words, "Believe me, I know."

Despite the sense of defeatism among intellectuals in this country, Eugen never once expressed any other sentiment but the will to fight back. "Bert," he would argue plaintively, "we must develop a strategy to save us from ourselves." Gene had such a strategy. It is based on the simple proposition that there can be no peace without freedom. Freedom is the indispensable condition of stability. It is therefore consistent with his logic that the Soviets, in accordance with the U.N. Charter, the Atlantic Charter, the Yalta Agreement; and the Helsinki Accords, all of which they signed, should permit free elections and self-determination in Eastern Europe as a condition for peace.

On the day that Gene left this mortal coil, President Reagan said that if Secretary Gorbachev were truly interested in peace, he would permit free elections in Eastern Europe and tear down the Berlin Wall. This was an unintended tribute to Eugen's memory. Yet this idealistic vision that Eugen conveyed to any interested party was tempered by realism. He knew the Soviets could not accept this proposition: To do so would destroy the empire and the privileges the *nomenklatura* have accumulated. He envisioned the proposal as a tactic in an on-going struggle. The way to Western solidarity, he maintained, was not through arms accords that, alas, have the opposite effect of what was intended, but through the assertion of principle on which all democracies are based.

When a detractor recently said of Eugen's idea that "It is something we will not see in my generation or my children's generation," Gene said, "He never lived in a box." Gene was not easily persuaded. During hours of conversation about economic theory, Gene would take my arm and say, "There is only one kind of economic theory—the one based on human behavior." It was sage advice from which most economists should take counsel. It was also consistent with Gene's unquenchable faith in people; he was forever an optimist.

When I would call to tell him an editor had rejected our manuscript, he would note, "So, is he the only editor? We'll keep trying." When I would tell Gene about my dismay with my colleagues in the academy, he would look at me and ask, "Would it be a better place without you?" Gene was a gentle warrior whose mind was affixed to grand ideas. He would look above his glasses; deliberately inhale his cigarette, then disarm you with the directness and clarity of his thoughts. Eugen didn't waffle. He was the senior partner in our collaborations; he always knew how to inspire me even when I was opposed to his position. One couldn't say no to Gene. In retrospect, I rarely wanted to say no. He was my friend, my teacher, my confidante. He brought wisdom to our meetings and strength to discussion. He gave love to his wife Greta and relentless energy to the cause of democracy. He was a European gift to this nation.

To paraphrase Browning, Eugen now rests in his heaven and we who survive are the better for having known him. One day, I suspect, the salvation of the West will be attributed to those anonymous men and women who had the courage to stand up to the commissars and speak the truth. Gene will always be counted among them.□

William Bennett in Perspective
"From the Editor," *Academic Questions,* Fall 1988

In 1980 a friend associated with the Reagan team asked me what the newly elected president should do with the Department of Education. My response was flip: I said the president could do the nation a service by eliminating this department. It was already apparent eight years ago that federal involvement in and expenditures for all levels of education had not served to improve the performance of American students. In fact, despite a 165 percent increase in federal expenditures in "real dollars," performance on standardized tests was lower than before the niagara of spending had begun. The Department of Education seemed like a logical candidate for budget cutting. However, eight years later I must admit that I was wrong.

What I didn't realize then was the extent to which this department, under the leadership of an extraordinary person, could by dint of his intelligence, determination, imagination, and integrity, change the nature of educational debate in our nation. William Bennett, more than any cabinet member in the Reagan Administration, used the bully pulpit to flush out the naive assumptions of his detractors. He simply won the debate. Instead of throwing money at our education problem—which simply is the inability of many Americans to read, write, and compute at a functional level, Dr. Bennett proceeded to espouse the educational approaches that work.

Where ideology stands in the way of sound approaches to learning, Dr. Bennett didn't hesitate to say so. He took on the NEA-sponsored "Choices" peace studies program. He railed against the influence of radical ideas insinuating themselves into the curriculum of higher education as an orthodoxy. He challenged the critics of Western civilization courses, raising the appropriate question: What will you substitute for the deposited wisdom of our civilization? He responded to teachers committed to the conversion of student attitudes by noting that anyone privileged to teach has a responsibility to tell the truth wherever that leads, including admiration for this country's institutions.

It is hard to believe that this young man, born in Brooklyn, who came to love football and Bo Diddley with equal passion, could turn out to be a powerful voice for the preservation of American traditions. At the Department of Education, Bennett invariably challenged the prevailing conventional wisdom, the educational establishment. He refused to comply with government-imposed affirmative action standards, yet hired more minority members than any of his predecessors, Republican or Democrat.

But from the point of view of this university educator, Bennett's singular achievement has been his articulate defense of Western civilization as pusillanimous and pragmatic university administrators succumbed to the pressure of post-sixties radical revisionism with respect to both the content of courses and the method of instruction. While many university presidents and faculty members rationalized the febrile action of their colleagues in an effort to keep campus peace, Bennett has had the courage to tell the truth. The center has not held at American colleges; on that point there is little disagreement. However, Dr. Bennett raised the banner of scholarly canons and academic freedom when there was little hope these traditions on which the academy rests could find a prominent or eloquent defender. For this William Bennett is owed a great debt of gratitude by serious scholars.

At some point, when sobriety reenters the academy, Secretary Bennett will be regarded as the Winston Churchill of American education. Derided by his critics, he refused to cater to the whims of fashion. University presidents found him to be a convenient target, but he gave them more in the form of upbraiding than he received. He, perhaps more than any person in the country, knows what is at stake in the campaign to recast the university into a propaganda center for molding the opinions of the young. It requires a special sensibility and strength to withstand the academic appeasers. Bennett has demonstrated these qualities in abundance.

Whether one agrees with all of Secretary Bennett's policy positions is somehow beside the point. He is the rod in educational institutions grown flaccid; he represents the inchoate development of a reassertive academic center. If this nation is saddled with a Department of Education, then I would hope that it can find another secretary like William Bennett. He served his country with honor. Clearly his role in national politics is only beginning. But now that his tenure as education secretary has come to an end, it is worth noting that William Bennett has set the standard for this office. From now on, his successors will be measured by Bennett's achievements and the tenor of his public proclamations. □

Remembering Allan Bloom
"From the Editor in Chief," *Academic Questions*

I first met Allan Bloom after the publication and startling success of *The Closing of the American Mind*. His candor was both amusing and disarming. He said that the first time he called the office of his publisher, Simon and Schuster, the secretary inquired, "Allan who?" When his book made the bestseller list, every time he called he was immediately connected with a senior editor. When the book reached number one, the president of the company answered his calls. After it remained at the top for several months, the chairman of the parent company, Gulf and Western, called him. When the book finally fell from the bestseller list, Allan had occasion to call the company only to be connected with the secretary he spoke to originally. After listening to his message, she asked, "Allan who?"

Allan was always entertaining. At several social events we both attended, he was the center of attention. Like Paul Heinreid in a scene with Bette Davis, he would drag on his cigarette before delivering his epigrammatic punch line. It was hard for me to believe that this gifted storyteller could become the *bête noire* of academic circles.

With the publication of *The Closing of the American Mind: How Higher Education Has Failed Democracy and Impoverished the Souls of Today's Students*, Bloom became the scholar university officials loved to hate. He's an "elitist," said one president of a major eastern university. That fatuous charge fails to distinguish democratic elitism from antidemocratic elitism. Rigorous standards of the kind advocated by Bloom enable newcomers to achieve success by work that benefits all of society, whereas lack of standards permits existing elites to entrench, securing privileges no longer earned. Thehu latter readily adopt the rhetoric of radical egalitarianism, which disguises their true motives, even from themselves. Whenever a commencement address derided Bloom's critique of higher education, in what I called Bloom-bashing, I found myself marveling at the extent to which radical egalitarianism has insinuated itself into higher education.

Although Bloom's book was embraced by conservatives, he was uncomfortable with that political label. He was a scholar whose translations of and commentary on Plato's *Republic* and Rousseau's *Émile* have had enormous influence. He was broadly cultured and entirely at ease not only with the philosophical classics but Mozart's symphonies and Shakespeare's plays and sonnets. Most of all, he was an inspiring teacher. He was not immersed in the world of politics. Perhaps that explains why he was surprised by the vitriol poured on his work.

Bloom answered his critics with an essay addressing their concerns, but remained baffled by his book's commercial success and the generally negative academic reviews it received. On one occasion, he asked me to speculate on the reason for the book's success. I argued that many middle-class parents spend $25,000 a year only to hear their children speak in a form of psychobabble, describe them as hopeless pawns of bourgeois culture, and denounce this democratic polity. "It is therefore not surprising that they would invest $20 in your book to discover why they are wasting $25,000." Bloom looked at me with a wry smile and simply nodded approvingly.

When I saw Allan at a conference in Washington a few years ago, he thanked me for my defense of his thesis. I noted then, as I have since, that his book was one of the most important written in the past two decades. It set the stage for the parodies of political correctness that appeared later and made legitimate an examination of the radical sensibility now reigning on American campuses.

There have been notable books written on higher education in the past few years, including those by Peter Shaw, Dinesh D'Souza, Charles Sykes, and Roger Kimball. These authors and all the others who have written about higher education work in the shadow cast by Allan Bloom and his extraordinary book. Until the university changes its direction, *The Closing of the American Mind* will stand as the most powerful excursion into the byways of the modern university.

Allan Bloom died last fall. He set the standard by which the university will be measured. Anyone who talks seriously about higher education today cannot ignore his comments. He inspired, he challenged, and he attacked. He was our Socrates on a journey from Cornell to Chicago, from anonymity to fame and back again, from the halls of ivy to the caverns of publishing. He jolted the academy out of complacency, and for that alone he will be remembered and sorely missed. □

Gathering to Look Back, An Introduction
The Peter Shaw Issue of *Academic Questions*

The articles and comments contained within this document bear testimony to Peter, the scholar, the man, the catalyst.

Jeffrey Hart provides an artful *tour d'horizon* of Peter's articles and reviews in *Commentary*, David and Stanley Rothman describe Peter's books as reflections of the *zeitgeist* and Gertrude Himmelfarb and Irving Louis Horowitz eloquently pit Peter's work against the dragons of postmodernism and historical revisionism, respectively.

Peter was an extraordinary scholar as these authors note, but it was his approach to scholarship that was as memorable as the scholarship itself. Contributor after contributor points to Peter's unwavering dedication to the pursuit of truth and the canons of scholarly discourse. If Peter rejected postmodernism, relativism,

Marxism, Lacanism, radical feminism, and the other fevers in con temporary academic life, it was not merely because he didn't share those ideologies. Rather, the rejection was his response to the intellectual sloppiness, soft thinking, and lack of rigor manifest in these upstart irrationalisms. Yes, it is true Peter could be polemical, but that was due to his uncompromising belief in the traditions of the academy, to the best that was written and thought.

Perhaps the most resplendent feature of the pages that follow is the reminder that Peter had a profound presence in the lives of so many distinguished scholars. As Joseph Epstein and others note, his enthusiasm was infectious. Peter had the rare capacity to restate ideas in a way that gave them more vitality than the originals. Because he could easily inspire, he could also easily deflate. Peter would disarm adversaries in debate with clever riposte and whimsical exchange, but he was always fair, always eager to listen to another point of view.

Those qualities of fairness and a willingness to listen obviously became a hallmark of his relationship with so many colleagues. Although Peter died more than a year ago, I along with several contributors continually ask in the midst of knotty intellectual problems, "What would Peter say?" For Peter was not only a valued friend, but for those who were graced by his gentle yet firm manner, he was a guide whose moral compass had unshakeable poles.

Ruth Wisse and several other contributors discuss Peter's ideological evolution from his days as a graduate student to the 1990s. For someone dedicated to fairness and reliance on evidence, an alteration in perspective is not unusual. Although several authors refer to Peter as a conservative, this label is not entirely accurate. Peter was different from most people devoted to an ideology. In the case of ideologists, evidence must conform to theory. With Peter the opposite was the case.

Johanna Kaplan calls Peter "the Fred Astaire of Jewish intellectuals." It is an apt description. Peter was effortless in discussion of almost any topic, from Mets baseball to Derrida's impenetrable logic. Like Astaire, Peter's passion for social dancing was based on the simple premise that two people moving together could, through subtle cues, produce elegance in motion. It's illuminating to contrast the social dancing that Peter and Penny enjoyed with the flamboyant and narcissistic dancing of the moment in which partners are not obliged to touch.

Peter's brush with the grim reaper after a severe heart attack in 1981 left him physically weakened, but morally resolute. As descriptions of his work suggest, Peter was unfettered from the demands of career enhancement. He said what had to be said without concessions to personal ambition. As much as anyone I have ever known, Peter was inoculated from academic preoccupations like tenure and promotion. He was truly his own man. He was not persuaded by flattery; nor was he impressed with pretension. He made the decision after his heart attack that he would pursue his goals without compromise. That pure sentiment, that sense of fearlessness, that independence, shines through every line of his later work.

While the National Association of Scholars has been a repository for scholars detached from the subjectivism that afflicts campus thought and is wedded in principle to the free and rational exchange of opinion, no one embodied the goals of this organization in praxis more than Peter. He was the exemplar. Those who have written for this edition confirm this sentiment in a variety of ways.

Peter Shaw was my guide through the thickets of academic irrationality. He was my best friend and my confidant. Most important, Peter was the eyes and ears on the world for a host of scholars. He was a human transponder feeding information to his friends, pointing them in appropriate directions, encouraging them with insights.

Peter eschewed the sentimental, and I won't taint his memory with reference to the many kindnesses he bestowed on me except to say Peter was my airwave. He kept me in touch with every dimension of higher education's reversion to silliness; he read the news with a microscopic eye, poring over a story to uncover any flaw in fact, logic, or structure.

His scholarship had the same artful foundation. Peter was among the first scholars to see through the absurd formulations of the deconstructionists. He had their number when it wasn't fashionable to decry their ideas. Peter didn't read a newspaper or a book the way the rest of us do. He read between the lines. He looked for assumptions and motives. He was the quintessential critical reader quite capable of writing a sequel to Mortimer Adler's *How to Read a Book.*

His biography of John Adams and his treatise on American patriots put in perspective the traits Peter most admired: reasoned argument, devotion to ideals, adherence to traditions. When it came to the defense of principles on which the academy rests, Peter was unwavering. He understood intuitively that sloppy thinking would result in undisciplined work and ultimately in the dissolution of standards. What he understood intuitively in the fifties became obvious in the seventies. For Peter, the surrender of academic rigor by normally engaged professors was one of the real tragedies of modern America.

Yet, through all the tortured debate, through all of his personal trials, Peter maintained dignity; indeed, I would employ the word nobility were it not for challenge by radical egalitarians. As editor of *Academic Questions,* he treated submitted articles fairly, but when they did not meet his high standard, he would call the author and gently upbraid him with the comment, "I think you can do better." Peter's instincts were impeccable.

There was another side to Peter often overlooked by the scholars who knew him only through his books. He was upbeat and playful. Peter could easily laugh at himself and at the absurd lengths his critics would go to challenge the debunking they received at his hand. If only Peter's academic critics could laugh at themselves the way Peter laughed at himself. Like most good critics he could frame stories so well I often thought Conrad, James, and Twain would have benefited from a conversation with him.

In the years Peter was editor of a newsletter I wrote, he had the unerring ability to clarify my thinking, a task I later learned he assumed with others. Peter enjoyed the act of editing because he enjoyed sharing ideas. He was and will always remain the most generous person I knew. Peter gave of himself in a way that only great scholars can conceive: he allowed his ideas to be shared freely without pride or passion, without barriers or invidious comparison. He was simply a scholar's scholar. This volume of essays and notes is not a *festschrift* in any strict sense. Peter would not have wanted one in any case. Nor is this volume a tribute to his writing, as insightful and illuminating as that is. This issue of *AQ* is dedicated to the spirit of the man, to someone who touched many and who built an edifice of ideals that will not pass from our memory. □

9

Scholarship and the Curriculum

Perhaps the central personal concern in my decades in university life is the nature of scholarship and the design of a curriculum. Why study X as opposed to Y? How does one determine what is important for students to know? When are changes in the curriculum needed? And under what circumstances are these decisions made?

Implications of the "New Demographics" and the "Information Explosion" for International Education
Education for America's Role in World Affairs

Harold Hodgkinson, former director of the National Institute of Education, wrote that, "The American public school curriculum is quintessentially European in nature, from the language it teaches to the music sung by its choirs. Although it is more relevant to blacks than in the past, there is still much to work on, and when we come to the curriculum *as it is learned* by all Asians and all the South Americans and islanders, we are truly flying blind." (emphasis in the original).

Here in rather unvarnished form is the view that the school curriculum must be responsive to a new set of ambient conditions summarized most often as the "information explosion" and the "new demographics." Presumably, computers, television sets, and the number of ethnics in our schools have rendered pedagogical assumptions of the past anachronistic. What educators in thralldom to changing conditions suggest is that new conditions call for a new curriculum, one based on interconnection, multi-culturalism, and "relevant'" materials.

Admittedly, this nation cannot tolerate the splendid isolation of the past. Our schools will inevitably spend more class time than has hitherto been the case on world history. Yet the essential character of this nation is as Western as ever. The philosophical precepts of the United States are based on tolerance for one's immigrant background and past and an expectation that the language, laws, and mores of one's adopted home will be embraced. There is the need for a canon to ensure acculturation, a canon that includes the *Magna Carta*, the *Constitution*, *The Federalist Papers*, the works of Shakespeare, Franklin, Jefferson, et al. For if the principles to which this nation adheres are to be accepted the provenance of individual rights and dignity, a belief in justice and equality and a faith in the rule of law must be imbibed.

The inference drawn from this proposition is not the abandonment of one's home of origin or a rejection of one's past. This nation has welcomed and continues to welcome people from diverse backgrounds recognizing the natural instinct for filial piety. But there should also be the recognition that to be a citizen of this nation all people must accept some minimal identification with and loyalty to the United States. A principal theme in US history has been hyphenated loyalty which permits a fondness for the Old World and a gradual blurring of ethnic, racial, and cultural distinctions within one's new home. That hyphen, which is unique to this nation, speaks volumes about American tolerance and interdependence, but it also demands one's allegiance to the adopted homeland.

It is certainly accurate to say we are living with an information explosion. But it is decidedly not true to contend—as many educators do—that more information implies more knowledge. Since information tends to be conveyed most effectively in the twin technologies of computers and television sets, it is worth noting that the primary uses of both machines are entertainment and organizing information. In neither case is it clear that the new technology has produced greater knowledge than we had before or greater wisdom than was evident heretofore.

In fact I would contend that curriculum designers have an obligation to knowledge that transcends the sciolistic and transitory. It is simply insufficient to argue that black students, to use one illustration, will be responsive to an Afro-centered curriculum. It is conceptually wrong-headed and it is patronizing to blacks precisely because of their race. If one curriculum goal is to explore the assertion of liberty among minorities, John Stuart Mill, a white Western male, speaks far more eloquently to this question than Malcolm X or Franz Fanon. It hardly bodes well for the future to assign to students already disadvantaged only those works or ideas consonant with racial and ethnic loyalties. These latter works may be relevant in some superficial sense, but in the long term a monopolistic dose of these readings will handicap students as assuredly as a lack of familiarity with arithmetic.

It has been argued that seven out of every ten new jobs in the beginning of the next century will be filled by women and minorities. This demographic condition has led some educators to the conclusion that the "new demographics" requires curriculum revision. But I maintain that students of any gender, racial group, or ethnicity require the knowledge and skills to be effective citizens in this polity. If relevance is the standard by which curriculum decisions are made, then one will teach students only what they want to learn. This proposition, as I see it, ensures marginal education and disadvantaged students.

It is instructive that several black organizations argued a few years ago that the Scholastic Aptitude Test is discriminatory. Cited as evidence for this claim was a verbal analogies question in which the correct answer was the word "regatta." It was alleged by black leaders that since blacks are often disadvantaged and culturally insulated, they could not possibly know what a regatta is. Yet it was at about the same time this incident took place that a recent émigré from Cambodia, who had been in this country only three years, won the national spelling bee with the word "daiquiri." What makes this illustration poignant is that this Cambodian girl entered this country without any knowledge of

English or American customs or any familiarity of our national drinks.

If the new demographics and the information explosion suggest anything at all for international education, it is the reassertion of basic national principles such as human dignity and the adherence to rigorous standards of achievement. After all, it is knowledge of what makes this polity unique that gives texture to the study of other states and organizations. The essence of international education is what students should know about other peoples regardless of those now enrolled in the schools, what appears on the Johnny Carson show, or how a computer pulse crosses national boundaries.

Understanding other people starts with knowledge of the self. But a sensible curriculum goes beyond that to inquire about the fundamental questions that inhere in the humanities, the questions that unite us as a people: Who are we? What are we doing here? Recognizing the inevitable derision of death, how can we leave our mark in this life? What is our relationship to others? How should we conduct ourselves? How do we wish to be governed?

There isn't any doubt that effective teaching-learning techniques vary. Students do not all learn in the same way. But it would be a gross mistake to confuse the technique of teaching and learning with curriculum modification. Curiously, the curriculum that is most effective for minorities and others, for females and males, for the poor and the rich is a curriculum that informs students about this culture and others, that offers the best that is known and written, that provides students with knowledge of truly great works, the deposited wisdom of our civilization. To deny the veracity of this claim by assigning marginal works that pander to those attempting to politicize the curriculum is, in effect, to handicap the very students who so desperately need our best counsel and most effective educational decisions. □

The Curriculum and the Census
"From the Editor's Desk," *Academic Questions*, Winter 1989-90

One condition that has insinuated itself into the college curriculum is the desire to be responsive to the ethnic composition of the student body.

Of course, our educational system should not be indifferent to the varied ethnic roots of the American people. Americans have long understood that "hyphenated loyalty," coupling a fondness for the "old country" with an aspiration toward eventual assimilation, represents a feasible and satisfying compromise between what otherwise might be considered warring psychological forces. What is wrong-headed and patronizing, however, is to argue that black Americans, to use one illustration, have a special need for an African-centered curriculum. Certainly, if a major curriculum goal is to explore the case for constitutionally guaranteed civil rights, John Stuart Mill, a white Western male, speaks far more eloquently than Malcolm X or Franz Fanon. Moreover, it hardly bodes well for the future to assign to those students who are already disadvantaged only works or ideas consonant with their visceral racial or ethnic loyalties. These may be relevant in some superficial sense, but in the long term an excessive dose of such readings will handicap them as assuredly as will a lack of familiarity with arithmetic.

If the new demographics suggest anything at all about the future course of American education, it is the need to reemphasize our traditional ideals of high achievement and preparation for common citizenship. This will not only preserve an American environment in which all can work and share in a spirit of brotherhood, but will also provide us with a frame of reference that will give refusal to legitimate meaning to the study of other societies. Moreover, our reasons for studying other societies are not primarily to be found in the changing mix of ancestral backgrounds that characterizes the national student body. Our interest in the experience of other peoples derives instead from a concern with the fundamental questions that affect all human beings: Who are we? How can we find enduring satisfaction in our lives? What are our responsibilities to other individuals and succeeding generations? How do we wish to be governed? What is the larger shape of the universe in which we live?

Curiously the curriculum that is most effective for minorities and others, for females and males, for the poor and the rich, is one that encourages reasoned to reflection about these commonalities of the human condition, that offers the best that is known and written and provides some knowledge of the deposited wisdom of civilization. To deny the veracity of this claim by assigning marginal works is to handicap greatly the very students who so desperately need our best academic counsel.☐

The Conversion of *Mother Jones*
"From the Editor in Chief," *Academic Questions*, Winter 1993-94

Mother Jones magazine—yes, the one dedicated to Mary Harris, "Mother" to the Jones, orator, union organizer, hell-raiser, and agitator extraordinaire. The magazine with reflexively radical views has a remarkable series of articles in the September-October 1993 issue. Although one might assume in reading them that history began in, say, 1991 and that no one had ever expressed such opinions before—after all, one must have a left-orthodox pedigree to get away with otherwise obvious arguments—it is remarkable that so many matters are discussed so sensibly in this issue.

Karen Lehrman, writing about women's studies, suggests that many classes alternate between the political and the personal, and many are filled with semiotic jargon and consciousness-raising psychobabble. While this argument has been made by Camille Paglia, Christina Sommers, and Elizabeth Fox Genovese among others, it is refreshing to read a first-hand report confirming it in the pages of *Mother Jones*. In fact, Ms. Lehrman has the temerity to note that the theories in the feminist classes she visited "have the potential to undermine· the goals not only of a liberal education, but feminism itself." Using emotional arguments to "validate" women risks reinforcing the stereotype of subjective, irrational female behavior that feminism is supposed to overturn.

As she notes, women's studies has become yet another example of oppression studies-academic analyses that invariably trace the ills of society to a patriarchal social system based on capitalism and Western values. Women, once they are enlightened, must engage in the struggle to reform the system and, of course, undermine male dominance. Ignored in this "academic" calculus are successful women who have succeeded by dint of individual merit and effort. Women, after all, must be seen as oppressed, forever victims of male bias. In fact, distinctions between societies like the United States, where a "glass ceiling" may exist, and Iran, where women are obliged to wear veils, are rarely made. Any example of bias merely reinforces the general sense of victimization.

According to one theorist quoted in the article, "Most teachers of women's studies presume that if you don't see yourself as a victim, you're in a state of false consciousness, you're "male identified." In this paradigm, to question or examine evidence is to assume the characteristics of a male-dominated order. Faith is what such courses often require; anything else reinforces female oppression. Yes, this admission appears in *Mother Jones*.

Next is an interview with David Osborne, author of *Reinventing Government* and friend of President Clinton. Osborne, it turns out, is an unabashed supporter of charter schools and school choice. As he notes, "the fundamental reason schools don't change rapidly is that they have the next best thing to a monopoly. The only way, in a traditional public-school system, that you can have your children go elsewhere than where they're assigned is by paying a lot of money." While this argument has been made by Chester Finn, Polly Williams, and Dennis Doyle for years, it is nonetheless refreshing to see it repeated by a contributor to *Mother Jones* and senior advisor to Vice President Al Gore.

Osborne realizes that in a truly competitive system of choice, if a school lost a significant portion of its student enrollment and money, the principal would be held accountable. "There would finally be a reason why somebody had to care about these schools."

Even more astonishing than the Osborne refrain is an article by Diane Brady titled "As the World Learns." Ms. Brady argues that access to a college degree shouldn't be our national goal; demanding excellence from those who choose to finish school should be. That reference to excellence made in a publication wedded to a form of radical egalitarianism is almost enough to restore my faith in the modern age. Moreover, the further claim is made that "the best course is to let the full force of international competition prod complacent American managers to try new ways of doing business." Who knows, perhaps in a succeeding issue *Mother Jones* will endorse free markets!

Is a new day on the horizon, one in which ideology takes a backseat to hard-headed reportage? If this recent issue of *Mother Jones* is an illustration, we may have some reason for hope. □

The Effect of Ethnic Studies on the University

It was recently reported that a City University of New York plan to restructure a program devoted to Italian-American students has led to an acrimonious exchange between the university's chancellor and some leading citizens of the Italian community. The university proposes to convert the program, the John Calandra Italian-American Institute, from a recruiting, counseling, and teaching program into a research center specializing in Italian and Italian-American issues.

Critics contend this change is a barely concealed effort to dismantle the organization and punish its long time director for participating in an anti-discrimination complaint filed by Italian American faculty members against the university. As one might guess, many prominent Italian-Americans are rallying for the preservation of the status-quo and, predictably, university officials deny any discrimination against Italian-Americans.

Jay Hershenson, a spokesman for the chancellor of the City University, said the reorganization was designed to give the program "academic" status by converting it to a research center which would be the catalyst for a doctoral program in Italian studies. The critics are unconvinced. They claim parceling out the institute's functions is tantamount to dismantling it.

It is instructive that the Calandra Institute, named after the former state senator, was established by the state legislature fourteen years ago after complaints of discrimination and neglect of the Italian-American community. However, what the state legislature, critics of the university plan, and university officials have overlooked is that any unit of the university organized to promote the interest of one ethnic group or race will invariably generate anger and frustration. In fact, if one gives this matter a little thought, it stands to reason that emphasizing one group over another is bound to result in turmoil.

Once the proposition of ethnic studies is recognized and given legitimacy by the university, there is no way to deny claimants for similar status. If one accepts Italian-American studies, Black studies, Hispanic studies, or Jewish studies, what rationale can be employed for denying the claims of Muslims, homosexuals, left-handed people, or any group organized by fate, culture, or history as distinctive? And if one does not deny these claimants, the university becomes Balkanized—organized solely around the superficial condition of what separates us.

Should the university continue down this path, it should change its name to the "diversity," since the conditions that unite students and are indeed universal will have been subordinated to that which separates and keeps us apart. Pandering to ethnic groups, politicians often contend such programs are needed to counter the effects of discrimination and bigotry. In fact, these programs often promote the very conditions they were organized to prevent. The very act of separation by ethnicity and the curriculum concession to cultural hegemony acknowledges the supposition on which discrimination is based.

If special interest could be examined dispassionately—a practically impossible situation—most sensible university administrators would admit that the university's willingness to redress the social ill of discrimination has contaminated the university with the views of multiculturalism for which there is no known inoculation. Ultimately, multiculturalism is a war of cultures. Since there are not ground rules for such competition, political influence is all that counts. Power, not scholarship, prevails; and politics, not the canons of scholarship, is the handmaiden of curriculum reform.

It is not surprising that the Calandra Institute has generated turmoil. Any other response would have been the real surprise. As long as universities deny the universal and emphasize the divisive, they vitiate an essential purpose for their existence. Universities don't exist to combat discrimination. In fact, no matter what steps are taken that goal is unachievable. Universities exist to promote learning, the search for truth, to consider what is universal and to transmit an understanding of the past. Any other mission imposed by political solons is likely to dilute the purpose of the university at best or generate anger and turmoil at worst.□

A Failing Grade for Changing Western Culture Curriculum
New York City Tribune, February 4, 1988

It is becoming increasingly clear that a campaign has been organized to delegitimize the literature of Western civilization at US colleges and universities. Perhaps the latest in a series of incidents is the willingness of the Stanford University faculty to introduce a replacement for Western civilization that includes equal time for minority contributions and women authors. Presumably, what the Stanford faculty has responded to is the charge that the reading list reflects a Euro-centered, male bias with sexist and racist stereotypes. Apparently, Plato, Aristotle, St. Augustine, John Stuart Mill, Shakespeare, and Dante have been reduced to stereotypes in the new age.

The argument employed by the opponents of Western civilization is that it is "too restrictive" to describe the diverse world in which we live and such courses demean those of color and femininity. While this curriculum turmoil at Stanford will be regarded by many as the febrile ranting of adolescents, there is a pernicious political side to the dispute. The anti-Western rhetoric reflects the views of some who would dismiss and replace the deposited wisdom of this civilization under the guise of fairness and equal rights.

What is at work at Stanford and elsewhere is the establishment of campus curriculum reform through intimidation. Those at the barricades tend to be the vocal reformers who claim that women, the poor, and blacks are insufficiently represented in course readings. As one student activist pointed out to me recently, "It is better to have one reading by a black revolutionary than all the sonnets of Shakespeare." Barry Katz, professor of history at Stanford and member of the academic task force responsible for the new course, contends that "the existing course requirement asserts that we have a common culture and it asserts that it can be defined by a bit of reading in the great works. This has been an affront to a large number of students and faculty, to women and members of minority groups."

As has been the case at many other colleges, the majority of faculty members at Stanford are disappointed with the curriculum reform but went along with it anyway out of a sense of compromise and because of excessive student pressure. However, once the compromise was accepted—namely the acceptance of a new course—the entire faculty can be held accountable for making a travesty of Western culture. Here is an unalloyed version of curriculum design by plebiscite; in fact, it may even be curriculum reform by a tyranny of the minority.

Writing in *The Wall Street Journal,* Isaac Barchas, a student, described the Stanford reform as an "impoverishment of the undergraduate experience." He writes, "For if the Western, intellectual tradition has a generally unifying theme, it is that incidental characteristics such as race are irrelevant. One's mind, not one's accidental existence, is the true measure of one's worth." Unfortunately, Barchas may be in the real minority at Stanford. Carolyn Longee, another faculty member and member of the task force, wrote, "The Western civ. course is not a timeless, eternal distillate of human wisdom." In her mind, this curriculum can be altered to accommodate the changing ethnic profile of the nation.

But even if one were to take this proposal seriously, how do you proceed? The novelist Saul Bellow implicitly addressed this question by asking where is "the Tolsoy of the Zulus, the Proust of the Papuans." This concern isn't easily dismissed. If one were to take seriously Matthew Arnold's admonition to teach the best that is known and written, one would be hard pressed to give equal weight to authors of color.

Yet in the long run the central desire of these activists—if achieved—will serve only to undermine the freedom they seem to admire. For it is in the Western tradition that one finds the concepts of civil rights, liberties, academic freedom. It is the West that created a civilization that permitted the quest for equality. To undo this tradition is to reintroduce the sentiment of bestiality, enslavement, and barbarism that characterizes so much of this globe. The tradition of Africa that many black activist students espouse is not a tradition that allows for inalienable rights or the free exchange of ideas that prompted a curriculum reform at Stanford.

If anything, the goal of refashioning Western civilization to satisfy feminists and activists demonstrates how ignorant of their own tradition many of these people are, it also demonstrates how much they depend on the rights granted through this tradition to voice their disapproval. □

Ipse Dixit Scholarship
The State of Scholarship: Political Science

The current issue of the *Political Science Quarterly* (Fall 1986) includes a curious article by William D. Anderson and Sterling J. Kernek, two scholars at Western Illinois University. According to these academics President Reagan is not the practitioner of realistic diplomacy that he says he is.

To buttress their contention they suggest that the president is a "a conservative American romantic with an unrealistic vision of the world, a taste for hard-line gestures of power politics and a talent for developing versatile rationalizations." Occasionally, these authors acknowledge, Mr. Reagan shows moments of sobriety, what they characterize as "political realism." They offer as evidence his recognition of "the central role that power plays in relations between competitive sovereign states" and his flexible diplomatic posture towards China.

But—and here is the rub—the president "is unlikely to reappraise his basic notions." These notions are the "romantic" and "unrealistic" visions presumably unattached to what the president claims is his "clear perception of the facts." One example is "his obtuseness about local conflicts in the Middle East." However, the "decisive" points in this article are scored by suggesting that Mr. Reagan's political faith runs contrary to political realism because he isn't cautious, is inclined to embrace moral crusades, and challenges the global balance of power.

Forget for a moment the many empty assertions in this article. What is of significance, it seems to me, is what passes for scholarship in a distinguished political science journal. Surely such articles must have undergone peer review. Does it follow that its scholarly reviewers accept *ipse dixit* as a reliable standard for scholarship when the assertions are designed to undermine the reputation of the president?

I am not trying to inhibit the work of scholars. The point of view expressed by Anderson and Kernek is not one I embrace, but that isn't the point of my argument. It strikes me as mind boggling that an article devoid of hard evidence and based on the arbitrary standard of what the authors call the "president's reluctance to reappraise his basic ideas" is published in a scholarly journal. What precisely does "a reappraisal of ideas" mean? Should the president change his opinion to suit these authors? Is that what they mean by "realism?" Why do they ignore as illustrations those times the president has changed his mind, e.g., South African sanctions? Or is it simply a matter of a president who has a point of view, perhaps a *weltanschauung,* different from the scholars'?

Certainly academics should feel free to be as critical of the president as they like. But I don't understand why criticism leveled at the president in the form of personal opinion and occasionally invective qualifies as scholarship. Does this case suggest something about political bias in the academy? Is scholarship itself so contaminated by politics that polemical and scholarly argumentation have become indistinguishable?

The article in question is of little consequence. It will quickly pass into the bowels of the bibliographical indexes. What is important, however, are the implications when a piece so devoid of hard-headed research can masquerade as scholarship. It may well be that the authors don't think of their work as scholarship, an admission I regard as unlikely. But what remains unanswered is why a refereed journal would consider this form of argumentation appropriate for publication. I wonder what justification for acceptance the referees would offer.

In the late sixties a prominent Australian political scientist told his American colleagues that it is our duty not to present balanced argument, "but to win." By winning he meant to change the terms of scholarship so that advocacy becomes the *sine qua non* of research. His view, to some degree accurate, is that if one relies on balance, fairness, and documentation in research the social order will not change, and change, he contends, should be the goal of scholars.

When I first read this statement I was bemused, believing that any serious scholar would dismiss it as the glandular rantings of a frustrated revolutionary. But I was wrong. The results of this theory can now be found in the *Political Science Quarterly*. A "new scholarship" is regnant that has little to do with what's new and less to do with scholarship.

In the good old days, one called this kind of work an opinion piece and it was usefully printed as such. Unfortunately scholars have lost their way and so have their journals. Now if an article appears to be an assault on the status quo it is *ipso facto* scholarship. One can only wonder what is said in classroom lectures behind closed doors. The thought should cause serious scholars to shudder. □

Sex Courses on Campus

It was once the case that universities were insulated from cultural faddishness. Even when Alfred Kinsey published his best-selling tome *Sexual Behavior in the Human Male*, scholars did not embrace courses on human sexuality.

Clearly, however, the fifties are not the nineties. Every dimension of sexual identity is now being explored in the academy. With catalogues swelling to unprecedented thickness, courses on sex account for much of this change.

The University of Minnesota, NYU, the University of California, the University of Chicago, and a host of other well known institutions have instituted gay, lesbian, bisexual, transgender—and any other permutation one can think of—programs.

In the era of "let it all hang out," the courses are invariably explicit. As the *New York Times* recently reported, undergraduates at the University of Virginia gather to sculpt genitals from Play-Doh. And at a recent conference sponsored by the State University of New York at New Paltz, sadomasochists demonstrated their "techniques" for interested students and sex toys were on display for the uninitiated.

Although one might make the argument that any subject might be considered in the curriculum if it meets rigorous academic standards and has an empirical body of evidence to substantiate its claims, most of these courses on sex have more to do with expression and feelings than research and scholarship.

Dr. John Bancroft, who heads the Kinsey Institute at Indiana University, contends that "there is still a lack of good, basic research into the fundamentals of human sexualities." Since there isn't a body of consistent scientific findings to build a discipline, it is appropriate to ask why there is current fascination with sexuality on campus.

The answer to that question like the answer to so many other questions in contemporary society is political. Invariably the instructors in these courses are trying to undo bourgeois morality. Susan Tate, an instructor at the University of Virginia, put it bluntly, "If we can discuss the heart, stomach, and elbow without embarrassment, we should be able to talk about the penis, clitoris, and vagina without laughing."

In other words, sex is to be treated without taboos like elbows. The only problem with this effort at proselytizing is that sex is not elbows and, even if it were, what do these classroom discussions have to do with an education?

I often wonder if parents who have sacrificed a great deal to send Johnny and Jane to college are pleased to learn that instead of reading Aristotle Jane is learning how to use a dildo.

Moreover, much of the programmatic basis for sex courses is the growing tolerance for and political muscle of homosexuals. Whether this movement serves the interests of the nation remains undetermined, but at universities homosexuality has become an extension of the civil rights movement. Hence, courses on sex assume that sexual orientation is a preference not unlike the selection of bow ties. Should one contest the claim by arguing homosexuality is a sexual aberration, insults and worse are forthcoming.

In this faux discipline all the questions have predictable answers which fit neatly into clearly defined political parameters. Same sex relations are natural, sex should be discussed openly and objectively, and there should be no shame in expressing oneself on this matter.

Since expression is the *sine qua non* of these sex courses, adolescents curious about sexuality gravitate to the classroom. What these classes often encourage is personal examination—as if self-absorption isn't already a national contagion.

In a higher education environment, in which students often do not know when Columbus came to the New World or how to find the area of a rectangle, it is astonishing that resources are being spent for courses on sexuality that have neither rigor nor an empirical body of evidence.

Professor George Chauncy, at the University of Chicago, notes that from 1987 to 1992 there was a ten-fold increase in the number of attendees at a conference on gay and lesbian studies. I would not question the veracity of this claim or his belief that this subject has new-found adherents. But what Dr. Chauncy has not noted is that the increased numbers at this conference may reflect the propaganda in sex courses, the legitimacy the academy has accorded the subject, the belief that homosexual rights are consistent with a civil rights agenda, and students inclination to express themselves rather than engage in the hard, painstaking effort of genuine scholarship. □

Subjectivism on the March in Law and Scholarship

Before the intrusion of subjectivism into every aspect of analysis, judges relied on legal precedents for their decisions submerging personal bias before the power of legal argument and historians and political scientists were obliged by the dictates of their disciplines to restrain their personal views within the parameters of available evidence. Alas those conditions have long passed.

It is now apparent that what one believes has been elevated to the station of "truth" and legal judgment. Two recent examples would seem to support this claim.

Federal judge Leonard Sand recently upheld begging in New York subways as a form of speech. In addition to the leap of faith implicit in this opinion is the extent to which Judge Sand substitutes his own personal view for legal precedent. He notes, "The simple request for money by a beggar or a panhandler cannot but remind the passerby that people in the city live in poverty and often lack the essentials for survival. Even the beggar sitting in Grand Central station with a tin cup at his feet conveys the message that he and others like him are in need. While often disturbing and sometimes alarmingly graphic, begging is unmistakably informative and persuasive speech."

While Judge Sand is certainly entitled to his opinion about begging, he is not entitled to transmogrify opinion into precedent. After all, observing able-bodied beggars suggests to some of us that the biblical admonition that he who doesn't work shall not eat, has retreated before self-indulgent logic. It does not strike everyone that a beggar is in need. Some would claim that the beggar would rather ask for assistance than work for a living. What the beggar informs us about is indeed subject to a variety of opinions.

This is not to suggest that Judge Sand is wrong—albeit, I'm convinced of that opinion—but to argue that Judge Sand's opinion is certainly no better than the opinion of anyone else. That his view is dignified by legal judgment does much to vitiate the meaning of the law for the average person.

Similarly, James David Barber, a professor of Political Science at Duke University, writing in the *New York Times* contends that George Bush "believes in aristocracy. He acts to advance the rich and powerful. Historically, aristocrats like George Bush have managed to ward off the challenge of real democracy, not by damning the people (at least in public) but by confusing them." Applying the canons of scholarship, this is an astonishing claim. For openers, how does Professor Barber know what President Bush believes? Has he talked to the president?

Furthermore, he claims the president advances the interest of "the rich and powerful." Yet, here again opinion substitutes for evidence. Is a proposal to lower the capital gains tax, an example ignored by Barber, evidence of supporting the rich and powerful? What can one possibly mean by the use of the word aristocrat? Has Bush ever described himself as an aristocrat? Indeed does anyone call himself aristocratic? And what is one to make of the argument that aristocrats like George Bush have managed to ward off the challenge of real democracy by confusing the people? What is real democracy? How is Bush warding it off by confusing the people? Who is confused?

By any scholarly standard these arguments are specious. Barber is as entitled to his views as anyone else, but if one applies scholarly analysis his views don't hold up. One would expect more from a scholar, as one I could expect more from a judge. However, this is the era in which every opinion counts and if one can disguise opinion behind the facade of legal judgment and scholarly discourse so much the better. The real casualties in these cases are the law and scholarship. They have not been the same in the era of subjectivism. □

Saving the Academy from Itself

Arguably the concept that has had the most profound effect on modern thought in the academy and in circles that imbibe radical theory is cultural relativism. As the label suggests, cultural relativists reject the notion that Western ideas provide any greater insight or are in any sense superior to those of other cultures, specifically indigenous cultures of the so-called Third World. Even Western knowledge and its empirical basis in rationality is interpreted as strictly limited by time and space without universal application.

Students with a rudimentary familiarity with logic and history now glibly assert the relativist platitudes of Foucault, Derrrida, Heidegger and their popularizers at almost every campus in the nation. I have been lectured by students from coast to coast on the need to recognize the idiosyncratic contributions of other cultures as we would our own. Yet while the wellspring of this sentiment is the recognition of universal human dignity, it ignores the unique, yes superior, contributions of the West in morals, politics, and epistemology.

Can one seriously conclude that the ritual execution and cannibalization practiced by pre-colonized Aztecs and Maoris—to cite two examples—should be treated in the same fashion as the Western humanist tradition, with all its flaws. Can logical exegesis permit an equation between "medicine men" and modern science? Can slavery in the Sudan be equated with freedom in the West?

Cultural relativism regards each culture as free to pursue its own goals within the confines of its own tradition. Hence, Western concepts like free speech or the rights of women are not perceived as universal principles, but rather the mere product of a specific time and place and inapplicable to other cultures. From this hypothesis, several dilemmas emerge.

For one thing, the cultures relativists wish to embrace generally do not share liberal openness. Islam, for example, isn't interested in relativism of any sort. The devout in this culture are confident of their beliefs, of an absolute authority. Relativism debases the culture for it assumes Islam is one of many equally valid paths to transcendence.

Similarly, if all cultures are equally valid, what standards can be employed for evaluation? And if one assumes each culture is unique, alien from anything we can understand or appreciate, the meaning of these cultures is *ipso facto* beyond our grasp. This, by the way, is the essential paradox in the discipline of anthropology. Without the existence of a universal culture, it is impossible to either understand or appreciate the meanings of specific cultures.

What cultural relativism has achieved is a withering critique of Western intellectual hegemony. The cultural relativist does not have to fear contradiction from defenders of the West. By and large, the defenders have succumbed to a false but persuasive epistemology. To suggest that cultures different from ours may be inferior is to invite the charge of racism, a debate stopper. Ironically, Western universalism that recognizes standards beyond idiosyncratic culture is the genuine anti-racist claimant. But that is a difficult sell.

Cultural relativism, with its roots in anthropology, was once only an intellectual critique of Western thought. Now that critique has emerged as a justification for political tribalism. Tribal cultures arguing that only their members can appreciate narrowly defined revealed truths insulate themselves from and compete with others. Africa, South Asia, and the Balkans are replete with examples of this phenomenon. Clearly, cultural relativism is an accomplice in international tribal bloodletting through its insistence on the integrity of any culture, no matter what practices are perpetuated. In a Kiplingesque world it was believed that the West brought civilization to the heathens; in the world constructed by Foucault and his ilk, it is the tribal cultures revered as humane. However, tribal culture, like all culture, must be evaluated against a backdrop of some standard before the attribution "humane" can be leveled.

The inference that political liberation of colonial people should be accompanied by epistemological liberation is illogical. It is one thing to remove the yoke of Western political control, but quite another matter to overturn intellectual instruments that could turn out to be the salvation of recently liberated peoples. Despite all of the rhetorical claims, there isn't a substitute for the Western scientific and rational tradition. To deny that truth is to impose a cruel hoax on the very people who can least afford it.

Since the university is in thralldom to an idea that directly assaults the traditional canons of scholarship, what can be done? What is the rejoinder to cultural relativists who claim that assigning Dante and Shakespeare merely imposes an Eurocentric ideology on the university?

Whether a spokesman for conservatives like Judge Robert Bork or for radicals like Richard Goldstein, on one point there is consensus: the left has won the culture war in the academy. A sixties generation weaned on polymorphous perversity is different from its ancestors. Believing that the self is the measure of all meaning and the arbiter of what is right, a generation arrived at adulthood worshipping the great demiurge solipsism. In its rejection of tradition, of all that came before, this generation assumed a societal *tabula rasa* that could be imprinted with self-expression. In this so-called post-modern period, what "I feel or think" is all that counts; "responsibility" and "duty" are words pegged into an anachronistic age. Many faculty members and most students worship the great god, Relativism.

Against this backdrop of self-expression is a technological revolution in which everyone is encouraged to express himself. The virtual super-highway leads directly to the Tower of Babel. There aren't any standards when radical egalitarianism demands that everyone is heard and the contemporary statues of Daedalus give every voice amplification. Amid the din, taste and probity are drowned out. A cultural Gresham's law is at work with the tasteless driving the tasteful out of existence. If this seems exaggerated, compare the popularity of gangsta rap with the financial struggles of most symphony orchestras.

An ample supply of illustrations demonstrating cultural deterioration merely confirms the proposition that for the time being the culture war is over and refinement, taste, and aesthetics are missing in action. For those who lament this outcome, little in the way of solace is available. Judge Bork, for one, says we should hope for the best; yet there is little besides hope that he prescribes. Suppose, however, that the ambiance of freedom, converted by radicals into license, were to be turned into a cultural instrument for rejuvenation.

In Ray Bradbury's classic novel *Fahrenheit 451*, outcasts defeated in a culture war retain a sense of the worthy by assigning to memory every one of the classic texts. This became a community of moral archivists with each person assuming responsibility for memorizing a text. In this way, book burners could not destroy the notable culture of the past. It seems to me that the Bradbury approach has much to recommend it. With Shakespeare increasingly unassigned at college campuses and Dante replaced on a classic reading list at Stanford by an Ecuadorian indigene, and Milton and Chaucer delegated to a category of irrelevant, dead, white, European males, the time may soon be approaching when reading the classics of Western civilization will be an act of rebellion, a guerrilla action in the remaining years of the culture war.

Since traditionalists are inept at engaging their adversary in the culture war, and since most conservatives are unwilling or unable to recognize the influence of culture on politics, a traditional media viewpoint was easily supplanted by radicals over the last four decades. Hence, a direct attack on cultural pollution is not likely to work. For those who determine programming, a moment of retreat today is worth a dramatic lunge forward sometime in the future. There is a growing recognition that the virtuecrats (this is not a term of derision) do not have staying power. Surely they do not have the influence of a growing market for the hedonistic, violent, and pornographic dimensions of culture. In Antonio Gramci's terms, the left has captured the culture.

In the cultural desert in which we find ourselves, it is incumbent on those with a traditionalist stance to assert it in modest but meaningful ways. A museum should be devoted to the best that has been achieved in artistic forms. By the "best," I am referring to that which is spiritually enriching, aesthetically pleasing, and technically uncompromised. A college should be established without any concessions to the *zeitgeist*. Students should meet rigorous requirements without electives. Moreover, they should read the great works of our civilization, be literate in two foreign languages, have numeric skill, and be familiar with scientific laws and methods.

If a college cannot be established because of financial limitations, a department or program should be organized that does not make any compromises with its belief in traditional principles of scholarship. Those that enter this program will know that no concessions have been made to the relativists.

A radio station should be organized that plays great music from shows, opera, and classical recordings disregarding popular music and vacuous palaver. A film company should be designed around family entertainment that neither patronizes nor depreciates the human experience. These films will not indulge the vulgar with coarse language, but instead will teach through great story telling and inspiring myth.

There are many other possible illustrations. My point is that when such a media institution exists—and there are already several examples—it must be publicized as the traditional response to cultural degradation, as the territory insulated from popular (read:

democratic) trends and devoted to excellence. Just as Bradbury's characters roam the forest primeval reciting their assigned books, traditionalists must resist sensate culture within the oasis where their culture flourishes. Notwithstanding the obvious charge that these institutions are elitist, traditionalists should be immune to this recently coined pejorative. Affirmative action and radical egalitarianism have no place in the oases; these are the institutions where merit and excellence count and are rewarded.

The best response to a degrading culture is its opposite forcefully defended within a psychological island of like-minded adherents occasionally unlikely visitors may find succor in the oasis possibly becoming converted. But the likely scenario is that the traditional cultural oases will be isolated and bereft of widespread support.

A lack of popular support does not suggest a lack of moral victories. As long as there are a few who recognize greatness, all is not lost. Being the last defenders of superior culture is an admirable calling to which some noble people will unquestionably respond. Now we must build the institutions, the programs, the departments to which these people can gravitate. Popular culture doesn't need traditionalists—in fact, it doesn't want us. Our duty is to reject what is demeaning and rest ore what is uplifting. It won't be easy, but it is certainly better than merely hoping for the best.□

Future Studies in the Academy
Academic Questions, Winter 1995-96

The French poet Paul Valery wrote, "The future isn't what it used to be." Indeed, that is true in more ways than Valery might have anticipated. In the sixties and seventies a cottage industry emerged called "future studies" with a specific target date, the year 2000. Like *"fin de siecle"* a century earlier, the phrase "the year 2000" assumed meaning unrelated to a date. The phrase was transmogrified into the mutually contradictory sentiments of hope, aspiration, change, a break with the past, restoration, and despair.

For a brief period in the late sixties and early seventies future studies penetrated the academy's walls into the curriculum. Programs were launched by such scholars as Kenneth Boulding. In most instances, courses were organized with proactive titles like "Search for Tomorrow" or "Do We Have a Future?" Herman Kahn gave a course at New York University in 1974; Julian Simon offered one in the late seventies at the University of Maryland; and Paul Ehrlich lectured at the University of California, Los Angeles, on his version of the future.

While social scientists initially dominated this area of study, humanists quickly jumped on the bandwagon. Professors of literature provided courses titled "Back to the Future" that featured the work of Jules Verne, Edward Bellamy, and George Orwell. One northeastern history department still offers a course with the title "The History of the Future." So compelling was this fad that several high schools, two in Nassau County on Long Island, used the future as a school theme.

The influence for this curriculum trend, like so many others in higher education, was exogenous. Think tanks such as Rand and the Hudson Institute, organizations such as the Club of Rome, and special interest groups such as World Watch had a profound effect on academic thought. To a degree impossible to determine, this influence still pervades many courses and programs.

The Gingrich agenda in Washington, representing a devolution of government, has been inspired by a Tofflerian scenario *(The Third Wave)* emerging from a discussion of technological change in colleges and universities. Presumably, the very air computer hackers breathe is cyberspace; the future has arrived in higher education in practical and figurative terms, even if the fad of future studies is in desuetude.

While Edmund Burke was probably correct in asserting that the past is not a guide to the future, it is also accurate to suggest that the way one thinks about the future helps to mold it. In *The Image of the Future,* Fred Polak makes the point persuasively by arguing that action and policy can have long-term consequences if linked to positive images of the future. William James's *Pragmatism* maintains that believing you are capable of achieving a goal is the essential catalyst for reaching it. In short, societies appear to flourish when guided by idealistic visions that negate the imperfections of the present.

This contention should give us pause. For every claim of guarded optimism there is a belief in what Max Weber called "the dark, cold, polar future." For every Julian Simon *(The Ultimate Resource),* who believes we cannot "run out of resources," there is a Paul Ehrlich *(Population Bomb),* who contends that scarcity of resources and violent competition are what await us. For every Herman Kahn *(The Year 2000),* who argues that the force of affluence is inexorable despite setbacks at any given moment, there is a Robert Heilbroner *(An Inquiry into the Human Prospect),* who holds a distinctly lugubrious view of the future. Can both the optimists and pessimists be right?

Franz Kafka quipped, "There is always hope-but not for us." And a friend often tells me that where the optimist believes this is the best of all worlds, the pessimist says, "You're right!" Perspective means a lot. The tenor of public opinion may be the key factor in determining which of the alternative images of the future prevails. However, public opinion is a fickle goddess.

In a 1981 article titled "Differing National Orientations toward the Future: A Comparative Examination Societal Characteristics and Public Opinion," Bettina Huber contends that Brazil, for example, has greater hope for the future than, say, South Africa. She based her conclusion on elaborate multivariate regression techniques. The evidence for this claim may have appeared compelling in 1981; it is certainly not compelling in 1996. The virtual collapse of the Brazilian economy and the dismantling of apartheid in South Africa since 1981 have unquestionably affected attitudes about the future in both nations, arguably reversing the trend lines reported by Huber fifteen years ago.

Similarly, Gary Spraakman, in a paper presented to the First Global Conference on the Future (1980), argues that the Western growth model accepted internationally after the Second World War cannot sustain itself into the future. "Low productivity improvement and high inflation appear to be in the offing for the foreseeable future." Dr. Spraakman contends that only through "conscientious cooperation" instead of "individualistic confrontation" can the future be hopeful. He goes on to say that, in the end, cooperation depends on faith in one another, which people in the West more than others probably do not have at this time.

Based on events of the last two decades, this is a strikingly naive claim. Inflationary pressures of the late seventies and early eighties have been harnessed. Productivity rates both in the manufacturing and service sectors have increased dramatically. And the Western economic growth model has been applied with startling success to Pacific rim nations, India, China, and several states that heretofore have known nothing but poverty.

Discussing the future is an intoxicating but highly elusive business, one that often says more about who is doing the talking than what is being talked about. After a period of unrelieved pessimism in the 1970s, when university professors routinely discussed the impending apocalypse, any expression of modest realism tended to be interpreted as manic optimism. To a degree, that mist of pessimism remains in the air today.

At the end of the film *Annie Hall,* Woody Allen says that his philosophy of life was developed when his mother—on one of the family sojourns to a Catskills resort—would argue, "The food is awful, just terrible, and the portions are so small." That was the mood of the era. The curious thing about it is that, in most instances, the food in the Catskills is superior and the portions are invariably too large. That may not be a metaphor for present conditions, but neither is Allen's analysis.

In 1972, when the Club of Rome report *Limits to Growth* was initially published the argument for disaster had reached the height of seemingly scientific validation. In fact, few studies have had as dramatic effect on the curriculum in higher education as this one. A research team concluded that if resources continue to be used at the current rate, the world will run out of food, be overrun with population and pollution, face a widening gap of rich and poor, and confront technology that is hazardous to our health and safety. To use the language of the report:

> If present trends in world population, industrialization, pollution, food production, and resource depletion continue unchanged, the limits to growth on this planet will be reached sometime within the next 100 years.
>
> The most probable result will be a rather sudden and uncontrollable decline in both population and industrial capacity.

This report had a profound effect on the national psyche. While serious scholars denounced the research methodology and its conclusions, the book's influence on public opinion was notable. Along with *Small Is Beautiful,* it sounded the alarm for imminent catastrophe unless we mend our ways and devise methods for living in harmony with nature.

Two years after issuing the report, the Club of Rome modified its findings, significantly recanting the earlier statements and calling them an "overreaction." Ten years later the principal author, Dennis Meadows, admitted that one of the things he would change from his 1972 study would be to "tell the people that the power to change lies with them." Although this may not seem like much of an admission, it dramatically alters what was done earlier. After all, *Limits to Growth* was a result of mathematical modeling that intentionally relied on the continuation of then present trends; human intervention, on the other hand, presupposes no such inevitability. In fact, it is precisely such human intervention that makes all trends unreliable. The late Rene Dubos, in an interview with Bill Moyers, contended:

> Present trends never continue....If there is something about human beings it is that they never stand idle in front of a situation that threatens them provided they can see the consequences of it. They start doing something about it.

But in the early 1970s, the Club of Rome report reinforced sentiments of fear, guilt, and shame that are still with us in many forms and still constitute much of what passes for environmental studies in universities.

Supporters of this point of view maintain that even if the arguments are wrong, the sentiments are right. Presumably, they feel that the fear of shortages will encourage public support for desirable policies—for example, conservation. But frightening people into "good" policies does not necessarily ensure desired results. By suggesting the inevitability of disaster one can also promote a "live for today, the hell with tomorrow" attitude, which is the antithesis of what the supporters want.

When previous generations of Americans learned about the triumph of American ingenuity and production, it gave them a sense of accomplishment and pride. Today, however, many college instructors suggest technology should be viewed as a menace; students are taught that US economic production is the cause of global problems and that this nation's technical and scientific ingenuity is a source of human woe. With this worldview, it is hard not to believe that America's role in history is malevolent.

In 1980, the National Education Association published a guide for teachers of future studies prepared by Draper Kauffman and titled *Futurism and Future Studies.* It was designed for high school students but has been employed in colleges as well. Among other things, this document makes the following astonishing claims:

> Food production is losing the race with the population explosion, and a massive famine within the decade seems probable. The main question remaining is whether famine will come in a single global disaster, or whether it will come as a chronic series of regional famines.
>
> The earth lacks the resources and the pollution-absorbing capacity which would be needed to support a situation in which all nations are developed to the economic level of Western Europe. Thus, economic development is likely to prove a false hope to many of the poorest fourth of the world's peoples...Every elimination of a habitat or species, every introduction of a new artificial chemical, and every increase in the demand we are already making on the environment represents an increased risk of unknowingly crossing some threshold which will cause the system to collapse.
>
> A shift to...slow-to-no-growth [is] likely for the economy as a whole. Although no-growth might be desirable for many non-economic reasons, it would give the developing nations among them the opportunity to catch up, it poses a serious threat to the economic stability of all industrialized nations.

Nowhere in this guidebook is there the slightest reference to the constructive role of wealthy nations in the global economy; to the rapid economic growth that has propelled many non-Western nations into the ranks of the middle-class; to the general record of declining resource prices and the reasons for it; to the reduction of air pollution in our major cities and the immensely successful program to clean our rivers and streams that has already borne dramatic results in the Great Lakes. What we have in Kauffman's guide is a return to the concept of "spaceship Earth," which depicts a limited universe with static resources and dwindling supplies that a few greedy bullies will gobble up to the detriment of the Earth's poor. There is no suggestion that the percentage of the world's poor has declined significantly in this century, or that "resources" encompass ingenuity, technology, and labor, not simply minerals in the ground.

Henry James once described unhappiness as a "disease." In our time it has reached epidemic proportions, and Typhoid Mary appears to us in cinematic entertainment, the late news, and teacher guidebooks. Predictions of doom have always been with us. The nostrums of Nostradamus and the prophecies of Cassandra have something in common: a belief that gloom, if not doom, is on the horizon. What distinguishes this era from others, however, is that gloom is often presented as a series of scientific verities, not as mere speculation.

While relativism and deconstruction have forced all philosophical discussion down a rabbit's hole in which truth is anyone's guess, when it comes to the future—an area of obvious indeterminacy—there is an ironic "certainty." Pelagian assumptions have forced the idea of original sin into subordination in every area of national thought except concepts of the future. To a surprising degree futurism has a neo-Puritan bias fraught with original sin and based on a belief that unless mankind recognizes its imperfectability and changes its ways, it is doomed.

What the neo-Puritans expect is an embrace of nature-modern pantheism—and a skepticism about technology. Although it has been fashionable for artists and literary figures to denounce technological advances as "a tyranny of body and mind," this view was almost exclusively restricted to intellectuals. Blake's famous line "these dark satanic mills" was a classic nineteenth-century intellectual's rendering of the factory system. Romantic literature and art may have condemned the machine and exalted rural life, but for the average person who experienced untold hardship and oppression in preindustrial society, such literature was dismissed to the dustbin of history.

Early factories were certainly harsh and dismal places to work, yet manmade cruelties, however severe, could not compare to the difficulties of eking out a livelihood on the farm. When Coleridge, Disraeli, and Carlyle, among others, criticized the factories, they did so without much regard for the people who enjoyed the benefits of longer lives, better food, and better housing than their forefathers, notwithstanding the many exceptions to the rule. Carlyle made the "machine" the symbol of the society he deplored, and nineteenth-century poets invariably represented fires in iron foundries as the cauldron of hell. For them, material progress was accompanied by a breakdown in spiritual values. This is also, of course, the argument of many twentieth-century environmentalists.

The intellectual of the nineteenth and twentieth centuries, especially in his role as literary spokesman, was and still is preoccupied with beauty and simplicity. This explains in part why, with very few exceptions, novelists are naturalists. But there exists a yawning gulf between the intellectual and the world's economic realities (although the successful writer is aware of the fact that his royalty checks are due to the economic prosperity he so glibly denounces). The intellectual usually scoffs at financial enhancement and thrives instead on "malaise," sanctified in his mission by what Lionel Trilling called "the adversary culture." The intellectual is the disturber of the peace, a rebel against creature comforts and technological advances.

One of these intellectual spokesmen, Dr. Bernard Dixon, expresses the extreme view that the environment must remain unchanged. In an article in *New Scientist* (1976), he argues:

> Some of us who might happily bid farewell to a virulent virus or bacterium may well have qualms about eradicating forever a "higher" animal—whether rat or bird or flea—that passes on such microbes to man....Where, moving up the size and nastiness scale (smallpox virus, typhoid fever bacilli, malarial parasites, schistosomiasis worms, locusts, rats...) does conservation become important? There is, in fact, no logical line that can be drawn. Every one of the arguments adduced by conservationists applies to the world of vermin and pathogenic microbes just as they apply to whales, gentians and flamingoes. Even the tiniest and most virulent virus qualifies.

This argument suggests that every creation, every microbe on God's Earth, has some purpose—sometimes hidden to us—that cannot be disturbed without significant harm to the future of the globe. Any technological change, however minor, is believed to modify the relationship of man to his environment and as a consequence uproot the essential balance in nature. If Prometheus is unbound, Dr. Dixon would have him pinned and tethered.

David Ehrenfeld, a professor at Rutgers University, writes in *The Arrogance of Humanism,* "Most scientific discoveries and technological inventions can be developed in such a way that they are capable of doing great damage to human beings, their culture, and their environments." Certainly, any reasonable person would admit that science and technology can do great damage and have been responsible for much environmental harm, but it is equally true that science has improved the material conditions of mankind, eliminated many of mankind's most dread diseases, and invited romantic visions heretofore considered beyond our imagination.

The idea of an ecology so fragile that it is unable to cope with human interference does not square with a global history that includes an ice age, flooding, worldwide pestilence, and every plague God could conceive of to impose on Pharaoh's Egypt. But a world in which mankind does not tamper with nature is a world in which insects, animals, and microbes declare war on their two-legged neighbors. Nature uncontrolled is not benign. What would be the price of an unspoiled wilderness? Aside from the millions of deaths caused by the diseases scientific advances have eliminated, the explosion in the insect population would be incalculable. The view of mankind as Tarzan or Robinson Crusoe is a marvelous literary metaphor but an impractical guide for human behavior.

For the anti-science and anti-technology advocates, the human spirit is static, frozen in time. Pleasures are or should be simple and our environment pristine. The only problem with this depiction is that human beings have a continual urge to improve their condition. To transcend the plight of animals subject to nature's whim has always been a human characteristic. It seems to me worth asking why, if God wanted the world unchanged, did He give people the power to think?

Robert Pirsig in his book *Zen and the Art of Motorcycle Maintenance* makes this argument:

> He [man] built empires of scientific capability to manipulate the phenomena of nature into enormous manifestations of his own dreams of power and wealth but for this he had exchanged an empire of understanding of equal magnitude: an understanding of what it is to be a part of the world, and not an enemy of it.

What, precisely, is being "a part of the world?" To Pirsig it is a transcendental feeling of harmony with nature combined with reason to create tranquility. However, nature isn't essentially tranquil; it is erratic and often violent. The idea of being part of the world generally includes some form of struggle with nature. Am I part of the world or an enemy of it when I step on a blade of grass? Am I an enemy of the environment when I ride in my car instead of walking? Is Jonas Salk an enemy of nature for finding a cure for polio?

For some people, any manifestation of nature from animal to microbe should be conserved because it exists and because this existence is a stage of a historical and majestic evolutionary process. Surely there is some validity to this claim—but only some. Is it not true that mankind's condition is evolving from one in which most people were impoverished to one in which most will be economically well off? As animals use nature for the survival of their species, so must man. Admittedly, humans can and do treat nature capriciously. Mine is not a defense of those who litter or kill animals frivolously. But I do not see the utility or good sense in ignoring man's unique role in nature and the history of natural adaptation to changing conditions.

C.D. Stone, scholar and lawyer, in a book titled *Should Trees Have Standing?* presents the case for the legal rights of forests, a position based on the view that forests should not be affected by human inadvertence. But what Stone ignores is that mankind can and does plant as well as cut down. People use the fruits of nature and replenish those fruits, sometimes improving the conditions that are found. Those trees can be used to improve the conditions of mankind, other animals, and much of the natural environment. Should we guarantee the rights of trees against lumberjacks? And if we do that for trees, why not streams, blades of grass, and even microbes? At what point does the legal protection of nature adversely affect mankind?

Charles Elton, in *The Ecology of Invasions by Animals and Plants,* proposes several reasons for conservation, including "because it is a right relation between man and living things, because it gives opportunities for richer experience." However, Elton does not tell us what "the right relation" is; nor is the "richer experience," as he observes it, a widely accepted view. Coexistence can take many forms, including a role for people in altering the natural setting for the benefit of nature and occasionally for the selfish benefit of mankind. It is also true that camping in a natural setting can be a very enriching experience. But that is generally because we can return to a warm room and a shower when the experience is over. Is it a rich experience to consider your camp your home? Is it a rich experience to be caught in a flood tide without a means of escape? Is being attacked by a shark the "right relation" with living things?

Admittedly, many of the areas of life that man has tried to harness have not yielded to his will. But it would require a very distorted imagination to ignore the very effective control we have established to reduce the high rates of infant mortality, bleak labor conditions, and the oppressive poverty of a scant fifty years ago. In some respects the world has not improved, but in most respects it has. And this improvement has been brought about by the human desire to reshape the character of the environment. Faulkner cautioned in *Go Down Moses,* that doomed wilderness whose edges were being constantly and punily gnawed at by men with plows and axes who feared it because it was wilderness.

Yet those same men overcame that fear to build temples of stone that reached the sky and let their spirits soar. Only an author living in twentieth-century affluence could so eloquently mourn the loss of wilderness. Yet Faulkner was on to something. He was wrestling with mankind's fundamental nature. Is our nature to reach an accommodation with those around us, to restore our relationship with the environment to one of "harmony," or is our spirit unbound, filled with promise to improve our conditions?

Some people, including many scholars, view life as limitation. For them, God's plan is not subject to alteration; science is the enemy of Providence. They view a land defiled as the result of "progress," and that price is unbearable. But what these advocates ignore is that this is the first generation in recorded time to so enjoy the fruits of technological innovation that a concern with nature is now feasible. The wilderness is appreciated because of our air-conditioned, insect-free homes and a transportation system that conveniently brings us to and returns us from its hostile fringes.

This evolutionary heritage will be preserved. But how much of it? At what price? Is conservation more important than the elimination of poverty? Do we subscribe to a standard of living that brings us closer to nature and closer to our animal instincts? Do we maintain nature's primordial condition, or do we change it to improve our lives? To see no difference between man and natural conditions is absurd and ultimately immoral. Nature neither thinks nor feels pain. It seems to me that if the choice must be made between mankind and nature, I am in the corner of my fellow humans, albeit the choice itself is a reflection of the impending-disaster scenarios of those convinced our tinkering with the environment will result in catastrophe.

As Eric Hoffer pointed out, "Faith in a holy cause is to a considerable extent a substitute for the lost faith in ourselves." Some futurists obviously have turned their backs on humanism. They see man in nature as Dr. Frankenstein's monster. Having decoded the secrets of science, Frankenstein loses control over his own creation. In this story, technology is the problem because once it has been unleashed it presumably can't be controlled. Mary Shelley's nightmare has been imposed on a generation of youngsters familiar with stories of technologically induced horrors. It is as if science were synonymous with horror.

In *2001: A Space Odyssey,* Stanley Kubrick has a computer, HAL, mutiny against the captain of the spaceship. Although this is typical science fiction material, it is also related to the belief that technology cannot be controlled, that once the genie is out of the bottle, human intervention can't be restored.

This fear is reinforced by the television news depiction of many current events. The Three Mile Island "disaster," for example, was a much-exaggerated description of a serious accident. According to the news reports, thousands of Harrisburg residents were threatened by an "imminent meltdown" and by the radiation vented into the atmosphere. In retrospect, we know there weren't any casualties. We also know that despite many unanticipated errors in judgment, the condition of the nuclear plant was far from meltdown. And we know that the level of radiation released during the height of this "manmade crisis" was lower than the routine daily expiration of radiation from Dutch and French nuclear energy reactors.

With a fear of technology rather pervasive in our news reporting, with some futurists of the Jeremy Rifkin variety encouraging the belief that we have no right to tamper with nature, with literary figures from two centuries cataloguing the horrible conditions brought about by technology, with scientists using models based on inaccurate assumptions to predict future gloom and perhaps doom including widely quoted "carrying capacity" scenarios, it is little wonder that many students cannot distinguish between imminent and possible threats to our future. As a result, they become part of a system that disseminates the currently popular, prevailing opinions.

When Herman Kahn and his associates wrote *The Next Two Hundred Years* they tested the scenario "that 200 years ago almost everywhere human beings were comparatively few, poor, and at the mercy of nature, and 200 years from now, we expect, almost everywhere they will be numerous, rich and in control of the forces of nature." According to Kahn and associates, this four-hundred-year period will have been as dramatic and important in the history of the world as the ten thousand years that preceded it.

While the Kahn thesis was published in 1976, Edward Bellamy in his novel, *Looking Backward: 2000-1887,* published in 1887, forecast changes he claimed were in accordance with the principles of evolution—Social Darwinism then being very much in vogue. The next stage of his evolutionary treatise was the dawning of a new era accompanied by widespread wealth, technological advances, and even moral development and human felicity unknown to his contemporaries.

Alvin Toffler, another prognosticator, predicts a break with the past, albeit the acceleration of this change leads to a psychobiological condition he calls "future shock." Presumably, the past is not a guide for the future since all that we know is being immersed in a strange, new culture about which we are unprepared. "[M]an either vanquishes the processes of change or vanishes...from being the unconscious puppet of evolution he becomes either its victim or its master."

For Lester Brown (in *The Human Interest*), we are bound to vanish or at least threaten our destiny unless there is the realization that we have reached the point where human demands on food, energy, and other resources cannot be satisfied. A crisis of massive proportions, on the order of what is predicted by the authors of *Limits of Growth,* awaits. For him, future shock is recognizing the "inevitability" of the massive problem we must overcome, albeit several commentators on the future, most notably Julian Simon, suggest there is insufficient evidence to sustain a neo-Malthusian scenario of the kind Brown proposes.

Another voice fearful of the changes wrought by technology is E.J. Mishan, who, in *Technology and Growth: The Price We Pay,* contends that we cannot yet conceive of the ecological consequences and effects on society of technological advances and economic growth, but he believes that unchecked growth and an obsession with affluence diminish the qualities of life? Television, to use one illustration, a "communications instrument," has actually limited human exchanges.

Wherever one stands with the optimists and pessimists and various shades of each perspective, the sources of change have been charted. Daniel Bell, in *The Year 2000,* which was prompted by the coming end of the century, maintains four sources of change that provide a framework for discussion of the future: technology, diffusion of goods and services, structural developments, and the relationship of the United States to the world. Some of this change, Bell argues, can be directed and some of it will be unanticipated. The future, to use his idiom, is a combination of serendipity and synergism.

As the end of the century approaches, it is possible to evaluate former predictions and quite possibly establish a new set of predictions for the future. While Francis Fukuyama argues we are at "the end of history," his Hegelian view only opens new, hitherto unexplored scenarios. Were futurists like Herman Kahn correct to be guardedly hopeful about the future? And if so, how do we define "hopeful" and how indeed do we measure success? It would be useful to look forward and backward simultaneously. But even then the rationalistic positivism and naive "progress" of the past seems implausible now. Nor would a doomsday scenario of the future appear plausible after so many nuclear weapons have been dismantled and a former militaristic Soviet Union defanged. Our tools of analysis are limited, which should give anyone in the business of prognosis pause. We should enter the world of futurism with humility, recognizing what we cannot know and being prudent about what we may know, i.e., demographic effects, whose consequences are beyond our ken. The fad of future studies has passed. But the ideas contained in these studies are very much with us. The tools of analysis may not be cultivated, but like tomorrow's weather prediction, every student has an opinion about the future. Imagination is often real to the one who imagines. If the twentieth century proves anything, it is whatever the mind can see, the hand will carry out. The question that remains is, What can we see and how close is our vision to 20/20? □

The State of Scholarship: Peace Studies in the Academy
Academic Questions, Summer 1988

The study of peace as a university discipline began to take shape during the late 1950s when it was fashionable to discuss a world polarized by two hostile camps, East and West. A view developed in the academy that there was a fragmentation of insight, based on national interests, that militated against giving due regard to more global considerations. This view evolved into a belief that by using the cools of various academic disciplines to examine the assumptions in rival camps, "depolarization" (this word appears in the literature of that period) might be promoted. But no one, as far as I can tell, gave any indication of when these benefits would accrue, nor whether the approaches advocated could engender the promised effect.

Perhaps this is the reason that there continues to be a very real void in the intellectual framework of peace education today. Few of the peace advocates have anything more than a vague, platitudinous idea of peace, encompassing a resolution of all human conflict and the establishment of utopian harmony. None of the program directors with whom I corresponded could even explain why certain characteristics, generally referred to by the Left as "the conditions of peace," are discussed in these programs. Moreover, not one of them would agree with Solzhenitsyn's claim that absolute peace is a chimera, a utopian state of mind unknown to human behavior. When I suggested that the opposite of war is stability, one director of a peace studies program responded by noting, "I don't think we'd get anywhere if we called this discipline 'Stability Studies.'" I suspect he is right.

In the evolution to the depolarized global peace that advocates discuss, there is a reliance on moral rhetoric which virtually excludes a consideration of the actual circumstances that prompt war. There is the ever-present insinuation that people who might wish to understand historical realities, particularly the causes and consequences of war, are those who want conflict. It is rare indeed for peace studies proponents to concede that a serious study of war might be the best intellectual preparation for those who wish to avoid it. And, as the syllabi collected from courses and programs indicate, the study of war has been subordinated to a gallimaufry of social paradigms, psychological musings, and trendy expressions of coexistence.

When the first peace studies programs were launched after World War II by pioneers such as the economist Kenneth Boulding their scope was modest and uncontroversial, at least compared to those that would follow. The courses were devised as supplements coexisting curricula in political science or international relations, and were based on the then-current set of theoretical propositions in these fields. During this period, peace studies tended to avoid raising ideological or schismogenic issues, seeking the promotion of international civility and consensus.

In the 1960s peace studies went through a significant transformation based largely on lessons learned or misunderstood from the Vietnam War. The formal considerations of law and comity as the requisites for peace were increasingly replaced by a focus on political questions, often couched as issues of "human rights." By the 1970s peace studies had clearly expanded to incorporate a variety of political concerns including, but not restricted to, ecology, hunger, and sex roles. The result has been the emergence of what peace acolytes describe as a "holistic," "process-oriented" study.

It is now readily admitted that what began as a theoretical examination of international conflict has become an argument for changes in global status quo, which asserts that unless inequality is removed, environmental conditions improved, and sex distinctions eliminated, peace cannot be attained. Accordingly, peace studies has incorporated into its curriculum the whole radical critique of society, which serves as the emblem of its "enlarged intellectual vision" as well as the means of encouraging global awareness and criticism of Western attitudes. It *is* interesting to note that national security studies, with its traditional focus on the causes and prevention of war, have to a notable extent been eclipsed by this radicalized approach to the study of peace.

According to a survey conducted by the *Christian Science Monitor* in 1986, more than one hundred colleges and universities were offering major, minor, and certificate programs in the subject of peace. Another study showed that about half of all American colleges and universities had at least one course listing in this field, as compared to the 14.6 percent of colleges and universities that reported having such courses in 1979. A number of institutions have also established special research facilities devoted to peace programs. The University of California, for example, has an Institute on the Study of Global Conflict and Cooperation to coordinate peace studies and research on its various campuses. As the Rev. Richard F. McSorely, a Jesuit and director of the Georgetown University peace studies program, notes: "We've spread everywhere. Universities that don't have peace studies courses are now ashamed of it." And, indeed, this sentiment was borne out by a number of responses. Thus, Harry Hamilton, Dean of Undergraduate Studies at the State University of New York at Albany, writes: "In response to your letter of 5 March concerning peace studies, please be advised that we have none here, though I wish we did. I hope to try to interest some faculty to begin at least a few courses."

There is certainly no dearth of funds for such programs. At least seventy-four private foundations contributed more than $52 million in 1984 for the promotion of peace studies. Michael Cirillo, a spokesman for the World Policy Institute—an organization supporting the spread of peace studies programs—claims that, "Money is plentiful. Foundation money especially." The Ford Foundation alone gave away $50 million for this purpose in 1987, while the Sloan Foundation is committing half a million dollars a year, for six years to train faculty members for undergraduate peace studies programs (420 people will be mined by the end of this cycle). The Carnegie Foundation has made a substantial grant to *Nuclear Times,* a journal critical of the weapons industry, to promote its dissemination within the academy. The MacArthur Foundation, second largest after Ford, has made a grant to National Public Radio for two fully-sponsored correspondents devoted to peace advocacy, and has helped sponsor a thirteen-part public television series called "The Nuclear Age," complete with textbook and supplementary materials. And Joan Kroc, owner of McDonald's, has given $6 million to Notre Dame for a peace studies institute.

To be sure, the peace studies community is not without its share of internal conflict. A struggle exists between those who favor a "holistic" approach, including under the ambit of peace everything from arms control and regional conflict, to world hunger, gender issues, and environmental matters—and those favoring a "conflict management" program of psychologically based studies, roughly equivalent to "I'm okay, you're okay" set on the international stage. On the basis of course and program titles it would appear that the "holistic" approach is winning the struggle, with programs often bearing titles like "Peace and Security Studies," "Peace and Women's Studies," "Peace and Global Issues," etc.

Beyond this is a still deeper difficulty. Peace studies remains a discipline in search of real scholarly respectability. Many in this campus movement (it has gone beyond the mere introduction of courses) admit that peace studies has a politicizing, indoctrinating dimension. Thus, Robert Ehrlich, a physicist at George Mason University and editor of *Perspectives on Nuclear War and Peace Education,* reports:

> There is an element that says, "It's impossible to be objective about these things, so why try:'" The real problem comes when they don't label advocacy as such. And, as a rule, most people in this business tend to take a more benign view of the Soviet Union and to be skeptical of U.S. policies.

A recent graduate of Mount Holyoke College observes that the students in such courses form cliques that "dominate classes," and tend to be "doctrinaire and intolerant." Another advocate of such courses admits that, "You get the single issue types who preach instead of educate." Asserts Georgetown's Professor McSorley:

> It's hard to say exactly what impact we've had. But we did stop the Vietnam War. We've kept Reagan from invading Nicaragua. We're helping to prevent World War III-to say that deterrence prevents war is simplistic.

Peace studies programs seek to transform traditional ways of thinking into a belief that war is irrational and that it can be prevented, not by national defense, but by pursuing peace as an attainable goal in itself. A set of rather dubious assumptions, sometimes tacit and sometimes openly stated, underlie many of these programs. War, for most peace studies advocates, is considered an unnatural condition, an aberration in human behavior, and variously described as atavistic, primitive, adolescent, and antithetical to society's interests. According to the faithful, war occurs because of accident and stupidity, militarism, the pursuit of national glory, or the selfishness of a small group who benefit from it. And, if people could be educated and made aware of its inherence irrationality, war would end. Since each of these memes appears and reappears in peace studies curricula, they are deserving of some comment.

A serious inquiry into the causes of war inevitably confronts human violence in general. Human conflict and the struggle for power are not confined to the global arena; they are present in the political and economic life of every nation, in every organization and family. To suggest that war is aberrational is to ignore human nature or ascribe to it more malleability than it ever has revealed.

The urge for war is not always or even usually a reflection of psychological deficiency. Wars can serve a purpose whether that purpose is plunder, territorial acquisition, or the quest for power, national liberation, or individual freedom. While war might well be deplored, it is by no means meaningless, despite often-cited illustrations that suggest the opposite. One could make the claim that surrender is to be preferred to all-out nuclear war—"Better red than dead." But most American blacks consider that their liberation was worth the carnage of the Civil War. Most Jews acknowledge that the defeat of Hitler came at a frightful price in death and destruction, yet was preferable to the fate that would have befallen them had Hider prevailed. Our Founding Fathers obviously thought that the political and economic benefits of American independence were worth a costly war against the British. It is simply absurd to contend that war never makes sense.

Not only do sensible people consider freedom worth defending, but historical events indicate that surrender to force not only fails to ensure security but often leads to an abject subjection in which death may be preferable to life. If education seeks to sensitize the young to the horrors of war, it should also instill in them an appreciation of what they have to defend. To neglect this is to leave their future hostage to the good will of potential enemies. Military valor, heroism, and courage can easily be sacrificed on the altar of sheer survival by a spiritually exhausted generation. Those who discuss survival at any price will sacrifice any principle or value for self-preservation.

The verities of international relations will not disappear because some people confuse wishful thinking with policy analysis. There are times when decent people must be ready to use force to defend themselves and the values they cherish. In the name of a just cause and with the restraint of honorable conduct, force can be morally justified. By ignoring these considerations or glibly neglecting them, or propagandizing in the name of international harmony, many peace studies programs (almost certainly the preponderance) fail to reveal the paradoxes and complexities behind international conflict.

F.R. Leavis, in his extended debate with C.P. Snow, made the observation that culture is not merely a body of knowledge or a stock of accumulated facts and theories. To be part of a culture is to be in possession of a sensibility, a way of seeing things, which in some way may be redemptive. It is also a matter of participation, a participation that alters one's beliefs and enters the realm of emotion. This cultural description explains the rise and success of peace studies on our campuses. For what is at stake is a perception of our national life. True believers assume that in the theory of conflict resolution they have unlocked the secret of war. In fact, what they have discovered is participation in a redemptive rite organized and given legitimacy by academic institutions. Colman McCarthy asked, "If peace studies or conflict resolution courses aren't needed or aren't credible, why are students enrolling in them?" The answer that Mr. McCarthy has probably not considered is woven into the *zeitgeist*. Peace studies students want a confirmation of their views. Taking the course is rarely related to its credibility or utility; it is a cultural ritual, analogous in many respects to attendance at a rock concert.

There are educators, of course, who resist the temptation to follow political fashion. In examining the specific cases that support my generalizations about peace studies programs and courses, I have excluded several exemplary programs dealing with national security. This review, however, is not intended to be a comprehensive survey. In the past, furthermore, there were forms of peace studies that often served students well, even though they have now been largely driven from elite campuses by the force of fashion. At one time most American students were obliged to take humanities courses in which they read about the central issues of war and peace in the Bible, *The Iliad, The Persian Wars, Antigone, Macbeth, The Trojan Women, The Peloponnesian Wars,* and *The Decline and Fall of the Roman Empire,* to cite several examples. While courses on the literature of war and peace are still taught, they are instead infused with contemporary politics. At Sarah Lawrence, where a freshman studies course called "Literature of War and Peace" is given, students are told that they will learn "about the awesome process whereby man turns man into a thing." Students are also assigned secondary readings about "culture and human nature," which address questions of gender, aggression, and nonviolence.

The new apostles of peace contend that the study of war, either through classical literature or through the examination of the tactics and strategy of war, undermines their efforts to curb the nation's martial spirit. As Colman McCarthy notes, students have the option of studying violence or nonviolence. It is not coincidental that during and after the Vietnam War national security studies and ROTC courses fell into desuetude. What is somewhat astonishing is the extent to which such programs have been replaced by peace studies offerings during the last decade.

Whether courses with a traditional outlook towards war and peace are reintroduced is somewhat beside the point. In the present climate even these courses are often slanted to accommodate the prevalent ideology on campus. In the war of scholarly ideas it would appear that peace studies has achieved a notable triumph. The question that remains is whether this triumph at our colleges and universities will in the end turn out to be a defeat for liberty and the principles that have made this nation an exceptional society.

In most programs bearing the title "peace" there is an implicit and occasionally explicit attempt to combine the study of military issues with so-called "social justice" matters. The attempt on the part of peace studies proponents to enlarge the intellectual vision of the curriculum has taken the form of incorporating economics, social activism, communications, gender studies, ecology, social psychology, and even filmmaking into its domain. In the examples that follow, it is apparent that the shadow of peace studies stretches across almost the entire range of undergraduate studies.

Cornell University, for example, publishes a catalogue of peace and social justice courses that includes an "Introduction to Peace Science"; "The Human Ecological Consequences of Nuclear War"; "Religion, Ethics and The Environment"; "Directions in Feminist Theory"; "African Socialism and Nation Building"; "Pan Africanism and Contemporary Black Ideology"; "Racism In American Society"; "Women in Revolution"; "Educating for Community Action"; "Power and Poverty In America"; "Power and Marginality: Women In the Third World," and many other offerings. It is instructive, as Michael Novak pointed out in a discussion of radical professors, that the word "freedom" rarely accompanies "peace" and "social justice" in the titles of such programs.

At the University of Chicago a course entitled "The Politics of World Prosperity and Peace" is offered in order to "examine economic issues such as aid, trade, debt, food, and security issues such as nuclear proliferation and arms sales." Presumably, there is a causal relationship between economic issues and nuclear proliferation. The dean of the college, Donald Levine, gives a course called "Conflict Resolution Practicum: An Aikido Centered Approach" that uses the martial arts as an "exemplar" for conflict resolution.

The School of General Studies and Professional Education at the State University of New York at Binghamton has organized a Peace Studies Education center that assumes nonviolent conflict resolution is achievable; that teaching should focus on the search for peace; that by learning to be a "planetary citizen," a student can help construct a just and peaceful world; that education for peace must take place in every sphere of life and that the individual working for peace is "empowered" through this activity to effect political change. Courses in the program include "International Politics," a survey of "why the world has been badly managed in spite of endeavors for peace and equality"; "Apocalyptic Cinema," an examination of the "criminal insanity" of Reagan's policies through the films of Steven Spielberg, Stanley Kubrick, and Francis Ford Coppola; and "World War III," an analysis of "how the next world war could happen." In a "Peace and War" course cross-listed with "Women's Studies and Mass Communication," the syllabus cites among many sententious questions, "Are Women More Peace-Loving Than Men: The Gender Question."

At Boston College the study of nuclear war is integrated into a consideration of the "broader political crisis rooted in the general problem of war and Empire in the modern era." As the instructor indicates in his description of a course called "Peace or War?" the way to solve the riddle of war is through "the exploration of the economic, cultural and political changes required to reduce prevalent militaristic adventures so common today." In a course entitled "Militarism and Its Alternatives," this same professor adds "racial and gender-based domination" to the topics that must be explored in an effort to find an alternative to war. In order to convince his students that the Soviet threat is misunderstood, he lectures on why "The Russians Aren't Coming: A Critical View of the Soviet Threat" with accompanying readings from George Kennan's *Nuclear Delusions*. In case students don't get the point, the last two lectures are devoted to "Steps toward a Non-Militarist Domestic Order: Conversion and an Economy of Peace."

At California State University, Sacramento, peace studies is described as "a partial response to the war in Vietnam." That war is viewed as symptomatic of a "larger reality"—a world in which warfare is commonplace and a threat to survival. In this program, war is seen as analogous to chattel slavery, an institution that requires elimination through the auspices of higher education. To achieve this goal, students take courses like "The Political Economy of Multi-National Corporations"; "South African Economics"; "Introduction to the Women's Movement"; "War, Peace, and the Mass Media"; "Inter-Cultural Relations"; and "Third-World Women."

A Colgate University brochure assures students that peace studies "is what a liberal arts education is all about." According to its founders, the program was established in 1970 in response to the war in Vietnam and the escalating arms race. The concentration consists of ten courses and an internship. Among those courses that can be taken to fulfill this requirement are: "Marxist Thought"; "Marxist Sociology"; "The Third World in the International System"; "Introductory Experimental Psychology"; "Peace"; "Views from Geneva"; "Theories of Peace"; and "Conflict and Global Violence." "Introduction to Peace Studies," the centerpiece in the program, is described as providing "perspectives on peace ideas and the dangers of violence and war" and offers an "analysis of the methods of constructive and nonviolent group and individual action to transform unjust, violent or oppressive situations, and the conditions for success of such an activity."

At the Maxwell School of Citizenship and Public Affairs (Syracuse University), a program in nonviolent conflict and change was created in 1987 to study "peaceful ways of dealing with conflict." Students enrolled in this doctoral program investigate such topics as "Political Protest at Seabrook, New Hampshire"; "Draft Resistance in World War I"; "Methods and Techniques in Community Dispute Settlement"; "Sir Liddell Hart and Nonviolent Civilian Defense"; and "'Cause/Effect Relationship Between Pre and Post Independence Violence and Nonviolence."

The Global Survival Studies Program at the University of Massachusetts is designed to give freshmen "exposure" to five broad areas of worldwide concern: war, peace, and alternative systems of world order; population; environmental deterioration and economic development; availability and distribution of world resources; and cross-cultural communication and conflict. The presumptive goal in this program is to "increase global literacy." As the program notes indicate, a student's response to the question, "Is there anything an individual can do about the issues of global survival?" is an important focus of his study. Clearly the question has some value and might be justified if it could be assumed that classroom deliberations would avoid a political agenda. There is nothing in the program guide, however, that elicits confidence that political tendentiousness will be avoided.

The Center for Peaceful Change at Kent State University is described by its founders as a "living memorial" to the May 1970 Kent State tragedy. Studies at the center focus on the dynamics of change in social settings. These dynamics are considered in such courses as the "Anatomy of Peaceful Change," "Concepts of Nonviolence," and "'Nonviolence Tactics in Peaceful Change and Field Study," which includes internships at Common Cause, Frontlash, and the Sierra Club. This academic program is designed, note its progenitors, "to accommodate some of the intellectual, emotional and action oriented goals of today's socially conscious students."

Due to the generosity of Joan Kroc, the Institute for International Peace Studies was unveiled at Notre Dame in 1987 offering an interdisciplinary Master of Arts degree in Peace Studies. New subfields have been introduced to supplement graduate offerings in political science, theology, and law. These include: "International Peace and World Order," "Cultural and Religious Dimensions of Peacemaking," "Conflict Resolution," and "Social Change."

At the University of Southern California, the School of International Relations offers several courses on the politics of peace and the resolution of conflict. In one such course, the instructor argues that he will introduce students to "the possibilities offered by the new technique of Conflict Analysis and a new approach to the study of bargaining, both based upon recent breakthroughs in the theory of games in social behavior." It is argued that the synthesis of approaches in this course will lead to "a unifying and empowering impetus to peace action."

The Institute for Research on Women at Rutgers University, using a curriculum development grant from the New Jersey Department of Higher Education, organized a course called "Peace, War, and Human Values" that has been offered since 1935. Included as goals in this course are: an effort to "help students understand how the ideology of individualism blunts our impulses towards communal values and activities and induces the belief that 'real life' must be lived in an atmosphere of aggressive competition" and an examination of "male-directed, class divided societies," which seem to produce the problems of violence, oppression, and competition. Several of the suggested readings in this course are: Ashley Montagu, *Learning Non-Aggression;* Roland Bainton, *Christian Attitudes to War and Peace;* Jonathan Schell, *Fate of the Earth.* Lest students arrive at their own opinions—a goal frequently mentioned in the course outline—the stated objective of a unit on nuclear deterrence is "to point out to students that at the height of the Cold War nuclear deterrence was not employed simply as a way of maintaining peace, but as an instrument of coercive diplomacy for specific goals."

At the University of Florida, Gainesville, a course entitled "Education and The World Community" was organized so that the "people possessed of a cosmopolitan disposition, i.e., people who are aware of, sensitive to, and committed to humankind as a whole" can devote themselves to the study of the planet's problems. The only prerequisite for this course is "an open, probing mind."

Stanford University offers a course called "Nuclear Weapons and U.S. Foreign Policy," which asks plaintively in the course description, "What are U.S. nuclear weapons for?" The course explores in detail "the numerous specific occasions when U.S. presidents—every one of them in every term of office since Hiroshima—have seriously contemplated or secretly threatened imminent U.S. initiation of nuclear war." According to the course description, in nearly every case, the anticipated first use of nuclear weapons was kept secret from the American public and scholars.

Middlebury College has organized a new course, which is subsidized by the Sloan Foundation's program on the New Liberal Arts, entitled "Nuclear Technology, The Promise and The Peril." According to the course organizers, "We confront the legacy of Chernobyl, Three Mile Island, and an unending increase in the world's arsenal of nuclear technologies." Topics in this course include "Nuclear Power and Nuclear Weapons," "Nuclear Waste Disposal," and "Political Issues Associated with Nuclear Technology."

At Tufts University, a team of instructors has organized a peace studies program based on the success of a course called "Toward a Just Society: Issues in Peace and Social Justice." The instructors note that "whatever the progress we have made as a species, it is hard to deny that our failures and our human made destructiveness have been prominent." Cited as evidence of this destructive character are racism, sexism, environmental decay, dwindling resources, starvation, poverty, inequality, the arms race, underdevelopment, and nuclear proliferation.

Manhattan College offers a multidisciplinary major in peace studies, which puts an emphasis on fieldwork for peace organizations such as the American Friends Service Committee and Bread for World Order. While aspiring to moral search for solutions to war and injustice, the program includes such courses as "Economics of Peace," which is devoted to the hypothesis that the inequitable distribution of natural resources and its resulting effect on economic development causes international conflicts.

These descriptions can be duplicated in dozens of cases. What is unusual is to find examples of peace studies programs that are not propagandistic, that do not have a barely concealed political agenda, or that attempt a fair pursuit of the truth. The issue of nuclear weapons has found its way into the undergraduate curriculum and is likely to remain there, but the discussion of these weapons should be a part of the backdrop of recent history and policies and should recognize the need for peace with freedom, it is absurd for instructors to create the impression that they have solutions that elude government leaders. Hegel once admonished teachers against the temptation of standing aloof from the grim realities of the human condition while prescribing cures for social problems. It appears that his admonition has gone largely unheeded.

While advocates of these courses and programs and their followers regard peace as the culmination of game theory, psychological theorizing, and efforts at cooperation, the real meaning of peace remains elusive. Rational discourse within the classroom cannot bring genuine understanding, tolerance, and mutual respect where the will to create these conditions doesn't exist. American students may be exposed to programs in which cooperation is enhanced through various scenarios, but their student counterparts in the Soviet Union are taught to despise and fear our society. While peace programs routinely suggest that Americans and Soviets do not understand the society of their adversary, this formulation, which apportions responsibility evenly, strains credulity. Genuine understanding will be impossible as long as Soviet education is characterized by the indoctrination of fear, and as long as much of what passes for American education is an expression of denial about our adversary's history and of wishful thinking about its goals. In one example after another, peace studies courses and programs resist the idea that there is an opponent whose ideology and values threaten freedom. Instead, in peace studies one invents the "real" threats to democracy, i.e., dwindling resources, inequality, or sexism that serve an enchanting mythology about the human condition. Invariably it is maintained that the "functional imperatives," e.g., ecological disasters, population growth, terrorism, will move the world willy-nilly to global interdependence. Yet this view denies the history of a century in which shared problems have not transcended ideological rivalries.

The reason peace studies does not fit nearly into academic departments suggests an essential flaw in such programs: the lack of an empirical body of knowledge that can form the basis of an academic discipline. As peace studies advocates admit, these programs are by their very nature "interdisciplinary." Moreover, the programs lack coherence because the meaning of peace isn't well understood. Is peace the lack of war or is it the affirmation of principles such as freedom, justice, and equality? Is a world kept stable through nuclear weapons at peace? Has the definition of peace, like so many other conditions, been psychologized? Who is qualified to teach peace? How does one select the instructors for this program? Is reading Gandhi or reading Herman Kahn a more reliable guide to peace? If government leaders can't find the solutions to the enigma of peace, why should sensible people believe it can be found in a college classroom? Is peace at any price better than war? Is war really a senseless act? Has the nuclear equation fundamentally changed notions of war and peace?

The fact is that most peace studies programs don't begin to address these questions. This is hardly surprising, since nonviolence has been elevated from an arguable theory of conflict resolution to a science beyond reproach among its followers. That college officials have suspended sensible judgment on these programs is illustrative of an inability or unwillingness to defend the principles on which the curriculum stands. It may well be that the effect of misrepresenting one's enemy, of institutionalizing amnesia, of inventing reasons for conflict, and of using relativism as the measure of all international disputes is ultimately the erosion of the will to defend the principles upon which our society rests, or to resist the encroachment of enemies whose intentions we have systematically denied.

Surely, this claim will appear as hyperbole for those who either actively accept or passively permit such programs. Yet, it was only six decades ago that the Oxford Declaration proclaimed the abysmal ignorance of world leaders who bring young men to the brink of war. These "well-educated" British lads would resist that martial spirit. The tocsin in the air would not affect them, for they understood what other generations did not: war is irrational; no one wants it and no one benefits from it. That Hitler didn't attend Oxford was a point lost on the youthful utopians. The Wehrmacht's invasion of Poland soon brought these students to their senses. One can only wonder what will bring peace studies instructors and their students to their senses now, and when the political center at universities—which represents the majority of faculty members—will assert itself and employ the canons of scholarship to scrutinize programs that promote propaganda and espouse untested assumptions of human behavior.☐

Education and American Values

Recommendations

1. We must recognize the limitations of technology as well as the advantages.
2. We should eliminate values clarification in education, for it raises moral awareness without providing any authority for making moral judgments.
3. We must reassert the Judeo-Christian ethic that undergirds the entire political and social system in America.
4. Education must respect American traditions, for the values of the past provide guidance in facing the complex issues of today.
5. Education must train students to be adaptable in a rapidly changing work environment.

Edited Remarks

There is no event that has shaped the character of this century as much as the introduction of technology. We are at a point in historical evolution when the myth of Daedalus is upon us. Machines, it has been argued, save us from ourselves. They are new slaves in a new world, a world in which personal fulfillment can be achieved as never before.

We are told that if we brush with one toothpaste as opposed to another, we'll have a better sex life. If we dress in fashionable clothes, we'll get better jobs. If we use the right deodorant, we'll be loved by our family. If we drive a sporty car, we'll have the glow of youth. Yet, after we've washed, brushed, dressed, sprayed, and driven with the right product, we find that we are no younger, no sexier, and no more desirable than we were before. The promise of the good life through the world of technology is true. The promise of the ideal life through technology is bogus. It isn't that technology can't deliver a fine car or a good soap. It can and does. The problem as I see it is we have so exaggerated the consequences of technology's products that it is impossible for our expectations to be realized. For many, the result is anguish.

Technology has created the illusion that anything is possible, even our collective salvation; but it has also increased our reliance on machines, and, as a consequence, has sometimes dehumanized our relations with other people. In a significant way we have let technology become our will. We rely on technology for the problems we can't solve and when we don't like the solutions, we simply describe the program as unsatisfactory or the machines inadequate. The problem is never diagnosed in ourselves. This situation is analogous to the addict who blames drugs for his addiction. It is true, of course, that the drugs are addicting, but in attributing powers of control to the chemicals, the addict has surrendered an ability to assert his will. He argues implicitly that the addiction absolves him from exercising his judgment. Yet, the drug itself is neutral; it is not the drug which is responsible for addiction, but the addict.

Machines are like drugs. We may increase our reliance on them, attribute grand powers to them, but in the end they are only an extension of ourselves. Ultimately control rests with us. Our technology may be able to produce the test tube fetus, but it cannot tell us whether life created in this way is desirable. The machine has made it easier to transmit information, yet it is increasingly more difficult to sort out the trivial from the important. In its way technology has forced us to examine the human dimensions of our decisions. At the moment we seem most reluctant to accept the responsibility.

We are instructed by the media everyday that there is no aspect of our lives that can't be improved through the use of technology's product. And to a remarkable degree, this is true seems enough. But the improvement, when it occurs, never seems enough. Raising the material level of millions of people beyond any expectation of the past is, indeed, the singular accomplishment of technology in the century. Yet, happiness does not abound. On the contrary, the search for happiness is more desperate because our technological gods have seemingly failed us. And this is particularly true among those who have a disproportionate share of technology's bounty.

We want to turn on our lives the way in which technology allows us to turn on our television sets. But life is not technology and all those psychic cures that simulate technology's methods inevitably end in disappointment. So, after you've decided input equals output; after you've been tested and analyzed, had your ego massaged and your back Rolfed, you are still the same person searching for answers to a world made treacherous by the erosion of traditions. Technology can't help, nor can the techniques of psychology that ignore the fundamental questions of existence.

The computer, for example, is a mirror of our systems it merely records what is observable affect the causes of despair and joy. It cannot possibly homogenize human emotions so that one answer is true for everyone. Its potential for growth is limited by our potential to unlock the mysteries of learning. And our potential is trapped by the unsolved riddles of our evolutionary history.

Yet comfort also creates spiritual discomfort. The itch for more is ever present. It is seen in the despair of those who have all that can possibly be consumed, yet remain dissatisfied. It is observable in a frantic search for recognition narcissism that is widely heralded as the era of narcissism.

It is found in the fatuous behavior of disco kings and queens who are burned out at thirty. Since meaning is not found in the superficial delights of life, something else must be found, a transcendence. The belief that we are only part of a grand design puts our humanity in an appropriate perspective. Even if one accepts the notion that God does not exist, divinity must still be sought.

I disagree with Kropotkin who said if there is a God we must destroy him. I would argue that if God is dead, he must be resurrected. Man must seek beyond himself to find his true self. That path is the way of faith. There is no other answer; certainly, it is not to be found in the myth of technology.

The French poet Paul Valery maintained, "There is only one thing to do—to redo oneself." It is none too soon for this action. Even if we are not sure of what we believe, we can still practice the exercise of faith. A Issac Bashevis Singer reminds us, in the act of continual prayer one's faith increases. That faith, along with our own will is the hold we have on technology. It is ours to control if we don't delude ourselves with unrealistic expectations and if we maintain humility about life's goals. Singer once said, "when I am in trouble I pray. Since I am in trouble a great deal, I pray a lot." There is a social prayer that can refashion our humanity. Treat technology as the material wonder it is. But don't confuse technology with humanity. Humanity is found in the pillars of faith and will. They are our salvation in a world of material wealth and spiritual shallowness.

What educators have created is the technological fix for a people starving for transcendence. It is surely not coincidental that US schools are being asked to stress moral values. When the home and church don't know how to cope with drug use and teen-age pregnancy, the buck is usually passed to the schools. This is somewhat curious since the schools have yet to demonstrate they can teach math, writing, and reading much less the vagaries of drug abuse.

Nonetheless the teaching of moral values is on the ascendancy. Both the Secretary of Education and Governor Cuomo of New York are talking about it. At New Rochelle High School, outside of New York, students watch a film and then discuss their responsibility for the homeless. In Maryland's Baltimore County, a parent-teacher committee was organized to draft a common core of values. In California, new textbooks are required to discuss ethical issues in science. Governor Cuomo said the essence of values education should be "Love thy neighbor" and a respect for the law and the environment. The governor also noted that he thinks it possible to teach values without linking them to religion and said it is necessary to avoid sounding "religious, moralistic, and unctuous." Superintendent of Public Instruction in Bill Hoenig, California said, "Education went along with all this craziness (in the sixties) so we've ended up with students who are ethically illiterate."

The current concern with values in schools was foreshadowed in the 70s by the introduction of "values clarification." With this approach teachers raise moral and ethical issues, e.g., a case of triage or the "life boat" example, and systematically refrain from taking any position themselves. Presumably in the exercise a student's level of moral consciousness is raised. But the problem with this approach is its lack of authority.

However, despite the well-meaning nature of these efforts and the occasional salutary result, it is virtually impossible to talk about personal and social values without discussing religion.

Yet the need to bring people together is inexorable. The more pluralistic the nation, the more there is an interest in values education. It is presumed to be the way to unite Americans under the banner of nationalism and respect for law. While "there certainly cannot be an objection to this goal, its pursuit without a firm grasp of the Judeo-Christian tradition is at its best a secularized version of the Ten Commandments and at its worst moral relativism.

What we need is the assertion of the Judeo-Christian ethic that undergirds our entire political and social system. From what other source can respect for individuals and commitment to decency come?

With teachers who have no formal study of religion, with textbooks that virtually ignore religion, and with many educators fearful of abridging the First Amendment, it is hardly surprising religion is removed from the school curriculum. But how then does one study values? It is a little like studying war without battles.

Technology may pose new problems, but those anchored in the Judeo-Christian tradition are more likely to have answers than their counterparts wavering on the shoals of moral relativism. In the last analysis there is no substitute for this .religious ethic as long as we wish to promote democratic values and the moral vitality in this nation.

Postscript

Anything you say about public education is true. There are fifty states in the USA and education in the USA is a local concern. it is not fair to say that education in the USA promotes the acquisition of jobs; nor is it fair to say that it is designed to promote a religious ideology or that it has any purpose except the purpose that is dictated by the local authorities.

What should the end of education be for the future? We are living in a world where change is the *sine-qua-non* of the future. We have to educate for adaptability. We have to make sure that students understand the kind of world they will inherit. This is one of the reasons that I believe in tradition. Tradition, by the way, can make a marriage with these changes. The changes that are occurring with us do not mean that we exclude the past. The past very often has an influence on our future. Nonetheless, we must be adaptable.

Why train people for a high-tech world when many of the jobs will be low-tech jobs? The answer should be an American answer: we want to give everyone an equal opportunity for the best jobs in this country. And if you want to give everyone an opportunity, you want people to read at a twelfth grade level and do higher math, because you don't want people left behind. We're not an America made up of a caste system. We're an America that believes in giving everyone an opportunity. Everyone will not have a high-tech job; but everyone should have a chance at a high-tech job—that's what I mean by adaptability.

Values and Common Learning

The Japanese have implemented the ideal of universal education and· seem to have resolved the quandary over equality and excellence. In short, the Japanese successfully practice many of our own ideals…we can do it too…and we can do it without sacrificing any of the values that America holds dear.—Secretary of Education William J. Bennett

If schools ignore or give minimal attention to transmitting the best of our moral and ethical heritage to the young, they are failing in their foremost responsibility.— Dr. Leo M. Christenson, McGuffey's Ghost and Moral Education Today

If values are crucial in the education of children and adults, one should seriously address the troublesome controversy about what values should be promoted. Moreover, all interested parties must evaluate the role of values in every facet of the curriculum. This leads to one basic question: What is the value of having a good education?☐

Marxism Thriving on American Campuses
"The World & I," *Commentary*, **January 1987**

Most people don't take Marxist studies seriously—not even academics, who are disinclined to accept its methodology and prescriptions. Yet while this statement is true, it is certainly not the whole truth. The strides made by Marxism at American universities in the last two decades are breathtaking. Every discipline has been affected by its preachment, and almost every faculty now counts among its members a resident Marxist scholar.

According to the editors of *The Left Academy,* four Marxist inspired textbooks on American government were published between 1970 and 1982. Before then, there were none. In the same period, three of the most prestigious university publishers, Cambridge, Oxford, and Princeton, issued books on Marx and Marxism, almost all of them quite sympathetic. There are more than 400 courses offered today on American campuses in Marxist philosophy; in the 1960s only a handful were being taught.

In addition, two self-declared Marxist historians, Eugene Genovese and William A. Williams, were elected president of the Organization of American Historian in successive selections, and Louis Kampf, a radical with Marxist predilections, was elected president of the Modern Language Association.

Although none of these Marxist intellectuals would claim to be using his professional eminence to subvert American political institutions, their academic success tells much about American university life. American universities have gone from discriminating against revolutionary socialists to embracing them as professional spokesmen.

When Secretary of Education William J. Bennett said he believes that "a significant body of opinion" had developed on college campuses that "openly rejects the democratic ethic," his comment was greeted by skepticism. John Chandler, president of the Association of American Colleges and former president of Williams College, said: "The situation he [Bennett] describes was a much more pronounced problem in the late sixties and early seventies than it is today."

Chandler's statement apparently refers to the egregious displays of student intolerance during that period. Admittedly, more disruption was going on in the sixties than today, but that observation overlooks the extent, to which Marxist courses have become a legitimate part of the college curriculum. In this sense, Bennett's concern about campus radicals at war with society and "raising a revolutionary consciousness" may be more pertinent now than in the turbulent sixties.

Professors More Liberal

In the period from 1967 to 1975, student disruptions were a rite of spring. Certainly, student attitudes have changed. Increasing numbers have become conservative and even larger numbers have become apolitical. But this is only one side of a complex picture. There are many faculty members with Marxist or radical predi-lections who are indeed at war with society, or, at the very least, with the Reagan government. As survey data by E.G. Ladd, S.M. Lipset, and the Carnegie Commission Report on Higher Education suggest, faculty members identify themselves as distinctly more liberal and somewhat more radical than the population at large. These people are now ensconced as senior members of our facul-ties with all the perquisites of academic power.

Before this analysis is interpreted as a crude McCathyist at-tack on Marxist professors, I hasten to note that these professors represent a minority of those in academe. If these people wield influence at our universities, it is because the large majority of non-Marxist professors either have abdicated responsibility or have come to believe that Marxism, even in the form or revolu-tionary agitation, is a legitimate form of scholarship that deserves their guarded approbation. I should also note for the record that I regard indoctrination as wrong and unprofessional, whether it is espoused by the Left or the Right. Attacks on academic freedom have come from both sides, although in recent years the assault has been primarily from the Left.

To an astonishing degree, the acceptance of radical ideas at our universities has been facilitated by the transmogrification of academic freedom. While the term was originally employed to allow professors freedom to teach within the boundaries of a discipline, it has been enlarged to include any position one wants to espouse. According to Marxist professors Berteil Ollman and Edward Vernoff, "Academic freedom, to the extent that it exists, should be supported, developed, and used."

Although the word "used" may in some contexts be innocuous enough, Ollman, particularly in his collection of essays, The Left Academy, leaves no doubt what he means by it. Classroom teaching is presented as an instrument for converting the young to revolutionary socialism; Ollman believes that body of ideas is being put into practice (with some imperfections) in communist states.

The presumption of campus Marxists is that, for universities to maintain legitimacy within a free society, opposing points of view must be presented, including those that challenge the prevailing values of society. Should Marxism be censored, the legitimacy of academe might be seriously undermined.

On the face of it, this is a compelling argument that has given Marxists a foothold on many campuses. Alfred North Whitehead insisted that "in a university, you must be free to think rightly and the variousness of the universe undisturbed by its peril....A university is imaginative or it is nothing—at least nothing useful."

While this statement stands as the essence of academe's mission, it is not responsive to ideological positions that threaten freedom.

Fear of Labels

Complicating the academic atmosphere is the fear of being labeled at McCarthyite. It is appropriate to reject the philosophy of a Nazi or even a supporter of the South African government, but it is hazardous to condemn a Marxist on campus. Arnold Beichman notes that, in 1978 at the University of Massachusetts in Boston, he discovered to his surprise the creation of the Henry Kersh Institute of Marxist Studies. Since the new institute has not been put to faculty vote, Beichman went to the vice-chancellor to inquire about its installation. The vice-chancellor responded by saying that, since no new courses were being offered, faculty senate approval was not needed. "Besides," he was told, "stop making trouble!" Today this Marxist Studies program includes seventeen professors and twenty-six courses. Since Beichman now teaches in Canada, it is unlikely that anyone at this campus is making trouble.

At public institutions that rely on tax dollars, Marxist studies have also had an influence. The Marxist Educational Press (MEP) operates out of the Anthropology Department at the University of Minnesota. A recent MEP conference of Marxist scholars was held at the University of Washington in Seattle with more than 500 registrants. This conference, at which Angela Davis gave the plenary address, was cosponsored by the University of Washington departments of philosophy and linguistics and the School of Social Work.

According to a report provided by Les Csorba III, editor of *Campus Report*, who attended the conference in Seattle, there were reports on American crimes and praise for the Soviet Union's "openness and scholarly freedom." A Canadian professor argues that "Afghanistan is better off" since the 1979 Soviet invasion; after all, they "paved the streets of Kabul." Another professor described the American belief in Soviet oppression as "nonsense." Herbert Aptheker, professor of law the University of California, called on the participants to engage in "illegal action, mass action, picketing, marching, demonstrating, sitting down, and interfering with the armed forces, interfering with the maneuvers, doing everything possible."

In what was perhaps the most important seminar, on "Teaching Marxism," one scholar, Ken Clatterbaugh, philosophy professor at the University of Washington and an event organizer, said he wanted "students going out of class and getting involved." When queried about indoctrination, he said, "If they want the other side, they should watch TV or read the newspapers."

Seeking Converts

This position is compatible with the one advanced by Bertell Ollman, politics professor at New York University (NYU), who once wrote, "If non-Marxists see my concern with such questions as an admission that the purpose of my course is to convert students to socialism, I can only answer that in my view...a correct understanding of Marxism (or any body of scientific truth) leads automatically to its acceptance." Once can only wonder what happens to the "dull" or "intransigent" student who does not accept the dogma.

One can also question Ollman's confidence in treating Marxism as "a body of scientific truth." Are Marxist revolutionary doctrines really as scientifically demonstrable as the law of gravity? Is Marx's labor theory of value of view of the inevitable and growing pauperization of the working class something provable by any commonly recognized standard of science?

Moreover, if this ideology masquerades as rational discourse, on what basis can a course be an open and fair exchange of viewpoints?

At the 22nd national convention of the Communist Party, USA, in 1979, party chief Gus Hall envisioned a bright future for communist ideas at college campuses where "Marxism -Leninism has emerged as a much greater influence." But the party, he chided, has not been diligent in taking advantage of this condition. He concluded, "The new Central Committee must make some decisions and plans that will correct this weakness in our work; if we do not, we are missing an historic opportunity."

At least one Marxist scholar, Michael Parenti at Brooklyn College, has seized this opportunity. He has described the university as "a corporation...protected by the power of the state. The function of academia...is to present the world according to those who own it." As a consequence, "our job in academia is not only to reach out to working people but also to remind our students that they're workers—so we must teach students that they're workers—that their struggle is also a labor struggle, that labor struggle is the most profound democratic struggle in our society."

Parenti is a former fellow of the Institute for Policy Studies and a contributor to the Communist Party journal *Political Affairs.* In his book, *Inventing Reality: The Politics of the Mass Media*, Parenti writes: "Far from lacking in benefits and rights...Soviet workers enjoy more humane and secure working and living conditions than their American counterparts."

In 1985 Saul Landau lectured at the University of California at Davis, where he dedicated himself to "making propaganda for

American socialism." This included showing pro-Fidel Castro films he had produced and making Sandinista diatribes.

Not to be outdone in the expression of radical opinion is Bradford Burns, professor of Latin American history at the University of California at Los Angeles (UCLA). Burns has expressed his support for the Sandinistas in his classes and acknowledged having Sandinistas and a representative of the FMLN communist guerillas of El Salvador as guests. He rejected a suggestion that a speaker from the other side be invited. According to one report, Burns discusses atrocities committed by the Contras routinely, but when asked whether he ever discusses Sandinista atrocities, he said "No" without any explanation. On various occasions he has acknowledged support for the communist guerillas in El Salvador, and he recently expressed pleasure over the *Challenger* shuttle tragedy, calling two of the astronauts "war criminals."

Despite these illustrations, a generalization is not yet in focus. Surely most professors, if forced to choose, would not condone such statements and actions.

However, what I find is that professors are *not* asked to choose. Radical opinion is as much a part of the university landscape as torn sneakers. Bard College, for example, offers a lecture series entitles "America after 1984." Topics in this series have included "The Underside of Justice in the United Stated," "American Cultural Imperialism," "Anticommunism in America: Its History and Functions," and "The Garrison State: The Cutting Edge of the Crisis."

Harmful Effects

Although it is impossible to establish a causal link, it is probably worth noting, for those who do not regard university programs as having consequence, that Bernard Coard, the founder of the Organization for Revolutionary Education and Liberation, which merged into the New Jewel Movement in Granada, studied economics at Brandeis University. A cofounder of the New Jewel Movement and foreign minister under Maurice Bishop's communist government, Unison Whitemen, studied politics at Howard

University. Both have asserted the influence of their education on their political views.

Admittedly such a claim is subject to easy criticism. I am not suggesting that revolutionary attitudes are necessarily cultivated in American universities or that there is a way to prove such a linkage. I do believe, however, that education with the specific motive of conversion can occasionally cultivate "true believers" whose subsequent deeds may have baneful effects on this nation and nations abroad.

Professor Guenter Lewy has written that "radical professors represent the most active and vocal group using the classroom for political propaganda." Curiously, the radicals agree. H. Mark Roelofs, NYU politics professor, writes, "political scientists are the high priests of the system, teachers who propound the truths and glories of American democracy to the young and thereby generate and sustain its myth." A Marxist sociologist argues, "It is not the accumulation of Marxist knowledge that is our aim for our students (or ourselves) but the development of revolutionaries, free of bourgeois values."

How does one counter this bourgeois ideology? The answer is apparent to any Marxist. Education is an exercise in conversion, a point that is readily admitted by some Marxist scholars.

Education vs. Indoctrination

If one accepts the argument that all teaching is indoctrination, then the radical approach to pedagogy has validity. It is simply the substitution of one myth for another. But as Sidney Hook has argues, "If all teaching entails indoctrination, what would the opposite of indoctrination be? Nonteaching?"

Surely a conceptual differentiation must be made. The fact that teachers—even good ones—don't always live up to standards of fairness and balance does not mean that the distinction between education and indoctrination can be ignored. Yet that is precisely what radical professors have attempted to do. It might be argues analogously that since germs can be found in even the most antiseptic operating room, it doesn't really matter where surgery occurs. Yet I doubt that anyone would prefer to be operated on in a sewer rather than in a hospital. It is also true that teaching doesn't always live up to a lofty ideal, but it is still possible to distinguish it from indoctrination.

Writing in the winter 1982 issue of *Policy Review,* Lewy quotes two Marxist professors who proclaim, "Radical ideas have spread and deepened. Nowhere is this more true than in the colleges and universities. There are hundreds, perhaps thousands, of openly socialistic professors...There is hardly a conventional idea that is not under radical attack."

To an extraordinary degree these Marxist professors are correct. The evidence is the array of revisionist theories—most relying on Marxist dogma—that have influenced all the disciplines. Professor Frances Fox Piven of Boston University, a Marxist and former vice-president of the American Political Science Association, noted "there is a growing acceptance of the critical approach taken by Marxists and other radical leftists as a useful means of advancing knowledge of society and its problems."

Whether this approach is useful in advancing knowledge is a matter of opinion, but the degree to which leftist theories have been employed as scholarly explanation is undeniable.

History, for example, has been overrun with radical theories. Professor Samuel Bowles at the University of Massachusetts at Amherst discusses "glaring American inadequacies" as a function of the private ownership of the means of production." E.P. Thompson's *The Poverty of Theory and Other Texts* and Perry Anderson's *In The Tracks of Historical Materialism* are two recent books by British Marxists that have had a profound effect on the discipline. Howard Zinn, author of *A People's History of the United States*, wrote: "The schools has taught whole generations the values of patriotism, of obeying authority, and has perpetrated ignorance, even contempt for people of other nations, races, Native Americans, women." Presumably, this evil could be undone with another kind of "education."

Frederic Crews, professor if English at the University of California, noted in his article "Dialectical Immaterialism" in *American Scholar* that "several fields of study have begun to practice what I will call Left Eclecticism, a welcoming of many styles of anti-establishment analysis—not just orthodox Marxist but also structuralist, deconstructuralist, feminist, gay, Lacanian, Foucauldian, and assorted combinations of these. The essence of Left Eclecticism is an understanding, ultimately borrowed from the Marxist ethos, that analytics and theoretic discourse is to be judged primarily by the evident, by the radicalism of its stance."

Critical legal studies have already had a profound effect on the teaching of law. The basic premise of such study is that the laws tend to follow from the social and economic organization of the nation. Law is, therefore, viewed as a means for maintaining the dominance of the powerful over the powerless.

That various disciplines have been affected by Marxist ideas and themes on leftist ideology is beyond dispute. What may be disputed is the extent to which these ideologies dominate academe.

Reject Rational Thought

From my point of view, what these ideologies have achieved is an unhealthy tension between the secular religion of Marxism—what A. Lawrence Chickering described as "attempts to objectify virtue and spirituality"—and rational thought. Most Marxists would reject rational thought as an expression of faith in evidence—presumably assertions of a bourgeois mentality. Yet if one dispenses with this means of acquiring knowledge, there isn't a way to search for truth.

Without some conviction of the value of rational thought there can be no defense of knowledge and, as a consequence, no basis on which the university can legitimately stand. This, of course, was once a self-evident principle. Before the gains made by Marxist theoreticians on our campuses, promoting ideological goals was deemed incompatible with scholarship. Max Weber wrote that the teacher "will beware of imposing from the platform any political positions upon the student, whether it is expressed or suggested...[T]he prophet and the demagogue do not belong on the academic platform." This may be honored more in the breach than in practice, but for the Marxist an ideological goal is the goal of teaching. That is what distinguishes him from his faculty colleagues who may have convictions and even ideologies that occasionally insinuate themselves into the classroom.

Walter Lippmann made the observation in *Commonweal* of January 17, 1941:

> That the schools and colleges have...been sending out into the world men who no longer understand the creative principle of the society in which they must live;
>
> That deprived of their cultural tradition, the newly educated western men no longer possess in the form and substance of their own minds and spirits, the ideas, the premises, the rationale, the logic, the method, the values, or the deposited wisdom which are the genius of the development of western civilization;
>
> That the prevailing education is destined, if it continues, to destroy Western civilization, and is in fact destroying it;
>
> That our civilization cannot effectively be maintained where it still flourishes, or be restored where it has been crushed, without the revival of the central, continuous, and perennial culture of the Western world.

Unwittingly, Lippmann posed what some scholars consider a pedagogical dilemma. If educators attempt to instill in students the virtues of Western civilization, they have thereby violated the Weberian test of objectivity. If instructors adhere steadfastly to this canon of pedagogy, there is the temptation to gloss over the "deposited wisdom" of Western civilization. In the first instance, the Marxist will say you have a mythology. In the second case, objectivity becomes neutrality—the terrain where views hostile to Western civilization prosper.

The Contest of Ideas

The way to resolve this conflict is to restore a belief—one that has unquestionably been eroded—that in a fair examination of the issues, in the contest of ideas, Western traditions will prevail. When faith in arguments sustaining Western civilization exists, objectivity is an advantage. The problem in recent years has been the diminishing faith in our values and the inability of scholars to counter the assault of radical theories. Academic freedom has become a refuge for radicals and an inadequate source of defense for faithless exponents of Western traditions.

Radical academics who disavow objectivity—what scholars have traditionally called the search for truth—and use the classroom for nurturing revolution violate the standards of professional competence. The problem, however, is not only with these radicals but with the ordinary sources of tradition support. That the capitalist class ever had cultural hegemony is a matter that is not easily resolved. Surely outside the radical camp, no one would argue that it maintains such hegemony today. In fact, the lords of capitalism don't act like capitalists and are often embarrassed by its defense. What one finds instead is that the style of radicals reigns even when their arguments aren't accepted. There is a reflexive disparagement of our institutions among many scholars and the use of the ritualistic disclaimers—"yes, of course, there are flaws in our system"—that are employed by the true believers in the radical camp.

Ortega Y. Gasset remarked more than fifty years ago that "the simple process of preserving our present civilization is supremely complex and demands incalculably subtle powers." As scholars we must be able to say what is just and admirable about the West and apply the canons of scholarship to that end. The belief of instructors that there is a standard to seek is infectious. For example, the study of ancient Greece is the study of life; it is not preachment or conversion. The ideas of this civilization carry their own persuasiveness. In the pursuit of evidence fairly obtained, one can indeed find affirmation of Western civilization.

The erosion of established authority has to an enormous degree been fostered in colleges and universities since the 1960s. Yet, as academics, we recognize that the "modern void" of which Lippmann spoke so eloquently can be filled with the liberation and rational thought that real teaching can encourage. Universities alone may not be able to fulfill this mission. But it is nonetheless a mission worth addressing at a time when missions are almost exclusively in the province of radical instruction. ☐

When Anti-Authoritarian Scholarship is Authoritarian
"From the Editor in Chief," *Academic Questions,* **Summer 1993**

The campaign to justify "political correctness" on college campuses and simultaneously to challenge the former chairman of the National Endowment for the Humanities, Lynne V. Cheney, continues. An illustration of how this campaign is proceeding can be found in "The Pursuit of Truth Is Inherently Disruptive and Anti-Authoritarian," by Professor Betty Jean Craige, in the January 6th 1993 *Chronicle of Higher Education.*

Professor Craige argues that, despite Mrs. Cheney's claim that the pursuit of truth has been subordinated to political goals on American campuses, students now "examine critically long standing 'truths' about race, gender, and our civilization's past." That's fine, of course, provided that the implicit assumption that American racism and sexism is "long standing," or in some way fundamental to our civilization, or was never questioned before the advent of academic radicalism, also is scrutinized. Needless to say, we shouldn't hold our breath.

The main ploy of Craige's article is to associate present-day leftist academics with the Darwinists of the late nineteenth century. Craige maintains that "conservative" scholars criticize feminism and multiculturalism for the same parochial reasons that Darwin was once denounced: "Conservatives fear a vision of human society as a continuously evolving system of interdependent individuals and cultures." (This betrays a profound ignorance of the views of such paradigmatic conservatives as Edmund Burke and Michael Oakeshott, whose conservatism emphasizes gradual, evolutionary change. If anything, it is the radical Left's contempt for cultural continuity that is antithetical to Darwinism.)

Craige then argues that conservatives resist change because change undermines a natural order: "No natural law decrees that whites should be considered superior to blacks or that men should be considered superior to women." I suppose this means that conservatives believe these things, and that non-conservative critics of political correctness do so as well. Nothing is more typical of the politically correct than this tendency to slur critics.

"Diversity is natural, even desirable," she continues. But who would disagree? Indeed, it is precisely PC's coerced conformity that we find objectionable. Craige, however, draws a different conclusion from this premise, namely that any ideal of the good, the true, and the beautiful is suspect. Her version of Darwinism is incompatible with a literary canon, indeed, incompatible with objectively ranking anything. "Humanists," she tells us, "are challenging the very possibility of objectivity." (Of course, by "humanists," Craige does not mean Petrarch and Erasmus, but those individuals who currently teach in academic departments in the humanities.)

After asserting that objectivity is a myth, Craige proceeds to announce that the pursuit of truth is inherently disruptive. Yet, if objectivity does not exist, what is there to pursue? And how could such pursuit be disruptive? At the most, it would be an amiable waste of time, yielding no results.

It is not most conservatives who adopt a static conception of society but the relativists who oppose objectivity. Consider that to be objective—one must be willing to subject one's opinions to the tests of evidence and logic. The road to objectivity is littered with the theories and opinions that have failed these tests. But that is the path to truth. Those who reject objectivity do so in order to reaffirm their present convictions. Thus, it is they who opt for stasis.

Yes, the academy must remain a site for vociferous quarrels over what is true. No one has a monopoly on its pursuit or acquisition. But it is not usually the academic "conservative" who wants to silence his academic foes; it is the academic relativist who wants to end the intellectual quest by expunging all distinctions. From the emptiness of relativism emerges a peculiar totalitarianism that rejects all views except those asserted by radicals as necessary to promote their "progressive" agenda. And this is called "anti-authoritarian." Of course, it may be called anything, but its fragrance is distinctly that of Orwell's *Animal Farm*. For those who listen carefully, the drumbeat heard is that of a rigid orthodoxy pounding not without but, alas, within the ivied walls. □

The Politics of the Core Curriculum
Change, September 1978

Like a "phoenix rising" from the ashes of the late sixties comes a concern for general education, the core curriculum, that now dominates faculty meetings from Cambridge to Berkeley. That this should be happening now is no accident. With the dust almost settled from the period of academic turmoil, it is only natural that faculties consider what damage they have willy-nilly wrought in academe. By adopting egalitarian values, they inevitably vitiated standards. By accepting the student demand for relevance, they abandoned area distribution requirements. And by concentrating their efforts on narrow scholarly areas to the neglect of academic disciplines, faculty members abnegated their authority to administrators and students. In a very real sense, the present concern for general education is not only a desire to reestablish purpose in the curriculum but an attempt by the faculty to reclaim its rightful university role.

This trend, it seems to me, is a healthy antidote to the previous era of vacuous faculty decision making. Recently national education bodies have unequivocally supported faculty plans to design a general education program. The American Council on Education issued a report in which it was quoted that "undergraduate degrees should not be awarded...for programs that lack a general/liberal education component." And the Carnegie Council on Policy Studies in Higher Education, while candidly describing general education as a "disaster area," argued that if colleges "cannot deliver an effective general education component, they should seriously consider eliminating it entirely."

Yet while I rejoice at the faculty concern about the curriculum, I remain uneasy about the outcomes. What has already emerged is not encouraging. Nowhere can one find a consensual view of appropriate undergraduate experiences. Instead of consensus, we see compromise that reflects the pluralistic attitudes of most university faculties.

Academics in technical areas of study, for example, who increased the proportion and importance of their courses as general courses lost their legitimacy and glamour have their own narrow interest in general education proposals. They continue to press for a wider array of specialized courses rather than for holistic approach. But even taken together specialized courses do not add up to a coherent undergraduate program. And the specialists are disinclined to go back to the drawing board to discover their shared assumptions. The result is that in those institutions that have promoted scholarly specialties the general education component reflects the specialized orientation of the faculty, whatever that may be.

Some academics (principally those in the behaviorist camp) distressed by the deterioration of basic skills competence have entered the general education debate as minimalists. "If you can train a pigeon to fly up there and press a button and set off a bomb," James T. Guines, associate superintendent of Washington DC schools mused to a Washington Post reporter, "why can't you teach human beings to behave in an effective and rational way?" This view translates into competency-based instruction, in which an area of learning is broken down into its component parts and each part has corresponding behavioral objectives that are carefully monitored and measured. There would be few critics of this approach if, like a simple equation, general education could be reduced to its component parts. But that isn't the case. What is worthwhile is very often not measurable; what is measurable is too often not very worthwhile. Researchers at the Educational Research and Development Center took the process of trivialization to its absurd conclusion by taking a simple objective—how to handle a book properly—and breaking it into its measurable components: keeping the book clean, holding it right side up, and turning the pages correctly.

Behaviorists have promoted a shift from the educational goals of the classical curriculum, which were noble but never quite attainable, to goals which are measurable and attainable but finite. In the attempt to apply minimum standards of competence to the general education discussion, they have inadvertently created a Gresham's Law of curriculum design: That which is measurable will drive what is not measurable out of the curriculum.

At a time when many departments are more concerned with survival than principle, the issue of the core curriculum becomes particularly touchy. A ballot to determine the complexion of the curriculum is very often simply a pork barrel bid. If department X can obtain two required courses in the general education program, it may bolster its sagging enrollment and thereby save several faculty jobs. To this end, it will court the good will of others by voting in favor of department Y's preferred course selection. Of what value is debate about academic issues in this climate of academic back scratching? Of what use are platitudes when jobs are at stake?

The proliferation of disciplines, subspecialties, and new courses along with ubiquitous fiscal retrenchment in higher education has made it virtually impossible to establish any system of genuine academic priorities. The reigning opinion in academic life is that one discipline is as valuable as another, so long as it leads to personal survival. In some circles it is even argued that one learning experience is as valuable as any other, though admittedly this is still considered a philistine philosophy. But how many contemporary academics would agree with Woodrow Wilson that it is the first duty of the university to bring older wisdom to its constituents: "The world's memory must be kept alive, or we shall never see an end of its old mistakes. We are in danger to lose our identity and become infantile in every generation."

We are well into what Gordon Craig called the age of the "Green Stamp University," in which a student receives as many stamps for T-groups, the Alexander technique, and self-awareness training as for classical philosophy. In such a world, it is difficult to know what degree means and even more difficult to reconcile competing disciplinary interests so that a coherent curriculum can be established.

There is one further complication. Since educators are now obliged to demonstrate how their degrees assist in securing jobs, the pragmatic dimension of training cannot be ignored in formulating a general education curriculum. It was undoubtedly appropriate for John Stuart Mill to argue that "universities are not intended to teach the knowledge required to fit men for some special mode of making their livelihood." In our own time, however, such neglect seems unconscionable.

The question is how to keep the career component from swamping everything else. Students arrive at the university so career oriented that attempts to discuss life activities other than law or medicine are futile. Since these students vote with their feet, the entire undergraduate curriculum reflects their prejudices. Even more distressing is the unwillingness of parents and legislators to encourage any change in attitude. As one parent put it, "I've lived through noble causes and high ideals; now I just want my kid to live comfortably."

If it was destructive for faculty to bow before every student demand of the last decade, it is equally wrong now to give in to the competing claims of specialists within the academy, of legislator, parents, or any other pressure group. The politics of designing a core curriculum will not disappear, but the effects may be mitigated if faculty remember what they are about. The university exists to train the mind, and that, it seems to me, is the reason for developing a core curriculum. Whether the core curriculum is ultimately effective will depend on the extent to which this vision of a university survives.☐

Loyalists vs. Shakers: The Campus Battle Is Joined
The Chronicle of Higher Education, November 1980

If one examines university administration today, as I am wont to do, it is obvious that there is a conflict of style and purpose between two ideological camps of administrators, camps whose members I call Loyalists and Shakers.

The Loyalist is a person who, after years of service to an institution, is rewarded with an administrative position that is regarded by critics as a sinecure. The Loyalist himself, however, regards his appointment as a commitment to the institution, rather than as a rung on the ladder to success. He has spent much of his professional life in the university and he knows its corporate parts well. His judgment of students, faculty members, and administrators is unerringly perceptive. His management skills, however, are limited. Although he is interested in making things work, his toleration of Byzantine practices sometimes turns out to be his undoing.

The Loyalist administrator does talk to his colleagues, although he often talks too much. After years of involvement with the old-boy network, he often forgets his new responsibilities when he gets together with a group of department chairmen. Sympathetic and sensitive, he simply can't be tough. Most faculty members will say of him, "He's not the most efficient person I've ever encountered, but he can be trusted." The presumption is, "trusted" to uphold faculty interests.

The Shaker, on the other hand, is invariably younger, bolder, more cost-conscious, and less sensitive than the Loyalist. His training was not in academic life but in business. He can design a clear organization chart of the university and develop goals statements for the next ten years with computer print-outs to support them, but the mores of academic institutions are alien to him. As his name suggests, the Shaker wants to turn the university topsy-turvy in the interest of efficiency, and to accomplish this task he has a virtual army of assistants reporting only to him. Their conversations, now called briefings, concern ways to get "them" (the faculty) to respond affirmatively to "us" (the new administration).Tension is the consequence of a Shaker administration. The Shakers, who acknowledge the condition, regard it as "creative" tension.

The rub for the Shaker is precedent. "I don't give a damn how things were done before," he is likely to say. The rejection of institutional history and its attendant policies is rationalized by the Shakers as "mental toughness." Old-fashioned, individualistic professors are pariahs for Shakers who put a premium on "playing ball," albeit to a whole new set of rules.

Faculty responses to the Shaker are mixed. Trust has become a quaint practice of the past in a Shaker administration, and an academic unfamiliar with management by objectives, charts, and print-outs is overwhelmed by the concern for cost efficiency, which he tentatively regards as good for him and the university. There are signs of improvement: The budget deficit has been reduced substantially; "cost-in-inefficient" departments (foreign languages, religion, and philosophy are always in this category) have been forced to retrench; and tenure is difficult, if not impossible, to achieve. In moments of privacy behind his office door, the professor is likely to ask himself if these improvements are worth the price of the tension, intimidation, and distrust that prevail on the campus.

There are issues that serve as litmus tests for discovering who is in which camp. One is the class schedule. Shakers would argue that a consistent schedule for the entire university, with classes beginning and ending at a given time for everyone, permits rational planning, effective utilization of space, and common meeting hours for faculty members and students. Loyalists say that such a schedule does not take into account the idiosyncratic teaching situation (such as longer periods for laboratory sessions), special constituencies (teachers who cannot begin classes until say, 3:30), or the faculty prerogative of determining the requirements for classes.

Another is the manner in which budget cuts should be instituted. Shakers have a simple and unalterable "objective" standard: Any course for which fewer than fifteen students are registered will be canceled. (The number may vary but the principle doesn't). Loyalists don't pretend to be objective in such matters. For them there are universal standards of liberal-arts educations that must be upheld even if attendance is woefully low. Philosophy must be offered even if only two students register for the course—it is simply an indispensable feature of the curriculum.

Still another is the matter of curriculum reform. Shakers are generally convinced that any reform that increases that attractiveness of university offerings is desirable. As a consequence, they endorse "early bird" courses that begin at 6:30 in the morning, "life experience" credit, junior-year-abroad programs, interdisciplinary programs, apprenticeships, and student-generated courses as "attempts by the university to be sensitive to the needs of new constituencies." This is, of course, a euphemism for "Let's get sexy programs that might appeal to potential students who are not now applying to our institution."

Loyalists contend that all the curriculum reforms and so-called new ideas that have been introduced over the last two decades have not altered the importance of the core liberal arts courses and of a vigilant concern for quality offerings. To convince them to support a curriculum modification, one must provide testimony from at least three leading academics that the introduction of the reform will not signal the decline and fall of a cherished discipline. Loyalist opposition is not based on a dispassionate analysis of the intended reform but on the feeling the loyalists—and perhaps they alone—have a responsibility to guard the gates of academe from the hordes of Philistines who wish to tear them down. If this analysis has any validity (despite the stereotypical profile of each camp) it is worth asking whether the university can survive the conflict, and whether one of the camps deserves to hold the reins of leadership.

I can unhesitatingly respond in the affirmative to the first question. The conflict will cause strain, but it will also force Shakers to consider not only what is "cost-effective" but also what is essential for the continuation of the university. And it will give Loyalists some perspective on the financial realities on which the university is predicated.

To the second question, my answer is that they will have to learn to live together. Signs of a *modus vivendi* are already apparent at some institutions—a condition, I suspect, directly related to the need for retrenchment. In the long run the university will require someone who understands management techniques and someone who recalls the traditions on which the university's existence rests. Without the former there will be no money to go on; without the latter, no reason to go on.

Cardinal Newman once said of higher education: "Its art is the art of social life and its end is fitness for the world." It seems to me that this vision of art and fitness applies not only to the university curriculum but to university administration as well. □

Social Science Scholarship: An Exercise in Formulas
"From the Editor's Desk," *Academic Questions*

After reading thousands of academic social science articles bearing a distinct policy prescription, I've discovered that they are almost entirely formulaic, and that even a cursory reading of the first paragraph usually suffices to predict the contents. What follows is the formula I've developed to test my hypothesis of predictability in such articles. Based on my empirical observation, it works.

The opening paragraph of the typical article of this genre is predicated on an observation: "Although it was once agreed that X is true, there is evidence to support the claim that Y is true."

Paragraph two poses the obvious resulting question, "If Y is true, then why is it that no one else has said so?" (Only one inference can be drawn from this self-serving paragraph: earlier scholars possessed neither the power of discernment nor the level of understanding of the article's author.)

Paragraphs three through seven regale the reader with the evidence for Y, which usually follows a did-you-know-that-such-and-such-is-true format. Paragraph eight contends that while many government and university experts believe that a key reason for the event in question is X, that assumption is naive.

Paragraph nine presents the foreign or cultural illustration that demonstrates the "surprising" thesis. "Yes, that event occurred before, but it was in Bulgaria. And it conformed to our hypothesis, Y."

Finally, paragraph ten offers the author's prescription: Based on what "we now know to be true," the following proposals should be considered, etc. One of these proposals is bound to advance the author's career and invariably takes the form, "higher priority should be given to" or "a comprehensive survey is called for" or "further support is needed for projects like...."

Of course, the author qualifies all of this by citing difficulties in obtaining evidence, complications in identifying priorities, and rapidly changing circumstances. Therefore, in the interest of honesty, the author should say, "Everything I've written enters the realm of speculation." Doing so, however, would make the article an easily dismissed opinion piece rather than an academic social science treatise.

Obfuscatory language helps to create an appearance of profundity. Every "effect" is an "impact" and sometimes (God help us) even "impacts." Every thought is "in terms of" even when thoughts don't have terms. Every preference becomes a priority, lifting it from the mundane to the ministerial. What is good is a "benefit," what is true is "genuine," and what is beautiful is "aesthetically tasteful." The result is that the reader often assumes an article is substantial when in fact it is merely the mechanical application of a formula learned in a graduate social science seminar.

Since this scholarly practice continues unabated, I can only conclude that these articles succeed in hoodwinking the reader or simply aren't read. Now that I can easily identify the formula, I am among the nonreaders. In part, what this conclusion suggests is that academic social science research is being produced by unimaginative scholars who have learned to make their work fit an academic Procrustean bed. And unless you are trained in this social science mysticism or obliged to read such articles for a class assignment, you are well advised to steer clear of any article that fits the formula outlined here. □

American Association of University Professors and Academic Freedom

The AAUP (the American Association of University Professors) has as its motto "Academic Freedom for a Free Society." While this motto rings with patriotic overtones, its application is often questionable.

Early this year the AAUP issued a statement supporting University of Colorado professor Ward Churchill, a tenured professor in the ethnic studies department. Churchill, as almost everyone knows, called the victims of the 2001 terrorist attack on the World Trade Center "little Eichmans"—a comparison to the infamous Nazi who organized the concentration camps where millions of Jews were murdered.

This remarked touched off an understandable firestorm. But the AAUP defended Churchill's right to his opinion. In fact, the professorial organization criticized the critics for their "inflammatory statements that...interfere in the decisions of the academic community."

However, it is worth noting that the AAUP 1940 "Statement of Principles on Academic Freedom and Tenure" sets out to describe and prescribe the nature of this freedom. This statement includes a brief for free speech outside the classroom, but it notes that professors should express opinions inside the classroom only on those matters in which they have scholarly competence. Moreover, "extraneous material unrelated to their areas of expertise" do not fall within the protective umbrella of academic freedom.

It would seem that in the Ward Churchill case the AAUP has been hoist by its own petard. Clearly, Churchill is free to express his opinions outside the classroom, however odious they may be. And just as clearly, he is not protected by academic freedom when he expresses these same opinions in the classroom. He has neither the scholarship to back up such claims, nor is this opinion consistent with his university appointment in ethnic studies. It is one thing to vouchsafe free speech to Churchill's rants, but quite another matter to suggest they are protected by academic freedom.

It is instructive that the AAUP General Secretary, Roger Bowen, has adopted a latitudinarian approach to academic freedom that is inconsistent with the organization's principles. When Jeremy Travis, the president at John Jay College of Criminal Justice in New York, decided not to offer a contract to Susan Rosenberg, a former member of the Violent Weather Underground, Bowen charged the president with "political persecution." Travis, of course, noted that Rosenberg has been indicted for committing a 1981 armed robbery of $1.6 million from a Brink's truck in which three people were killed. He noted as well that AAUP principles indicate that criminal activity is a valid reason for dismissal or, in this case, not offering a contract.

It is increasingly obvious that the AAUP has become politicized. The once pristine organization designed to protect academic freedom, has veered into the fever swamps of left wing advocacy. Cary Nelson, for example, second vice president of the association, argues that the AAUP should be "following the example of the activist group Move On.org." He explains: "We need to send e-mail to members to involve them in petition signing and letter writing campaigns." I wonder how John Dewey, founder of the AAUP, would have responded to this campaign.

Of course, Dr. Bowen and his claque deny any left-wing bias in higher education. But the "rose colored glasses defense" is increasingly challenged by the rush of events. Ward Churchill is merely the thin edge of the political wedge. It is noteworthy that even Castro's brutal repression of academic dissent was insufficient to raise AAUP censure.

In the "new age" academic freedom is defended selectively. Despite claims of nonpartisanship, the organization designed to protect faculty members from political black listing and government intrusiveness has a political agenda of its own. Interestingly that agenda often puts the AAUP in the position of repudiating the very principles it was organized to defend. This isn't the first, and it probably won't be the last, association that has lost touch with its own principles, but as someone associated with the academy for four decades sees it, this isn't a pretty picture.□

What Universities Must Do for the War Effort

The American Council of Trustees and Alumni (ACTA) recently issued a report criticizing colleges and universities for their failure to defend Western Civilization and recommended that American History and Western Civilization be required courses of study. In this report entitled "Defending Civilization: How Our Universities Are Failing America and What Can Be Done about It," the authors outline the yawning gap between the academy and the public at large on the transmission of the history and heritage of the United States.

Now more than two months after terrorist attacks, "it is clear that college and university faculty members have been the weak link in America's response," wrote ACTA president Jerry Martin and vice president Anne D. Neal, authors of the report. "While faculty should be passionately defended in their right to academic freedom, that does not exempt them from criticism. The fact is: academe is the only section of American society that is distinctly divided in its response to the attacks on America," noted the report.

The message from the academy has been distinctly equivocal. While there are groups on campus that have supported the war effort, the "blame America first" organizations have been equally influential. The Martin-Neal Report cites over one hundred examples of anti-US sentiment at colleges and universities. Most significantly, the top-ranked fifty-five colleges and universities in the country no longer require the study of Western Civilization or American History. To redress this deficiency, ACTA has called on institutions of higher education to include such required courses in the core curriculum.

There is little doubt that the nation's first line of defense against terrorism is a knowledge about and faith in the unique institutions that serve as a foundation stone for the nation. Ignorance is a great weapon for America's enemies since it can be deployed to undermine confidence and shake the stamina needed to sustain battle readiness.

"It has never been more urgent for education at all levels to pass on to the next generation the legacy of freedom and democracy. What is not taught will be forgotten, and what is forgotten cannot be defended," the report notes. Alas, for a generation American History has either been ignored or eviscerated of its accomplishments. For revisionists, America is a land of colonialists, imperialists, warmongers, and paranoid reactionaries. To the astonishment of many, this one sided interpretation has taken hold.

Hence, Hugh Gusterson, professor of Anthropology at MIT, argues, "The best way to begin a war on terrorism might be to look in the mirror." Kevin Lourie, a scholar at Brown University School of Medicine contends, "This war can end only to the extent that we relinquish our role as world leader, overhaul our lifestyle, and achieve political neutrality." And to cite merely one more example from the report, Walter Daum, math instructor at the City University of New York, maintains, "The ultimate responsibility lies with the rulers of this country, the capitalist ruling class of this country."

Here in unadulterated form is the echo of the hate-America position reverberating through the corridors of US history. Even as flags are exhibited throughout the nation in this time of grief and conflict, naysayers on campus have their acolytes. In many instances, they point an accusatory finger at America, not the terrorists.

While these radical professors are free—and should remain free—to express their point of view, they should not be inoculated against criticism for their moral relativism and their hatred of the nation that offers a sanctuary for the pursuit of their scholarship. Moreover, Americans should realize that these instructors have an obligation to transmit to our children the heritage of the nation, including both accomplishments and failures.

The United States is an imperfect nation, but it is also the last, best exemplar of a democratic republic. To suggest the US is the primary source of the world's ills—as many professors do—is simply misguided. Frequently students are told that America's failure to understand and appreciate Islam accounts for the terrorist mind-set. Yet there is a failure to note how the US supported Islamists in the Gulf War, Kosovo, and Bosnia.

Restoring confidence in our way of life and giving students the intellectual tools to defend the nation should be part of the educational mission. In my judgment, it has never been more urgent for institutions of higher learning to pass on to adolescents the legacy of liberty and constitutionalism.

ACTA should be commended for taking a stand on this matter. Lynne Cheney, chair of the ACTA, put it well when she noted, "We need to understand that living in liberty is such a precious thing that generations of men and women have been willing to sacrifice everything for it. We need to know, in a war, exactly what is at stake." I say amen.□

Curriculum by Plebiscite
"From the Editor's Desk," *Academic Questions*, Fall 1990

In this era of radical egalitarianism it is hardly surprising that, at least at one large university, education by student plebiscite has become a reality. For the last ten years, students at the University of California at Irvine have been regularly voting on the subjects they want the institution to offer. Under this system, a student committee makes an initial survey of the institutions fifteen hundred undergraduates, asking them to identify subjects for university-sponsored courses, including those in the core curriculum. The top listings are then put on a ballot and the four with the most votes are submitted to university officials for approval. Finally, a student committee recommends lecturers to teach the designated subjects.

Alas, not all the chosen courses actually can be offered because, as the director of the program points out, "We just don't have the resources to offer them. We try to do what we can." On the other hand, according to the university's financial planning department, the program is privileged to draw upon a budget of $140,000, and the faculty members selected are paid $34,000 to teach two courses each quarter. Barbara Bertin, the director of undergraduate studies, maintains the program is a significant benefit to the university, observing, "We're really adding to the diversity here."

While there have been many aberrations in the history of academic life, it is undoubtedly the case that the role of students, particularly student influence over the curriculum, has become grossly distorted. An outgrowth of the egalitarian sensibility, which gained its foothold on campuses in the late sixties, these distortions reflect the idea that students are as qualified as faculty members to make judgments about their course of study. Since present faculty members are often the student activists of two decades ago, and frequently remain immersed in a radical agenda, there indeed maybe a degree of ironic plausibility to this contention. Nonetheless, if students select the courses that should be offered and identify the faculty members who will teach them, what is left of the intellectual authority on which the existence of colleges and universities is ultimately predicated?

Education by student plebiscite is one of those ideas that sprang from the fertile imagination of people like Margaret Mead, who argued that the young should teach the old. But looked at realistically, colleges are by their very nature undemocratic institutions. Teachers know, or should know, more than students. Teachers should determine grades. And a curriculum should reflect the thoughtful influence of faculty judgment.

Admittedly these conditions don't always prevail. But, if institutions like the University of California at Irvine decide that students can determine their own program, parents are certainly within their rights in asking why they are paying good money to send their offspring there. Presumably those capable of approving a curriculum do not require the counsel of faculty members.

It is only a short step from the selection of courses to the determination of grades by students—a stage we are fast approaching in light of the number of colleges with undifferentiated grading. The application of the egalitarian spirit to college life has obscured the critical difference between the status and knowledge of faculty members and students. While many faculty members may think and act like adolescents, this shouldn't entitle them to avoid their responsibilities as professionals and adults. Nor is there any reason to believe that eighteen year-olds, weaned on television, are prepared to make decisions about what should be taught and who should do the teaching. □

Oasis Strategies

In *Slouching Towards Gomorrah,* Robert Bork makes the claim that "Decline runs across our entire culture." Having described a book burning at Yale, Bork concludes with the comment that "the charred books on the sidewalk in New Haven were a metaphor, a symbol of the coming torching of America's intellectual and moral capital by the barbarians of modern liberalism."[1] Alas, the barbarians at the gates and, despite an occasional cultural victory by the Right, any realistic assessment of American cultural life today must acknowledge that Left has utterly triumphed in the *kulturkampf.*

Richard Goldstein recognizes this when he exults in the pages of the *Village Voice,* "The Culture War is Over! We Won!" There is no question about the "we" to whom he refers. As Goldstein notes, "in the other America...the nation of home entertainment centers—the Republicans have no legs. Their roiling attacks on Hollywood and gangsta rap, their crusade against the evil empires of Levin and Eisner...their jeremiads against Jenny Jones, have all but on deaf ears."[2]

Among conservatives and liberals, there is consensus on this one point, that the Left has won the culture war. A 1960s generation weaned on polymorphous perversity is different from its ancestors. Believing that the self is the measure of all meaning and the arbiter of what is right, the 1960s generation arrived at adulthood worshipping the great demiurge solipsism. In its rejection of tradition, of all that came before, this generation assumed a societal tabula rasa that could be imprinted with self-expression. In this so-called postmodern period, what I feel or think is all that counts; "responsibility" and "duty" are obsolete words from an increasingly anachronistic age.

Against this backdrop of self-expression is a technological revolution in which every individual is encouraged to express himself without restraint. Thus, the virtual superhighway leads directly to the Tower of Babel. Standards are impossible when radical egalitarianism demands that everyone is heard, amid the din, taste and probity are drowned out. A cultural Gresham's Law is at work: the tasteless driving the tasteful out of existence. If this seems exaggerated, compare the popularity of gangsta rap to the financial struggles of most symphony orchestras.

The unfortunate truth is that traditionalists are inept at engaging their adversary in the culture war, conservatives with money and power are too often co-opted by media panjandrums, and most conservatives are unwilling or unable to recognize the influence of culture on politics. Thus, traditional viewpoints in the media have been easily supplanted by radicalism over the last four decades. A direct assault on cultural pollution is therefore unlikely to succeed. For those who determine programming, a moment of retreat today is worth a dramatic lunge forward sometime in the future. There is a growing recognition that the virtuecrats (this is not a term of derision) do not have staying power. And surely any cultural influence they do have pales before the growing market for the hedonistic, violent, and pornographic.

When the university is in thrall to the symbolic and ephemeral and freedom is denied to those with views in disfavor, there can be little doubt that a cultural shift has occurred. Relativism is the handmaiden of complacency with any belief system, and vitiating standards have been the catalyst for the dumbing down of American students. If students rarely read good books, how will they know what is good? If they are told that truth is an illusion designed to reinforce the status quo, why should they pursue truth, and if they are led to believe that beauty is only in the eye of the beholder, why should they accept the judgment of the past?

The modern museum, presumptively the repository of cultural artifacts that should be preserved, has become a center for the storage of detritus. Instead of offering what may be uplifting, the modern museum provides a menu of the shocking, degrading, and politically correct, and its myrmidons defend its shows as manifestations of "anti-art" or as a critique of the bourgeois sensibility. Curators don't defend shows as another form of beauty, but as intentionally ugly and deformative.

Similarly, language has slid down the rabbit hole of deconstruction. Words are now whatever you want them to mean, and every form of language, even the most crude, is accepted in this era of democratization. Coarse language has been accompanied by coarse behavior, its natural outcome. As a consequence, manners have been relegated to the ash heap of a bygone age.

This litany of cultural deterioration merely confirms that the culture war is over for the time being, and that refinement, taste, and aesthetics are missing in action. For those who lament this outcome, little in the way of solace is available. Judge Bork, for one, says we should hope for the best, but he prescribes little besides hope.

The Oasis Strategy

As prisoners of the culture war, cultural traditionalists, like all prisoners of war have few options available. We can leave this nation, but there are few places inoculated against American popular culture. We can surrender, but this is acceptable only for those who do not understand culture. We can fight back, but the odds against success are formidable. What can be done, in my judgment, is somewhere between retreat and resistance. I call it an oasis strategy.

In this cultural desert, those with a traditionalist stance must assert it in modest but meaningful ways. A museum should be created devoted to the best that has been achieved in artistic forms. (By the "best," I am referring to that which is spiritually enriching, aesthetically pleasing, and technically uncompromised.) A college should be established without any concessions to the *zeitgeist*, where students would meet rigorous requirements without electives, read the great works of our civilization, be literate in two foreign languages, have numerical skill, and be familiar with scientific laws and methods. A film company should be designed around family entertainment that neither patronizes nor depreciates the human experience. These films will not indulge the vulgar with coarse language, but instead teach and edify through great storytelling and inspiring myth.

In some respects the oasis strategy recreates the approach of Antonio Gramsci's progeny who "infiltrated" institutions until their numbers represented a critical mass. Wherever there are openings, traditionalists today should try to advance their agenda by ("leavening" institutions now dominated by the Left. For example, if affirmative action judgments militate against fair play and the pursuit of excellence, these arguments should be emphasized and perhaps fictionalized into film and television programs. How can a society with our legacy resist appeals to fair play?

As cultural consumers, traditionalists should shun the bad and embrace the good pointing out—for those who care—what is meant by true, good, and beautiful. When there is a sound adaptation of a Henry James novel into film, one that avoids the gratuitous sex and vulgarity James himself would have deplored, traditionalists should go out of their way to praise it as a hopeful cultural indicator.

There are many other possible illustrations. My point is simply that edifying examples do exist, and that they must be the traditionalists' response to cultural degradation. Just as Bradbury's characters roamed the forest reciting their assigned books, traditionalists must resist sensate culture within the oasis where their culture flourishes. They should be immune to the charge that their institutions are elitist. Affirmative action and radical egalitarianism have no place in the oases; these are institutions where merit and excellence count and are rewarded.

The best response to a degrading culture is its opposite, forcefully defended within a psychological island of like-minded adherents. Occasionally, unlikely visitors may find succor in the oasis and may even be converted. But the most likely scenario is that the traditional culture oases will remain isolated and bereft of widespread support. A lack of popular support, however, does not suggest a lack of moral victories. As long as there remain a few hardy souls who recognize greatness, all is not lost. Being the last defenders of superior culture is an admirable calling to which some noble people will unquestionably respond. Now we must build the institutions to which these people can gravitate.

Building the Institutions

How we build these institutions isn't obvious. Even if like-minded people congregate, that in itself won't change the barren landscape of culture. What is necessary are models. A few faculty members devoted to the restoration of Great Books can forge a new department without an enormous financial investment. All that is needed is evidence that students will embrace the idea. Surely if radical faculties can influence students, moderate faculty members should be able to do so as well.

Based on all the audio tapes of superb books now available in the Blackstone catalogue, it would not be difficult to syndicate a series of radio programs that give audiences a chance to hear several of Jane Austen's novels in a given weekend, perhaps *The Iliad* and *The Odyssey* the following week. As a refreshing change from the many culturally-degrading stations in the country, this could be a commercial success in addition to being a cultural break through.

In the Internet age, there are virtually no impediments for establishing a "chat room" devoted to the serious exchange of ideas. Assignments could be given and papers "delivered."

A catalogue of national museums devoted to aesthetically pleasing and uplifting works could be created. How many cultural sophisticates are aware of the extraordinary Hudson River collection housed in the Hastings-on-Hudson Newington Cropsey Museum?

If the *Blair Witch Project* could become an overnight box office sensation by relying on cheap thrills, it seems that films can be made inexpensively and still find an audience. Perhaps more edifying films could also be made inexpensively; a film based on the life of Teddy Roosevelt as a child, for example, would have visual appeal and powerful moral lessons.

The purpose of such projects is to create a beachhead on the hostile cultural landscape, a safe place for experimentation with worthy artifacts and wholesome ideas. Naturally, critics will decry such efforts as the *cri de coeur* of Babbits. But that's okay; they don't have to participate.

My suspicion, however, is that in time skeptics will become converts. When the Goodspeed Opera House in Connecticut first opened, audiences couldn't be found for the musical theatre productions of yesteryear. That has changed. Today there are sellout crowds for virtually every performance.

Moreover, the projects to which I refer need not be stolid or boring. What is culturally uplifting is often surprisingly enjoyable even for audiences weaned on violence and sexual perversion. As I see it, shifting the culture is not unlike turning a battleship in mid-ocean. It's hard, it requires skills, and it demands determination. Recognizing the goal, of course, is ultimately what is critical, and the goal is producing what is worthy for those who will appreciate it and developing models for those who can be converted.

Can an Oasis Strategy Be Successful?

If the oasis strategy can be successful is not clear. Despite my ardent belief that it is worth trying (What else can a traditionalist do?) the strategy has its weaknesses.

For one thing, there is the argument that these tactics cut traditionalists out of the so-called mainstream. That stream, of course, is polluted and it doesn't welcome anti-toxins, but it is what Americans consume and that cannot be taken lightly. While I would welcome an elitist label, it should be noted that in a radical egalitarian environment, elitism is a pejorative. As a consequence, even popular culture that attempts to be uplifting is swimming upstream.

Second, in our morally indeterminate climate, judgment about what is worthwhile and what is degrading is relativistic. The contagion of moral libertinism has turned the public's passion against truth and coarsened the culture to such a degree that the Nike ad to "Just do it" is the existential calling card for the entire society.

Furthermore, the nihilism of out capitalist culture makes it difficult to even attempt and oasis strategy. Unless you can demonstrate beyond a shadow of a doubt that there is a commercial market for an uplifting cultural product, financial investment will not be forthcoming.

Last, the assault on moral indeterminacy and cultural suicide by the virtuecrats has not resulted in a cultural retreat. On the contrary, appealing to shame in a shameless environment doesn't work, and appeals to religious principle in an increasingly nonreligious climate are regarded as mere superstition.

The dawn of a new era catalyzed by oases of renaissance culture faces formidable obstacles that cannot be overlooked. They key to this struggle—which is both moral and aesthetic—can perhaps be found in religious institutions. If they can reclaim the terrain once appropriately held, culture might go through efflorescence. If not, oases might be trapped by isolation in an increasingly hostile climate.

The struggle in which traditionalists are engaged requires moral regeneration, which, although very hard, is not impossible. Working for cultural change won't be easy, but it is certainly better than merely hoping for the best. As I see it, cultivating little gardens of cultural beauty in the vast contemporary desert is a worthwhile activity despite the impediments that stand in the way of successful cultivation. Rejecting what is demeaning and restoring what is uplifting may be a Sisyphean task; nonetheless, in a nation with increasingly fat wallets and hollow souls, it is the right thing to do. □

The Traditional Curriculum as Fable
"From the Editor's Desk," *Academic Questions*, Summer 1989

What is an appropriate curriculum for our students? What happened to the consensus on which the college curriculum once rested? Together these comprise two of the most urgent questions in contemporary American higher education. It seems to me that the criticisms of Allan Bloom's *The Closing of the American Mind* are symptomatic of the problems we are facing.

High standards are described as elitism, a pejorative of scathing proportions. A call for the assertion of Western traditions is characterized as racist and anti-democratic. And Bloom's critique of radical feminism as a virus let loose on the curriculum is greeted with cries of "phallocentrism."

The college curriculum as the source of youthful enlightenment free of the impediments of bias and prejudice has unraveled. While Stanley Katz, president of the American Council of Learned Societies, recently noted, "scholars are less politicized in the United States than in any other country in the developed world," he neglected to point out that a profound and revolutionary change has occurred on American campuses since the 1960s, resulting in the institutionalization of a radical agenda.

Even if one agrees with Dr. Katz, or considers my description somewhat exaggerated, there are certain assumptions about higher education that are likely to be accepted: one is that some matters should be studied by all students and another is that the welfare of society depends on some knowledge and appreciation of the basic ideas that undergird this democratic polity. These generalizations, in themselves, rarely cause a heated reaction, but their application in a society as diverse and perhaps as atomistic as ours makes them intrinsically volatile.

William Bennett in *Our Children and Our Country* noted that there is no longer an overarching, well-understood purpose for the university. In the past—some distant, imprecise past—all activities were ancillary to teaching, including research and publication. Today, however, the university's purpose is manifold: research, administration, publication, affirmative action, redressing real and perceived social ills, therapy for middle-class kids suffering the ravages of divorce and neglect, ideological indoctrination (what I have called in another context "the Derridaization of the curriculum"), and occasionally teaching. The honored disciplines are still taught and some are less contaminated by the political virus than others, but along with them is a heavy overlay of deconstruction, Lacanism, Marxism, semiotics, minimalism, hermeneutics of everything except the Bible, self studies, ethnic studies, and theory—theory about every matter to which a theory can be applied.

Let me illustrate this point with a Hasidic tale recounted by Martin Buber. The story involves the consuming desire of Reb Yitzak Yaakov of Poland to encounter the prophet Elijah. Elijah, according to the Bible, did not die. He was carried off to heaven in a fiery chariot and ever since, Jewish tradition has it, he has regularly been sent on various missions throughout the world, under disguise, to hasten the coming of the Messiah.

To satisfy his desire, Reb Yitzak Yaakov would dress himself in peasant's garb, and with a companion wander through the streets and markets of neighboring villages, hoping by chance or by God's grace to meet the prophet Elijah.

One day, as they were walking down a typically unpaved and sandy street, they met a peasant walking towards them leading a donkey on a halter. Yitzak grabbed his companion's arm in deep agitation: "There he is!" he cried.

But the peasant glared at him with fiery eyes: "Yehudi!" he thundered (Yehudi means Jew), "Yehudi, if you know, why must you speak?" And in an instant, Elijah disappeared.

Now, as I see it, the encounter with Elijah in this tale conveyed the assurance so ardently desired by Yitzak that a divine purpose exists. It was a dazzling sign that there is a latent meaning and a body of principles governing the world, which to many seems devoid of both.

But why, one may well ask (although Buber does not) was Elijah angry? Why did he disappear as soon as he was identified? And, to ask a third question, which on first blush may seem frivolous, what happened to the donkey?

I shall return to these questions in due course, but first I would like to ask why the curriculum consensus on our campuses has unraveled. Some might be tempted to argue that this situation is a reflection of the disorder of our times, in which false and perverse notions are employed in order to enhance faculty authority and preferences. Others argue that the curriculum has been undone by a process of academic logrolling among the established disciplines, unfettered by any transcendent idea of the good or even the desirable. Still another view has it that the instability of the curriculum reflects a desire to keep up with shifting tides of intellectual fashion.

Clearly, it would be unwise to argue that the curriculum should be narrowly sectarian. I'm reminded of Colonel Muammar Qaddafi's response to a French ambassador who earnestly spoke of friendly relations between the two countries. Qaddafi nodded and then said, "It would be so much easier if the French were to convert to Islam." As professors we are constrained by the reality of cultural, religious, and ethnic differences that make an inflexible curriculum improbable. But that in no way obviates the need for a common core that transmits the deposited wisdom of our civilization and poses the essential questions of life—How should I live? What is the good life? What can I hope for? What must I do? How do I find the truth? (questions raised by Allan Bloom)—or that provides students with knowledge about the democratic polity of which they are citizens.

Though we are all living in a durably enigmatic universe and following paths through life that lead each one of us to death, we all want, or should want, to know what we are doing here and what we must do to give our lives value to overcome the apparent derision of death, which threatens to deprive all our efforts and accomplishments of any lasting significance. Higher education, in itself, cannot address this yearning. At its best, it refines the questions and establishes a path for the pursuit of answers. Yet my concern is that the typical college curriculum does not ask the important questions, does not encourage the quest for real self and community knowledge, and substitutes the wisdom on which this civilization was founded for that which has current and evanescent meaning.

It is ironic that at the moment we have eviscerated meaning from the curriculum, academics are urgently calling for "values education," a recurrent phrase in the pages of the *Chronicle of Higher Education*. But what is this values education to be? The emergence of cultural relativism has elicited the belief that our culture is one of many others deserving no particular praise or even attention. As the web of symbols, which in every culture designates the ultimate values from which moral rules are derived, is subject to rational exegesis and then refutation, a vacuum results that most high-minded scholars don't have the foggiest idea how to fill. Moreover, the scientific worldview on which scholarly discourse depends provides only one—and by no means the most important—dimension of values.

This leaves us in a double bind. The call for values in the curriculum occurs in a social setting characterized by accelerated change, a scientific worldview, skepticism towards religion, a fascination with that which is fashionable, and the emergence of a peculiar orthodoxy which relies on relativism—except when it comes to women, blacks, and the Third World. One cannot bring back the past, despite my wish. But neither can one forget the past. While there are obviously many ways to pursue curriculum reform and many viewpoints on any direction taken, I would argue that the way toward the reassertion of common sense involves a renewed consideration of those questions that deal with our fundamental humanity.

Rejecting the compromise of standards that has afflicted higher education since the 1960s, we should carry the torch—like a government in exile—for the highest value, that which is irrefutably common to all students: the desire to question and to know. In that sense, we are all like Reb Yitzak Yaakov wandering through the streets in search of a presence that will confirm our faith and our humanity that will certify we are not adrift in an inhuman and meaningless universe headed for a meaningless death. This is the common bond we share, and it is upon this search that the curriculum must be constructed.

This brings me to another of my questions from the allegorical tale: Why was Elijah angry? He was angry, I contend, because while people may be allowed to sense his presence, they cannot presume to point it out and give it a name. The time was not yet ripe for revelation because in the Jewish tradition the Messiah had not come and preparation for his coming made everything precarious. Hence, one should not designate this hidden force, nor utter the name of God capriciously. Elijah disappeared because he was designated and named. Yitzak said aloud what should have been left unspoken and acknowledged only in the heart.

If I may apply Yitzak's dilemma to the academy, the highest value is potentially ripened within the walls of our colleges. The nostalgic need often expressed for a "human world" will find its expression only in the quest for what is most authentically human. That is not a quest limited to the last two decades, or even the last two centuries; it is a search for answers to those universal questions that transcend the latest cause or ''ism'' and go right to the essence of being human.

The nineteenth-century Polish poet, Cyprian Norwid, faced with the crude demand for a "truth," saved his neck by replying that "man is not yet ripe—he is a priest without knowing it." What I think he meant by that phrase is that, like Yitzak, each of us is a questioner, a mediator between the highest value and the banality of quotidian responsibility, between a world that is dreadfully predictable and a future charged with possibilities. Those are the real parameters of curriculum decisions; not whether the voices of femininity, color, or the Third World will be represented in a reading list, but whether those readings and questions bring us closer to the true source of our humanity.

Now for the last of my questions: What happened to the donkey that Elijah was leading down the dusty village street? I suspect (since I don't have this from a higher authority) that when the prophet disappeared the donkey ambled down the street and stopped at the water fountain. There he was picked up by a man who had witnessed the encounter and knew the donkey belonged to the prophet Elijah. Realizing the animal was granted special powers, he was sent to the United States where he was given an endowed chair in semiotics at the University of California at Berkeley.

While Elijah in my story is the searing; unrelenting, illuminating questioner, the donkey is no more than a precocious and false answer. One might say the donkey is the Golden Calf—a firm answer to a question that requires no answering. Like so many subjects in the contemporary curriculum, there are questions that don't deserve our attention. For example: Can peace be established through the elimination of nuclear weapons? Is race the only way to evaluate societies? Should hermeneutics be reduced to gender? I can go on. The essence of the curriculum is desire: the desire to go beyond oneself and to ask the questions that cut across time and place. The extent to which scholars can revisit the issue of the curriculum with this desire in mind is the test of whether true educational attainment is being encouraged. I am not sanguine about the prospects, but like my belief in Elijah, some matters are better left unsaid and faith is still the great harbinger of change.☐

Notes

1   Robert H. Bork, *Slouching Towards Gomorrah: Modern Liberalism and American Decline* (New York: Reagan Books, 1996), pp. 342-43.
2   Richard Goldstein, "The Culture War Is Over! We Won! (For Now)," *The Village Voice*, 19 November 1996, p. 51.

Index

academic credits,
academic journals, 15-17, 41, 242
Academic Questions, 6, 61-63, 70-74, 139-144, 150-164, 188-192, 213-228, 233-236, 251-280, 297-298, 305-307, 311-313, 320-325
Accuracy in Academia (AIA), 10-11
admissions, 3, 38, 50-51, 56, 65, 101, 122, 141, 148, 166-167, 169-173, 175-178, 209-210
American Association of University Professors (AAUP), 11-12, 33, 157-158, 307-309
American University, The, 35, 50, 53
Association of American Colleges, 12, 286

B.A. in a Box, 73
Babel Index, 41
Balch, Stephen H., 6, 9-33
Barnard College, 150-152
Barzun, Jacques, 35-37, 41-47, 50, 52, 57-59
Bennett, William J., 20-21, 54, 57, 220-222, 285-286, 320
black studies, 21-23, 187, 237
Bloom, Allan, 39-40, 49, 222-224, 320, 322
Boston College, 273
Boston University, 31, 42, 293
Brandeis University, 90-91, 291
Brown University, 142-144, 310
Burawoy, Michael, 17-18

Calhoun, Paul, 72
Cameron, Alan, 72
campus protests, 10, 15, 73, 146-148
campus Red Guards, 66-68, 75, 84, 184
Carnegie Commission Report on Higher Education, 128, 287
Carnegie Council on Policy Studies in Higher Education, 296

Carnegie Council on Teaching, 57
Carnegie Foundation for the Advancement of Technology, 14
censorship, 64-65, 69
Chandler, John W., 12, 286
college dorms, 68-69, 196, 205-209
Columbia College,
    author as student, 1-2, 7
    endowments, 89
    sports, 134-135, 165, 169-172
Columbia University,
    experimental education, 125
    parietals then and now, 192-197
    student riots, 36-37
commencements, 3-4, 40, 68, 144-145, 179-183, 223
Commission on Undergraduate Education, 3
Communism, 74-77, 133-134, 179-180, 201, 216-217, 290-292
Cornell University, 11, 206-207, 272
credentialism, 58, 90-93
cultural revolution, 13

deans, 5-7, 44-45, 108, 121-122, 141, 143, 153-154, 194, 201, 208, 210, 273
divestiture movement, 9-12, 27
diversity, 68-69, 144, 146, 237, 298, 312
Draper, Mark, 70-74

experimental colleges, 3-5, 98, 128-129
experimental programs, 95-96, 99, 102-109, 111-122, 124-126

Fellows, James, 58
Finn, Chester Jr., 43, 236
Freud, Sigmund, 49, 199

Gallatin, Albert, 4-5
Gallatin School, 123, 201
Georgetown University, 64-65, 267, 269

Gibbs, Graham, 71
Gramsci, Antonio, 2, 43, 316
Grove City College, 144-146, 194

Handler, Evelyn, 90-91
Hartley, James, 72
Harvard Divinity School, 139-141
Harvard University, 11, 19, 38, 194, 196-197, 203
homosexuality, 62, 66, 68-70, 84-85, 183, 194-195, 205-207, 243-249
honorary degrees, 69, 179-183
Hook, Sidney, 4, 6, 77, 126, 190, 292
Hunter College, 154-155, 204

Ivory Tower competition, 78-80
Ivy League,
    admission standards, 179
    elitism, 181
    sports, 171

Jameson, Frederic, 19-20
John O'Sullivan Law of Institutions, 7

law schools, 3, 65, 97, 114, 128, 131-134
Left, The, 12-17, 25-27, 30-33, 217, 264, 287-288, 294, 297, 313-316
Lewontin, Richard, 19
liberal arts, 14, 24, 47, 52-57, 62, 73, 101, 108, 118, 121-129, 149, 274, 304

McCarthy, Colman, 271-272
McCarthy, Joseph, 76-77, 134, 185
McCarthyism, 12-13, 53, 133, 157
Macmanaway, Lancelot, 71-72
Marxism, 16-22, 27-28, 31, 33, 75, 136-137, 217-218, 225, 274, 285-295, 321

National Association of Scholars (NAS), 63, 141-142, 159-161, 189-190, 215-216, 226
National Education Association, 54, 256
New York University (NYU),
    enrollments, 55
    experimental college, 95, 99, 102
    political professors, 291-292
    sex courses on campus, 242-243
Northwestern University, 76, 97

Oasis strategy, 315-317
Ollman, Bertell, 18-20, 287-290

Parenti, Michael, 18, 290
political correctness, 7, 64-68, 75, 141-142, 144, 147, 156-159, 183, 224, 297
Princeton University, 20, 134-137, 286
professors,
    anachronistic, 72-73, 87
    as merchants, 54
    declining industry, 57
    freedom to teach, 185-188, 307-309
    grants, 151-152
    liberal, 287-288
    McCarthyism, 12
    Marxist, 20, 75, 288, 293
    popularity, 111, 115
    radical, 2, 7, 16, 272, 292

radicals, 13-15, 21, 27, 31, 36, 44, 63, 65, 146, 161, 201, 249-250, 286, 292, 295-296, 298
Rorty, Richard, 74-76

scholarly associations, 12, 16-17, 21, 26-28, 48, 157
Scottish system, 81-85
sex,
    courses, 242-244
    lectures, 64, 135-140, 150
    openness, 156, 187
    sexual harassment, 83-84, 194
silent revolution, 70-73
sports, 165-178
Strategic Defense Initiative, 53, 56
students,
    alcohol drinking, 208-209
    and reading, 3-4, 5, 7, 39, 125, 145, 151, 162-164, 283-284
    and sexuality, 84-85, 135, 243-244
    arrests, 135-136, 152-154
    as "customers," 209-211
    athletes, 165-178, 182
    class attention and participation, 24, 71-72
    complacency, 57, 113-114, 126-129, 221
    demands, 154-155
    during trying times, 66-68
    emergent technologies, 72-74
    ethnic studies, 236-238
    freedom, 188-192
    lacking college preparation, 54-55, 82-83, 118, 302

liberal arts, 121-123
military action, 202-204
parietals, 144-145, 192-197
protests, 11-12, 20, 36-37, 43, 62,
    142, 146-148, 160-162, 183-184,
    287
prototypical student radical, 44, 200
relationship between teacher and
    student, 89-90, 200-202
shaping their beliefs, 74-76
skeptics, 53, 204-205
social transformation, 2, 10, 95-105,
    106, 221

technological revolution, 249, 314
tenure, 6, 16, 42-43, 52, 62, 69, 79, 84-86,
    158-159, 186, 216, 304, 307-308
Trilling, Lionel, 1, 258
Tufts University, 23-26, 277

undergraduates, 3, 46-47, 54, 57, 78, 89,
    101-102, 107, 117, 136, 153, 191-197,
    203, 239, 291-302, 312

University of Pennsylvania, 144-146,
    193
University Without Walls (UWW), 96-
    102

Vassar College, 21-22, 39, 52, 218
Veblen, Thorstein, 39, 163
Vietnam War, 2, 10, 266, 269, 272

Weber, Max, 18, 253, 294-295
Welch, Jack, 74
Whitehead, Alfred North, 48-40
Wittgenstein, Ludwig, 49
women's studies, 22-23, 25-26, 65, 137-
    138, 234-235, 268, 273

Yale University, 11, 142, 148-150, 203,
    208, 313

zero budgeting, 45-46
Zinn, Howard, 31, 42, 293

For Product Safety Concerns and Information please contact our EU representative GPSR@taylorandfrancis.com Taylor & Francis Verlag GmbH, Kaufingerstraße 24, 80331 München, Germany

Batch number: 08153774

Printed by Printforce, the Netherlands